Framing Crime

In a world in which media images of crime and deviance proliferate, where every facet of offending is reflected in a 'vast hall of mirrors', *Framing Crime: Cultural Criminology and the Image* makes sense of the increasingly blurred line between the real and the virtual.

Images of crime and crime control have become almost as 'real' as crime and criminal justice itself. The meaning of both crime and crime control now resides, not solely in the essential – and essentially false – factuality of crime rates or arrest records, but also in the contested processes of symbolic display, cultural interpretation, and representational negotiation.

It is essential, then, that criminologists be closely attuned to the various ways in which crime is imagined, constructed, and framed within modern society.

Framing Crime responds to this demand with a collection of papers aimed at helping the reader to understand the ways in which the contemporary 'story of crime' is constructed and promulgated through the image. It also provides the relevant analytical and research tools to unearth the hidden social and ideological concerns that frequently underpin images of crime, violence, and transgression.

Framing Crime will be of interest to students and academics in the fields of criminology, crime and the media, and sociology.

Keith J. Hayward is Senior Lecturer in Criminology and Sociology and Director of Undergraduate Criminology at the University of Kent.

Mike Presdee (1944–2009) was Senior Lecturer in Criminology at the School of Social Policy, Sociology and Social Research at the University of Kent.

Framing Crime

Cultural Criminology and the Image

Edited by Keith J. Hayward
and Mike Presdee

First published 2010
by Routledge
2 Park Square, Milton Park, Abingdon, Oxon, OX14 4RN

Simultaneously published in the USA and Canada
by Routledge
711 Third Avenue, New York, NY 10017

A GlassHouse book

*Routledge is an imprint of the Taylor & Francis Group,
an informa business*

Typeset in Times New Roman by Keyword Group Ltd

British Library Cataloguing in Publication Data
A catalogue record for this book is available
from the British Library

Library of Congress Cataloguing in Publication Data

A catalogue record for this book has been requested

ISBN13: 978-0-415-45903-7(hbk)

ISBN13: 978-0-415-45904-4 (pbk)

ISBN13: 978-0-203-88075-3 (ebk)

This book is dedicated to the memory of Mike Presdee
11.11.1944–10.7.2009

Contents

Contributors

Michelle Brown is Associate Professor in the Department of Sociology and Anthropology at Ohio University and Director of Ohio University's Center for Law, Justice and Culture. Her research examines media, culture, and punishment, including the ways in which pain and exclusion are structured through social practice and its representation. She is co-editor of *Media Representations of September 11* and author of *The Culture of Punishment: Prison, Society, and Spectacle* (NYU Press, 2009).

Alexandra Campbell is an associate professor of sociology at the University of New England. She completed her graduate studies at the University of Cambridge at the Institute of Criminology. Alex has researched and published in the areas of gender and crime, identity, nationalism, and deviance, and is currently working on a manuscript which focuses on representation, crime, and suffering.

Phil Carney trained in medicine and psychiatry, took degrees in sociology and criminology, wrote about photography, and was involved in the making of a documentary before undertaking doctoral research. In the process of conversion to a book, his PhD thesis, *The Punitive Gaze*, uses photographic, critical, and cultural theory to examine case studies in which the photograph is both the scene and means of punishment and terror. Recently, he has written about 'Vague Spaces' (with Vince Miller) and the figure of Enrico Ferri. His current research interests include the relationships between power and desire in the culture of crime, control, and punishment. A lecturer at the University of Kent, he teaches in the fields of crime, media and culture, the sociology of crime and deviance, and coordinates the international Common Study Programme in Critical Criminology. He is currently Co-Director of Studies for the MA programme in criminology.

Chris Cunneen is the NewSouth Global Professor of Criminology at the University of New South Wales, Sydney, Australia. He has published widely in the area of juvenile justice, policing, criminal justice policy, restorative justice, and Indigenous legal issues. His books include *Indigenous*

Legal Relations (Oxford University Press, 2009), *The Critical Criminology Companion* (Federation Press, 2008), *Juvenile Justice: Youth and Crime in Australia* (Oxford University Press, 2007), *Conflict, Politics and Crime* (Allen and Unwin, 2001), *Faces of Hate* (Federation Press, 1997), and *Indigenous People and the Law in Australia* (Butterworths, 1995).

Jeff Ferrell earned his PhD in Sociology from the University of Texas at Austin, and is currently Visiting Professor of Criminology at the University of Kent, UK. He is the author of the books *Crimes of Style, Tearing Down the Streets, Empire of Scrounge,* and, with Keith Hayward and Jock Young, *Cultural Criminology: An Invitation*. He is also the co-editor of the books *Cultural Criminology*, *Ethnography at the Edge*, *Making Trouble*, and *Cultural Criminology Unleashed*. Jeff Ferrell is the founding and current editor of the New York University Press book series *Alternative Criminology*, and one of the founding and current editors of the journal *Crime, Media, Culture: An International Journal*, winner of the Association of Learned and Professional Society Publishers' 2006 Charlesworth Award for Best New Journal. In 1998, he received the Critical Criminologist of the Year Award from the Division of Critical Criminology of the American Society of Criminology.

Keith J. Hayward is Senior Lecturer in Criminology and Sociology at the University of Kent, UK. He has published widely in the areas of cultural criminology, criminological theory, popular culture, social theory, and terrorism. He is the author of *City Limits: Crime, Consumer Culture and the Urban Experience* (Routledge-Cavendish, 2004), the co-author of *Cultural Criminology: An Invitation* (Sage, 2008), and the co-editor of *Cultural Criminology Unleashed* (Routledge-Cavendish, 2004), *Criminology* (Oxford University Press, Second Edition 2009), and *Fifty Key Thinkers in Criminology* (Routledge, 2009). Dr. Hayward is also the founder of the International Cultural Criminology Conference Series and runs the website: www.culturalcriminology.org.

Bruce Hoffman is Associate Professor in the Department of Sociology and Anthropology at Ohio University. His work lies at the intersection of criminology, science studies, socio-legal studies, and social theory. His research on the cultural boundaries of criminology and the subtle ways in which law and science shape social movements are themes of recent articles in *Contemporary Justice Review, Law & Social Inquiry*, and *Law & Society Review*. He is currently completing a manuscript exploring how the identity and organization of midwives and birth activists in California, Oregon, and Washington differentially developed in response to diverse state regimes of criminal and regulatory law.

Philip J. Jones' research examines the relationship between media representation, personal identity, and popular opinion. He is a research student at the Graduate School in Life Long Learning at the University of Roskilde,

Denmark. Philip is currently involved in a research project funded by the Danish Agency for Science, Technology and Innovation. The project collects the life history portrayals of people with an incurable illness and examines them with reference to external media representations. Philip's research interests include journalistic representation, crime in the media, life historical and biographical research methods.

Tom de Leeuw is junior lecturer and PhD candidate at the Department of Criminology, Erasmus University Rotterdam. His primary research interest thus far has focused on the cultural meanings surrounding the production and consumption of football hooligan identities in the Netherlands. His more recent doctoral research is an ethnographic study of the social construction of safety in disadvantaged neighborhoods in Rotterdam and Antwerp, and in particular the everyday practices and experiences of social actors in the context of urban revanchist rhetoric.

Wayne Morrison is Director of the University of London External Undergraduate Laws Programme and professor of law, Queen Mary, University of London. His research and publications span criminological and legal theory. Recently, he has worked towards a more global criminology that includes topics traditionally excluded from the canon, such as genocide. His most recent book in criminology is *Criminology, Civilization and the New World Order* (Routledge, 2006).

Stephen L. Muzzatti is Associate Professor of Sociology at Ryerson University in Toronto, Canada, where he teaches courses in media, crime, and popular culture. He has written extensively on the news media's criminalisation of youth culture, as well as on terrorism, crimes of globalisation, motorcycle culture, and street racing. He is the past Vice-Chair of the American Society of Criminology's Division on Critical Criminology, and former editor of *The Critical Criminologist*.

Mike Presdee (1944–2009) was a Senior Lecturer in criminology at the University of Kent and author of *Cultural Criminology and the Carnival of Crime* (Routledge, 2000). He was a sociologist of international acclaim and considerable personal magnetism. His work focused on the sociology of youth and cultural criminology. He was fascinated by the way in which young people are criminalized and controlled; of youth being seen as the problem rather than young people being the locus of the problems of the system.

Cécile Van de Voorde is Assistant Professor in the Department of Criminal Justice at John Jay College (CUNY). She earned her PhD from the University of South Florida, where she conducted research on suicide bombings. She is currently developing multi-site ethnographic projects regarding genocide, human rights violations against refugees and internally displaced persons, and child soldiers. Her research also focuses on gender-based abuses and persecution, notably the use of rape and other forms of sexual violence as a weapon of war. An avid documentary photographer, Dr. Van de Voorde has been actively promoting the integration of visual methodologies such as photoethnography into empirically novel and theoretically rigorous research.

Claire Wardle is Lecturer at the School of Journalism, Media and Cultural Studies at Cardiff University. Her research focuses on journalism studies, particularly press constructions of high-profile crimes in both the UK and the US.

Majid Yar is Professor of Sociology at the University of Hull, UK. His research interests include the Internet and new media, popular culture, criminology, and social theory. His works include: *Cybercrime and Society* (2006), *Criminology: The Key Concepts* (2008) (with Martin O'Brien), *The Handbook on Internet Crime* (2009) (with Yvonne Jewkes), and *Community & Recognition: Ethics, Inter-Subjectivity and the Grounds of Political Life* (2009).

Alison Young is Professor of Criminology in the School of Social and Political Sciences at the University of Melbourne. She is the author of *Judging the Image* (2005, Routledge), *Imagining Crime* (1996, Sage), and *Femininity in Dissent* (1990, Routledge), in addition to numerous articles on the intersections of law, crime, and culture. She is currently completing a book, *Visions of Violence: Cinema, Crime, Affect* (2009, Routledge-Cavendish), on spectatorship, cinema, and violence. Her other area of research concerns street art and city spaces, and is funded by the Australian Research Council.

Damián Zaitch is Lecturer and Researcher at the Willem Pompe Institute for Criminal Law and Criminology, University of Utrecht. He has published on social control and terrorism, police co-operation in Europe, critical criminology, and, for the past 10 years, on organised crime and drug trafficking in the Netherlands and Latin America. He is the author of *Trafficking Cocaine* (2002, Kluwer Law International), for which he obtained the Willem Nagel Prize in 2003. Since then, he has conducted qualitative research on drug smuggling in the port of Rotterdam, synthetic drugs markets in Amsterdam, virtual hooliganism, and the trafficking of women. His current research interests include new forms of cross-border transnational crime, corporate crime in the food industry, virtual ethnography, and visual criminology.

Chapter 1

Opening the lens

Cultural criminology and the image

Keith Hayward

> Do you want to acquire power through the image? Then you will perish by the return of the image.
>
> (Jean Baudrillard, 2005)

Five years ago now, in the edited collection *Cultural Criminology Unleashed* (Ferrell *et al.*, 2004), we commented that the true meaning of crime and crime control was to be found not in the essential (and essentially false) factuality of crime rates, but in the contested processes of symbolic display, cultural interpretation, and representational negotiation. Images of crime, we claimed, were becoming 'as "real" as crime and criminal justice itself', with mediated anticrime campaigns, visually constructed crime waves, and media fabrications of countercultural imagery all circulating in 'an endless spiral of meaning, a Möbius strip of culture and everyday life' (ibid: 3–4). At that time, our intention was to be controversial; the goal being to play with the parameters of the discipline and challenge the staid conventions of orthodox criminology. However, surveying the world five years on, such proclamations appear less irreverent flights of futurological fancy and more commonsense observation. While the everyday experience of life in contemporary Western society may or may not be suffused with crime, it is most certainly suffused with images and increasingly images of crime.

However, it is not just a case of image proliferation – contemporary society's keen sense of the visual demands that images also be both mutable and malleable. Here the 'logic of speed' (Virilio, 1986, 1991) meets liquidity of form, as images bleed from one medium to the next. Uploaded and downloaded, copied and cross-posted, Flickr-ed, Facebook-ed and PhotoShop-ped, the image today is as much about porosity and manipulation as it is about fixity and representation. This, of course, poses a question: what does the term 'image' actually mean under contemporary conditions?

The word 'image' is utilized and etymologically defined in a number of ways. However, from a pictorial perspective, image traditionally refers to a representation of the external form of an object. This remains the case, of course, but for the purposes of this collection, we have deliberately sought to expand and enhance the term. Just as cell phone photos migrate from street to screen and 'user-generated-content' websites set video clips loose from their origins, traditional conceptual understandings of the term image are also set in motion. One such example is the increasing interchangeability of the terms 'image' and 'visual'. If the former relates to representation, then the latter (traditionally at least) relates to 'seeing'. However, consider our mass-mediated society, what Appadurai (1996: 35) calls the late modern 'Mediascape' (that bundle of media that manufactures information and disseminates images via an ever expanding array of digital technologies). Here, much of what we 'see' is actually mediated by the image. On the internet, for example, the photograph and the icon function as navigational devices, allowing us to 'see' virtual worlds and traverse the endless pathways of cyberspace. Likewise, while TV, film, and video all incorporate sound and broadcast technology, they are by definition primarily photographic experiences. Hence the increasing use of terms such as 'visual culture'[1] or 'imaged form' as ways of explaining and understanding a world in which the collective conscious is now shaped and manipulated by the digital image-making machinery of the Mediascape.

This blurring of representation and seeing, of image and visual, is never more apparent than when we consider how crime is imaged in contemporary society. While mug shots, surveillance photographs, and newspaper pictures of notorious criminals have long featured as part of the 'spectacle' of crime and punishment in modern society (see Carney, this volume). Today, as criminals videotape their crimes and post them on YouTube, as security agents scrutinize the image-making of criminals on millions of surveillance monitors around the world, as insurrectionist groups upload video compilations (filmed from several angles) of 'successful' suicide bomb attacks and roadside IED (Improvized Explosive Device) detonations, as images of brutality and victimization pop up on office computer screens and children's mobile phones, as 'reality TV' shows take the viewer ever deeper inside the world of the beat cop and the prison setting, there can be no other option but the development of a thoroughgoing *visual* criminology.

For some, such a 'visual criminology' is already with us. After all, phrases like 'images of' and 'media constructions of' are now common and commonly accepted prefixes to conventional criminological categories such as policing and prison studies. However, as I have stated elsewhere, '[t]his disciplinary drift into the realm of the image hardly constitutes an adequate visual criminology… Simply importing images into a discipline defined by words and numbers is in fact likely to *retard* the development of a visual criminology, since it will leave in place the ugly notion that written or numeric analysis can somehow penetrate

1 I use the term 'visual culture' here in its general sense and not as it relates to the distinct subfield of social and cultural study that draws together cultural studies, art history, philosophy, and critical theory (see e.g. Mirzoeff, 1999; Dikovitskaya, 2006 for introductions to the academic discipline of visual culture).

the obfuscation, conquer the opaqueness, of the image' (Ferrell, Hayward and Young, 2008: 184–6). Instead of simply studying 'images' we need a new methodological orientation towards the visual that is capable of encompassing meaning, affect, situation, symbolic power and efficiency, and spectacle in the same 'frame'. This new approach must seek to fuse precise visual attentiveness with politically charged analysis, to be as attuned to representation and style as it is to the way visual culture impacts on individual and collective behaviour. As David Freedburg (1989, xxii) makes clear in his book *The Power of Images*: *Studies in the History and Theory of Response* (itself a work that urges art historians to take their analyses beyond traditional understandings of the 'image'): 'We must consider not only beholders' symptoms and behaviours, but also the effectiveness, efficacy, and vitality of images themselves; not only what beholders do, but also what images appear to do; not only what people do as a result of their relationship with imaged form, but also what they expect imaged form to achieve, and why they have such expectations at all'.

In keeping with such a philosophy, this book aims to help cultural criminologists go beyond simple analyses of the static image/picture and develop the theoretical and methodological tools needed to understand the dynamic force and power of visual culture. Such a task is now urgent. Contemporary visual representations of crime, transgression, and punishment take us far beyond the realm of the criminal justice system or law and order politics; even beyond established understandings of the media's role as 'a storehouse of illicit excitement', a ready resource for the voyeuristic consumption of violence and tragedy. Today, our world might best be described as a highly mediated 'crime fest', where the visual representation of crime and punishment plays out in reality TV theatres of the absurd and mediated spectacles of punitiveness. To paraphrase a famous quote by Gianni Vattimo and Wolfgang Welsch, over the last few years, the (visual) media has changed from simply conveying information or telling entertaining stories about crime, to actually shaping and producing its reality (Vattimo and Welsch, 1998: 7).

This is exactly the point at which cultural criminology enters the frame. Over the last decade or so, cultural criminology has emerged as a distinct theoretical, methodological, and interventionist approach that situates crime, criminality, and control squarely in the context of cultural dynamics (see e.g. Ferrell and Sanders, 1995; Presdee, 2000; Ferrell, Hayward and Young, 2008). From this view, crime and the agencies and institutions of crime control operate as cultural enterprises – that is, as richly symbolic endeavours created out of ongoing human interaction and power relations. As such, they must be read in terms of the contested meanings they carry; they must be interrogated as key social sites in which rules are created and broken, and where moral entrepreneurship, political innovation, and experiential resistance intersect. In undertaking this interrogation, cultural criminology often focuses theoretically on situated meaning and constructed social identity, and methodologically on forms of ethnography predicated on the Weberian tradition of 'verstehende sociologie' (see Ferrell, 1997). However, while early cultural criminological research emanating from the United States focused predominantly on rich, indexical cultural accounts of marginal deviant groups (e.g. Ferrell, 1993/1996; Hamm, 1995: see also Ferrell and Hamm, 1998), more recently, it has expanded its focus to include space, place, and cultural geography; the ongoing transformations and fluctuations associated with hypercapitalism; the vicissitudes of power, resistance, and state control; concepts of risk and embodied practice, and a whole host of other areas. The strength of the 'cultural approach', then, is the way it seeks to tackle the subject of crime and criminalization from a variety of new perspectives and academic disciplines. In effect, as I have stated elsewhere, its 'remit is to keep "turning the kaleidoscope" on the way we think about crime, and importantly, the legal and societal responses to rule-breaking' (Hayward and Young, 2007: 103). In all of this, cultural criminology attempts to reorient criminology to contemporary social and cultural changes, and so to imagine a 'post' or 'late modern' theory of crime and control. In this regard, cultural criminology conceptualizes many transgressive behaviours as attempts to resolve internal conflicts that are themselves spawned by the contradictions and peculiarities of contemporary life; put in different terms, 'cultural criminology seeks to fuse a phenomenology of contemporary transgression with a sociological analysis of late modern culture' (Hayward, 2004: 9).

Concepts such as situated meaning, symbolic richness, or cultural flow are, of course, meaningless unless they incorporate a thoroughgoing consideration and appreciation of the visual. Thankfully, cultural criminologists have had a long-standing interest in both symbolic interaction and the way meaning and power are negotiated and displayed through the efflorescences of mass-produced imagery. Similarly, from a methodological perspective, cultural criminology embraces visual analysis, with readings and counter readings of images and imaginative media/textual case studies and deconstructions featuring from the outset (see Ferrell, 1999: 406–8 and the international journal *Crime, Media, Culture*). How could it really be any other way? In our contemporary world of media festival and digital spectacle, the 'story' of crime and crime control is now promulgated as much through the image as through the word. Hence, cultural criminologists use the visual evidence of crime as a critical and pedagogic vehicle to illuminate the power of images in shaping popular understandings and social constructions of crime, deviance, and punishment.

From cell phone photographs and video footage shot in the combat zones of Iraq and Afghanistan and then posted online, to the grainy CCTV footage that drives the slurry of primetime 'cops and robbers' compilation shows (Fishman and Cavender, 1998; Rapaport, 2007), from unreal 'reality TV' moments that shape moral values and social norms, to stylized representations of crime and power in comic books (Nyberg, 1998; Williams, 1998) and even criminology textbook covers (Ferrell, Hayward and Young, 2008: 101–2), ours is a world in which 'the street scripts the screen and the screen scripts the street; [where] there is no clearly linear sequence, but rather a shifting interplay between the real and the virtual, the factual and the fictional. Late modern society is saturated with collective meaning and suffused with symbolic uncertainty as media messages and cultural traces swirl, circulate and vacillate' (ibid: 123).

Needless to say, such concerns are seen by some as a frippery, a marginal concern well beyond the scope and remit of mainstream (state-sanctioned) criminology. Nevertheless, as cultural criminologists have said many times before, dismissing this focus on visual imagery as a decorative or 'aesthetic' criminology is to mistake method for meaning. In a world where power is increasingly exercised through mediated representation and symbolic production, battles over image, style, and cultural representation emerge as essential moments in the contested negotiation of late modern reality.

However, if cultural criminology is keen to break free of the constraints of orthodox criminology, it is equally keen to escape the limitations associated with the existing scholarship on 'crime and the media'. To my mind, this relatively formulaic body of work (be it the 'objective' quantitative study of media forms associated with 'content analysis'; the decades old 'media effects' literature that attempts to unearth tangible causal linkages between media representations and subsequent audience behaviour; or the tradition of 'cultivation analysis' which seeks to explain how an excessive fear of crime is produced by a surfeit of 'anxiety-inducing' violent crime stories) is in desperate need of creative reinterpretation and reinvention. The goal must be to move beyond this static received body of knowledge and strive instead to understand and identify the various ways in which mediated processes of visual production and cultural exchange now 'constitute' the experience of crime, self, and society under conditions of late modernity. This is now an essential task for criminology. For while, traditionally, criminology has typically denied the visual and the sustained attention it deserves,[2] elsewhere in the ever-mutating world of the 'Mediascape' others working both within and against the criminal justice sphere are only too aware of 'the power of the image' and how it can be used both as a tool of control and resistance.

Consider, if you will, the extent to which contemporary Western police forces (along with the ever-expanding battalions of security and parapolicing agencies) now utilize camera technology and image monitoring in their everyday practice. Whether it's identifying 'known offenders' via 'algorithmic surveillance' systems; using dashboard-mounted cameras in police squad cars; the use of video recording in custody suites and during police interrogation; the photographing and videotaping of crowds and individuals at political demonstrations and protest marches; acting as consultants on the installation and operation of public and

2 Of course, criminology is not the only social science guilty of this charge. With few exceptions, sociology has also long ignored the visual as a primary source of data, prioritizing instead the two pillars of social scientific research, text and statistic. Thankfully, recent years have seen the flourishing of a fully fledged 'visual sociology' (see Harper, 1998; Papedemas, 2002; Stanczak, 2007; and especially the journal *Visual Studies*). One noteworthy exception within criminology is the expansive three volume set *Images of Crime* (2001, 2004, 2009), edited by Telemach Serassis, Harald Kania, and Hans-Jörg Albrecht.

privately funded urban CCTV systems; the deployment of mobile and static car license-plate recognition cameras; the use of TV shows like *C.O.P.S* and *L.A.P.D: Life on the Street* by certain police forces as both recruiting tools and informational devices to keep up with developments in other police departments;[3] and now even the deployment of miniaturized uniform and helmet-mounted personal video cameras by beat officers, it's clear that police work is now very much visual work. Indeed, one might even venture that we are fast approaching the point where prospective police officers might be better off enrolling on a media studies course than a criminal justice degree!

But the power of the image – be it a crime scene photograph, a slice of low-res CCTV footage from a surveillance film, or a car chase shot from a police helicopter cam – is not something that the State and its agents can ever fully own or control. Far from it – the force of the image, the power and spectacle of the visual is simply too multidimensional. Images permeate the flow of cultural meaning in any number of ways, and just as they can be used to serve the State, they can also be used to critique and undermine it. One of the tasks of cultural criminology, then, is to insinuate itself into this flow. We must begin to use images and visual culture for our own ends, to make hard turns towards uncertainty and surprise amidst the saturating spiral of mass culture. For example, just as one interest group seeks to control or possess an image for its own purposes, another group can steal it right back and subject it to a cultural hijacking and a radical reversal of meaning.

Anyone who has attended a protest march, a political demonstration, or even a football match in the UK over the last few years will no doubt be familiar with the sight of police officers photographing and filming the scene for surveillance and crowd control purposes. Now while, for some, such practices are just further evidence of an all-consuming Big Brother state, for others, it's the trigger for organization and resistance; a way of practically invoking Jean Baudrillard's (2005) portentous statement that '… those who live by the spectacle will die by the spectacle' (see also Retort, 2004).

Heading out for Sushi on Second Avenue during the summer of 2004, New Yorker Alexander Dunlop inadvertently stumbled upon a demonstration against

3 And then, of course, there's the troubling (and largely unremarked upon) relationship that exists between police forces and TV executives involved in the production of 'reality' policing shows – a strand of programming that has become so popular it now constitutes its own genre: the so-called 'criminal vérité' format (one example, the 'real life' police show, *C.O.P.S.*, has spawned over 600 episodes, and grossed in excess of $200 million in the process). While many of these shows such as *World's Wildest Police Videos* and *Police, Camera, Action*, are little more than tawdry compilations of sensationalist car chases or traffic stops gone bad, there's also the phenomenon of the police 'ride along' show, where a TV crew follows and films officers involved in every aspect of police work, from traffic cop, to dog handler, to helicopter squad. What's interesting about these shows is the way they are used by the police forces themselves both as a visual recruiting sergeant and as a form of 'image management' – 30-minute, media-friendly police promo videos.

the Republican Party's National Convention. Realising his mistake, Dunlop tried to extricate himself from the area but found his path blocked by riot police setting up a perimeter around the area; a process that, in a bizarre physical manifestation of Stan Cohen's (1985) famous criminological dictum 'widening the net and thinning the mesh', involved the deployment of an eight-foot-high plastic mesh fence and the subsequent arrest of anyone found on the 'wrong side' of the temporary barricade (Clancy, 2007). Within minutes, Dunlop was arrested, handcuffed, manhandled onto a bus, and transferred to a temporary holding facility at Pier 57. Held overnight, he was eventually charged with disorderly conduct, resisting arrest, parading without a permit, and obstructing government administration. When Dunlop's attorney, Michael Conroy, challenged the arrest, he was provided with an official police video tape of the demonstration showing his client's arrest and subsequent processing. However, as an evidential record, the tape was seriously flawed. It contained a number of jump cuts that omitted Dunlop asking for police advice about how to exit the demonstration and also the key moment when he ultimately, very calmly, resigned himself to the spurious arrest. In short, the tape had been selectively edited. Enter Eileen Clancy, one of the leading figures of *I-Witness video*, an activist group who specialize in videotaping events that have the potential to spark civil liberties infringements. Expecting trouble, *I-Witness video* had been organising workshops and training up teams of videographers to shoot footage that could be used as part of a legal defence against mass arrests. This resulted in a 'treasure trove' of hundreds of tapes, including one that contained the vital missing moments in the Dunlop arrest. Conroy subsequently used the footage to successfully defend his client, but it did not stop there. As a result of the coordinated efforts of *I-Witness video*, the National Lawyers Guild and others, the vast majority of the cases brought against those arrested at the convention protest were subsequently dismissed.

A year or so later, a separate but not totally unrelated incident occurred that illustrates how the power of the image is being further democratized as a result of the panoptic gaze of digital citizenry. It is 28 July 2008 and Times Square is deluged by hundreds of bicyclists as the activist group Critical Mass holds one of its monthly rides. During the ride, committed urban cyclist Christopher Long, 29, is involved in a collision with Rookie NYPD officer Patrick Pogan. Tension has been running high between the NYPD and Critical Mass since 2004, when 250 riders were arrested for parading without a permit during a protest rally against the aforementioned Republican National Convention. Perhaps no surprise, then, that Long was arrested on charges of 'Attempted Assault in the Third Degree', 'Resisting Arrest' and, 'Disorderly Conduct'. However, within days of the incident, a video of the collision (shot by a tourist) surfaced. It revealed that, far from being Long's fault, the 'collision' had been caused deliberately by Officer Pogan who violently body slammed Long off his bike and onto the pavement (Eligon and Moynihan, 2008). Within days, the story was taken up and publicized by video activists such as the Glass Bead Collective, the TIMES UP Video Collective, and *I-Witness Video*, all groups who know more than a thing or two

Figure 1.1 Two wheels bad for Officer Pogan.
Source: YouTube.com

about using the image in defence of civil liberties. This small collision became big news (at the time of writing over 1.6 million people had viewed the YouTube footage of the incident) – and ultimately big trouble for Officer Pogan. In an incredible volte-face by the NYPD, Pogan was first suspended and later indicted by a Manhattan grand jury for falsifying a police report and assault. In the words of *I-Witness's* Eileen Clancy, 'This indictment is a signal event for video activists. Despite the abundance of video showing that police officers have fabricated charges against people arrested at demonstrations, in New York City at least, we have never before achieved an indictment of a police officer for lying in a sworn statement' (Clancy, 2008).

Like these video bloggers and activists, cultural criminologists must also work to 'become the media' and use the power of the image as a tool for understanding and monitoring issues surrounding crime and criminal justice (see Hoffman and Brown, this volume).[4] That said, the focus of this book is not on video activism per se (see Gregory *et al.*, 2001 and Harding, 2001 for useful introductions to this

4 At this point, one is compelled to mention the work of Hughes Leglise-Bataille, the photographer who shot our cover image. A specialist in protest and riot photography, Hughes' work consistently transcends the division between art and politics.

field; and relatedly David, 2007).[5] Instead, as stated earlier, the goal of this collection is to make a case for *the importance of the image within criminology more generally*. It is my belief that, given the ascendant position of the image/visual in contemporary culture, it is increasingly important that *all* criminologists are familiar with the various ways in which crime and 'the story of crime' is imaged, constructed, and 'framed' within modern society. This collection therefore offers criminologists, be they academics or students, policy makers, or theoreticians, a more general overview of this relational dynamic, as theorized through the critical paradigm known as 'cultural criminology'.

However, it is not enough simply to theorize or interrogate the visual. Whilst this collection will certainly help the reader unearth the hidden social and ideological concerns that frequently underpin images of crime, violence, and transgression, it has another aim: to point the way forward for those keen to embark on their own cultural criminological visual analyses. Given that many academic criminologists and the vast majority of criminology students have little if any experience of media studies, let alone visual cultural analysis, this book will outline and articulate some of the methodological strengths and conundrums associated with research into the 'looping' and 'spiralling' processes of the crime-media nexus (see Manning, 1998; Ferrell, Hayward and Young, 2008: 129–37). To this end, each chapter has a short 'Methodological Reflections' section offering some thoughts and advice for those wishing to conduct their own visually focused criminology project.

So to the various chapters that comprise this collection. However, before introducing the individual essays, a brief word about what you will *not* find in this book. As with any text, there is only so much that can be addressed in any meaningful detail and thus inevitably certain related areas of interest are not covered. You will not, for example, find any sustained attention paid to subjects such as the 'psychological' and 'behavioural' responses surrounding the relationship between image and beholder, or film-theoretical issues such as cinematographic technique, the psychoanalytic interpretation of semiotics,[6] interpellation, or 'narrative desire' etc. The mandate of this book likewise does not extend to include aesthetics, art history, or the changing relationships between images and people over history. Neither does it attempt to resolve the theoretical imbroglio surrounding the 'media effects' debate, or the ongoing dispute within cultural studies about the distinction between so called 'high' and 'low' culture(s). Similarly, we make no claims to summarize the voluminous body of research produced by the many disparate fields that constitute visual media studies.

5 See also Alfonso *et al.* (2004) and Pink (2006) for introductions to the field of video ethnography, a social research method that aims to 'capture the detail and nuance of social interactions in context more intensely than audio or written description' (Rhodes and Fitzgerald, 2006: 351).

6 For a thoughtful primer on how to understand and employ semiotics in (visual) criminological research, see Mariana Valverde's *Law and Order: Images, Meanings and Myths* (2006, Chs 2 and 3).

Nor do we attempt to condense the criminology-specific empirical research on the media representation of crime (see Ericson, 1995; Kidd-Hewitt and Osborne, 1995; Reiner, 2002; Carter and Weaver, 2003; Jewkes, 2004; Boyle, 2005; Trend, 2007; and Carrabine, 2008 for eloquent and comprehensive summaries). Instead, we have stuck to our stated aim of understanding the theoretical and methodological nuances involved in the relationship between *cultural criminology and the image/the visual*. To this end, we have gathered together an impressive roster of academics well known in Australia, Continental Europe, North America, and the United Kingdom for their insightful works on cultural criminology. However, *Framing Crime*: *Cultural Criminology and the Image* is not just another collection of 'sexy' essays wherein each author is afforded free range to indulge their own gaze. Rather, we have sought a degree of consistency; the goal being the creation of a cohesive collection of topics that, when taken together, break new ground for cultural criminology without ever becoming esoteric or abstract. Yet a word of caution: these twelve essays are not meant to be 'the' definitive statement on cultural criminology and the visual – far from it. Instead, they should be seen as more suggestive than diagrammatic; a series of metaphors rather than an accumulation of static models. Otherwise, in the very attempt to engage with the fluidity of contemporary culture, we risk reifying our own understandings, risk forgetting that these understandings are at best useful ephemera in the emergent construction of collective meaning.

The collection opens with two chapters on the photograph/photography. Constructing a picture of the photographic 'spectacle' and its practices in the arena of crime and punishment, Phil Carney's opening essay takes us on a historical journey from the invention of photography in 1839, through to our contemporary mediated world of late-modern digital entertainments. In a rich account of how colonial anthropologists, criminal positivists, and others sought to use the photograph as an aid to the scientific science of identification, the rise of newspaper photography, and the emergence of paparazzi, Carney asserts that what is omnipresent in this history is the way the photograph has functioned as a 'social practice of production'. In this case, the production of a modern *spectacle* that turns around theatres of crime and punishment constituted from the performative force of the photograph and its associated festive dynamics of desire and power. Staying with the modern image par excellence – the photograph – but changing the focal lens, Jeff Ferrell and Cécile Van de Voorde's chapter explores the photodocumentary tradition. Reviewing the work of celebrated photographers such as W. Eugene Smith, Robert Capa, and Henri Cartier-Bresson, the chapter shows how in the hands of a skilled practitioner, the photograph becomes an archetype that captures and condenses visual knowledge. However, this is no didactic history. In a comprehensive methods section, Ferrell and Van de Voorde offer advice on how cultural criminologists might undertake their own photodocumentaries; to click the camera shutter on their own 'decisive moment', whether that moment is found at the soup kitchen, the political demonstration, the street corner, or on the steps of the criminal courts.

Continuing the analysis of how photographs are used to frame social and personal life in specific ways and from particular angles, Philip Jones and Claire Wardle's chapter highlights how photographic representations of criminals (when juxtaposed with text, headlines, and accompanying captions) are manipulated by tabloid newspapers to shape popular opinion about crime, justice, and wrong doing. Focusing on the pictorial press coverage of three centre-right British newspapers of the high profile Soham Murder Trial, Jones and Wardle unearth disturbing evidence of how newspaper-formatting techniques encourage readers to draw entirely misleading conclusions about the case and its prosecution. Given the influence of the tabloid press, it is perhaps strange that media scholars have tended to overlook the powerful role of page layout and image montages in the news-making spectacle. This chapter provides a much-needed corrective.

A second batch of three chapters, in the words of Majid Yar, takes cultural criminology to the movies. Yar sets the scene by arguing that a thoroughgoing understanding of the cinematic construction of crime (in all its manifold dimensions) must play a central role in the project of cultural criminology. His essay starts by reviewing the established social science approaches to film study (content analysis, the Marxist tradition of film analysis, and, finally, an overview of the postmodern approach to reading film), before suggesting that the best way forward for cultural criminology is to transcend these models and develop instead a new 'synthetic critical framework for crime film analysis'. In a sweeping critique of Hollywood crime movies that encompasses such diverse offerings as *Bad Lieutenant* and *Catch Me If You Can*, Yar maps out a distinctive, alternative approach to reading crime film that captures the richness and diversity of film texts, whilst simultaneously discerning the ways in which they play a role in the wider politics of law, order, and punishment. Staying with Hollywood film, but changing tack, Alison Young's chapter turns more around the relationship between the spectator and the image. Drawing on the tradition of 'criminological aesthetics' (see Young, 2004), Professor Young aims to 'discover how law, violence and justice appear and re-appear in the image on screen, in order to open up and give access to the *affective* dimension of crime and its structures of identification'. For Young, the emotions that haunt the public imagination are interlaced with media dynamics – something she calls the *affective processes* associated with crime representation. Her chapter therefore urges, or perhaps more accurately, challenges cultural criminologists to follow her lead and make the affective dimension the starting-point for future interrogations of the cinematic imagination of justice and injustice. In the final chapter on film, Alexandra Campbell uses the Hollywood movie *The Siege* as a case study to illustrate how political and nationalistic ideologies circulate in the 'cultural script'. For Campbell, the meanings contrived through films such as Edward Zwick's 1998 'terrorist cell thriller', *The Siege*, do not remain confined to the world of fiction. Instead, they provide a lens or framework for interpreting events and identities, insidiously compelling us to understand the world in particularized ways.

Campbell asserts that *The Siege* is a classic expression of an age old 'orientalist' Hollywood gaze that stereotypes Muslims as a 'dangerous Other' or 'enemy'. Drawing on semiotic and textual analysis to deconstruct the film, Campbell's thoughtful chapter illustrates how such images and narratives of the 'Muslim-Other' ultimately serve to reaffirm misguided understandings of terrorism and counter-terrorist measures within the public imagination.

Moving from Hollywood film to images of crime and law in artwork, Chris Cunneen's chapter argues that cultural criminology opens a new space for understanding crime where the image is produced by those who are victims of crime and, at the same time, without access to other channels of communication within mainstream social and political institutions. Using a fascinating series of Australian Aboriginal artworks as his research data, Cunneen shows how one can use these images to both critique the unthinking imposition of colonial law on the Aboriginal way of life, and, importantly, as a powerful medium for expressing the oft-neglected nuances and subtleties of Aboriginal law and culture. Stephen Muzzati also embarks on a nuanced reading of cultural artefacts, only this time his chosen subject matter takes an all the more ubiquitous and corrosive form. While advertisements envelop our every turn, occupying the pages of newspapers and magazines, saturating our television programming and web surfing, and increasingly transforming public spaces into corporate billboards, they have been subject to surprisingly little criminological analysis. Some, of course, will assert that there is good reason for this: what, after all, have commercials got to do with criminology? Cultural criminologists take issue with such a position, and Muzzati's engaging essay contributes to a growing tranche of cultural criminological research that explores and critiques the increasing use of transgressive visual imagery in contemporary advertising (see e.g. Presdee, 2000; Hayward, 2004). Focusing specifically on automobile commercials, Muzzati shows how, in a desperate bid to boost the flagging sales of increasingly redundant Sports Utility Vehicles and fuel-inefficient luxury cars, late-modern advertisers now regularly base their advertising and marketing campaigns on romanticized tropes of transgression and crime, allied with visual motifs of conspicuous disobedience.

Bruce Hoffman and Michelle Brown's chapter turns our attention away from figurative and imagined representations of crime and resistance and directs us back to an earlier theme of photo (or more accurately visual) documentary. Employing the 'new technologies of digital filmmaking' Hoffman and Brown show us that, as a consequence of the 'digital revolution', it is now possible – indeed wholly advisable – for cultural criminologists to think about producing their own short or feature length 'newsmaking' documentaries. Drawing on their own experiences of videoing the media circus that engulfed the execution of Oklahoma Bomber Timothy McVeigh in 2001, Professors Brown and Hoffman offer reflections and advice about how documentary filmmaking can function to challenge and destabilize the dominant frames of meaning that underpin the mainstream broadcast media.

No collection concerned with how crime is imaged would be complete without a chapter on the representation of transgression and deviance on the internet – surely now society's most fecund seedbed for the spread of violent imagery. Damian Zaitch and Tom de Leeuw analyse the construction, performance, and recreation of identity by football hooligan groups (specifically Dutch '*Casuals*' or 'hard-core' football supporters, and Argentinean *Barras Bravas*) on the internet. Closely Dissecting photos, photomontages, video posts, and other forms of 'bricolaged online iconography', Dutch criminologists Zaitch and de Leeuw take us inside the *sub rosa* world of subcultural football violence; highlighting a number of critical issues about the cultural performance of football supporters rarely addressed either by mainstream 'hooligan' research, or by internet violence studies.

Bringing the collection to a close, the criminologist and legal scholar, Wayne Morrison, continues his campaign to develop a more global criminology capable of encompassing topics traditionally excluded from the canon, such as the crimes of war and genocide. Here, he focuses on four harrowing images of human suffering that span the Spanish conquest of the Americas in the fifteenth century, nineteenth-century colonial exploitation of central Africa, and the low point of twentieth-century genocidal history, the Nazi Holocaust. Morrison's goal is twofold: to illustrate the complex processes by which such 'atrocity images' are produced, collected, and edited; and to offer a series of challenging reflections about the role of the visual within criminology. Traversing both historical epoch and the disciplinary divisions that exist between criminology and juridical-legal analysis, Morrison's essay adroitly illuminates the power of the image, but it also raises unsettling philosophical questions about the nature of the relationship between the spectator and the image of atrocity.

It is established academic convention for opening chapters of edited collections to introduce and summarize the essays that follow. However, it is less common to reflect on how the reader might 'see' the volume as a conceptual whole. When taking in a landscape, billboard, or photograph, one approaches the image from different angles, focuses on different aspects, sees within it different things. It is hoped that the same is true of the eclectic mix of critical articles, case studies, and visual deconstructions that have been gathered together here. As mentioned above, cultural criminology's goal is to keep 'turning the kaleidoscope' on the way we think about crime, and this is never truer than when we try to make sense of the ever-mutating world of the late modern Mediascape. If we are to broaden and enliven criminological teaching and research in the area of visual culture, we cannot afford to regress to simplistic, monolithic methods. It is no longer sufficient just to count or codify images, or even to strive to unearth spurious *causal linkages* between media representations and subsequent human behaviour. Instead, we must approach our subject matter as a person studies an album of photographs or as a visitor approaches a painting in a gallery – from various angles and from diverse perspectives. If images are creatively constructed, then we must study not just the image itself, but also the process of construction and the subsequent processes of production, framing, and interpretation. In other words, cultural criminology's relationship with the image/the visual must be a creative one that recognizes images as carefully crafted moments (see relatedly, Nisbet, 1976).

Perhaps, then, it is fitting that this introduction concludes on an artistic note. The Canadian art photographer and academic Jeff Wall is frequently described by critics as 'a storyteller'. He describes himself as 'a painter of modern life'. Since 1977 he has used backlit transparencies and large-format black-and-white photographs mounted in light boxes to create a series of extraordinarily intense, almost cinematographic images that challenge social reality, explore the phenomenology of experience, and champion the lives of oppressed groups in American society.[7] In a short essay celebrating the visual force of Wall's work, the art historian Jean-Christophe Ammann makes the following important observation: documentaries, he asserts, have shown us the difference between a picture and a document: *a picture is always likewise a document, but a document is certainly not always a picture*. 'Jeff Wall operates with both types, transforming pictures into documents and documents into pictures. He achieves this dialectic tour de force – which links history, narration, art history, and everyday life to the present – with a masterful feel for the picture' (Ammann, 2001: 11). If cultural criminology is to move forward in the study and interpretation of images of crime and transgression, and if it is to develop new theoretical expressions of discovery and documentation, it too must strive to achieve 'a masterful feel for the picture' – a mastery that is at once both creative and critical.

In another time, Erving Goffman (1974) famously wrote that 'frames' both organize the past and help shape and determine how new experiences are felt and interpreted. The hope for *Framing Crime* is that it will also help shape and interpret cultural criminology's future experiences, as it strives to make sense of a world in which the image is truly ascendant.

7 Wall also knows something about the immediacy of crime, having had a gun pulled on him by a disgruntled student during a brief stint as a professor of photography at the Düsseldorf Academy in 1996.

References

Alfonso, A.I., Kurti, L. and Pink, S. (eds) (2004) *Working Images: Visual Research and Representation in Ethnography*, London: Routledge.

Ammann, J-C. (2001) 'Jeff Wall Opened My Eyes', in R. Lauter (ed.) *Jeff Wall: Figures and Places – Selected Works from 1978–2000*, Munich: Prestel.

Appadurai, A. (1996) *Modernity at Large*, Minneapolis: University of Minnesota Press.

Banks, M. (2001) *Visual Methods in Social Research*, London: Sage.

Baudrillard, J. (2005) 'War Porn', *International Journal of Baudrillard Studies*, January Vol 2 (1) Trans: Paul A. Taylor.

Boyle, K. (2005) *Media and Violence*, London: Sage.

Carrabine, E. (2008) *Crime, Culture and the Media*, Cambridge: Polity.

Carter, C. and Weaver, C. K. (2003) *Violence and the Media*, Buckingham: Open University Press.

Clancy, E. (2007) 'Documenting Transgression: Filming the Streets, Filming the Cops', Paper presented at *On the Edge*: *Transgression and the Dangerous Other Conference*, John Jay College of Criminal Justice and The CUNY Graduate Center, New York City, 9–10th August.

Clancy, E. (2008) 'Indicted! NYPD Officer who Tackled Cyclist', <http://iwitnessvideo> (info accessed 20 February 2009).

Cohen, S. (1985) *Visions of Social Control*: *Crime*, *Punishment and Classification*, Oxford: Polity Press.

David, E. (2007) 'Signs of Resistance: Marking Public Space Through a Renewed Cultural Activism', in G. Stancak (ed.) *Visual Research Methods*, Los Angeles: Sage.

Democracy Now (2005) 'NY Law Enforcement Caught Doctoring Video of RNC Arrests', <www.democracynow.org> (accessed 18 February 2009).

Dikovitskaya, M. (2006) *Visual Culture*: *The Study of the Visual after the Cultural Turn*, Cambridge, MA: The MIT Press.

Eligon, J. and Moynihan, C. (2008) 'Police Officer Seen on Tape Is Indicted', *New York Times*, 15 December.

Ericson, R. (1995) *Crime and the Media*, Aldershot: Dartmouth.

Ferrell, J. (1993/1996) *Crimes of Style*, New York: Garland Publishing/Boston: Northeastern University Press.

Ferrell, J. (1997) 'Criminological *Verstehen*: Inside the Immediacy of Crime', *Justice Quarterly*, 14(1): 3–23.

Ferrell, J. (1999) 'Cultural Criminology', *Annual Review of Sociology*, 25: 395–418.

Ferrell, J. and Hamm, M. (1998) *Ethnography at the Edge*, Boston: Northeastern University Press.

Ferrell, J. and Sanders, C. (1995) *Cultural Criminology*, Boston: Northeastern University Press.

Ferrell, J., Hayward, K.J. and Young, J. (2008) *Cultural Criminology*: *An Invitation*, London: Sage.

Ferrell, J., Hayward, K.J., Morrison, W. and Presdee, M. (2004) (eds) *Cultural Criminology Unleashed*, London: GlassHouse

Fishman, M. and Cavender, G. (1998) *Entertaining Crime*, New York: Aldine de Gruyter.

Freedburg, D. (1989) *The Power of Images*: *Studies in the History and Theory of Response*, Chicago: Chicago University Press.

Goffman, E. (1974) *Frame Analysis*: *An Essay on the Organisation of Experience*, Boston: Northeastern University Press.

Gregory, S., Caldwell, G., Avni, R. and Harding, T. (2001) *Video For Change*: *A Guide to Advocacy and Activism*, London: Pluto.

Hamm, M. (1995) *American Skinheads*: *The Criminology and Control of Hate Crime*, Greenwood Press.

Harding, T. (2001) *The Video Activist Handbook*, London: Pluto.

Harper, D. (1998) 'An Argument for Visual Sociology', in J. Prosser (ed.) *Image-Based Research*, London: Routledge.

Hayward, K. (2004) *City Limits*: *Crime*, *Consumer Culture and the Urban Experience*, London: GlassHouse.

Hayward, K. and Young, J. (2004) 'Cultural Criminology: Some Notes on the Script', *Theoretical Criminology*, 8(3): 259–73.

Hayward, K. and Young, J. (2007) 'Cultural Criminology', in M. Maguire, R. Morgan, and R. Reiner (eds) *The Oxford Handbook of Criminology*, 4th edn, Oxford: Oxford University Press.

Jewkes, Y. (2004) *Media and Crime*, London: Sage.

Kidd-Hewitt, D. and Osborne, R. (1995) *Crime and the Media*, London: Pluto.

Manning, P. (1998) 'Media Loops', in F. Bailey and D. Hale (eds) *Popular Culture, Crime and Justice*, Belmont, CA: Wadsworth.

Mirzoeff, N. (1999) *An Introduction to Visual Culture*, London: Routledge.

Nisbet, R.A. (1976) *Sociology as an Art Form*, London: Heinemann.

Nyberg, A. (1998) 'Comic Books and Juvenile Delinquency: A Historical Perspective', in F. Bailey and D. Hale (eds) *Popular Culture, Crime, and Justice*. Belmont, CA: West/Wadsworth.

Pademas, D. (2002) *Visual Sociology: Teaching With Film/Video, Photography, and Visual Media*, American Sociological Association.

Pink, S. (2006) *Doing Visual Ethnography: Images, Media and Representation in Research*, London: Sage.

Presdee, M. (2000) *Cultural Criminology and the Carnival of Crime*, London: Routledge.

Rapaport, R. (2007) 'Dying and Living in "*COPS*" America', *San Francisco Chronicle*, 7 January.

Reiner, R. (2002) 'Media Made Criminality: The Representations of Crime in the Mass Media', in M. Maguire, R. Morgan, and R. Reiner (eds) *The Oxford Handbook of Criminology*, Oxford: Oxford University Press.

Retort (2004) 'Afflicted Powers: The State, the Spectacle and September 11', *New Left Review*, 27 May/June: 5–21.

Rhodes, T. and Fitzgerald, J. (2006) 'Visual Data in Addictions Research: Seeing Comes Before Words?', *Addiction Research and Theory*, 14(4): 349–63.

Serassis, T., Kania, H. and Albrecht, H-J. (2001, 2004, 2009) *Images of Crime* (Vols I, II and III), Berlin: Max-Planck-Institut.

Stanczak, G. (2007) *Visual Research Methods*, Los Angeles: Sage.

Trend, D. (2007) *The Myth of Media Violence*, Oxford: Blackwell.

Valverde, M. (2006) *Law and Order: Images, Meanings, and Myths*, New Brunswick, NJ: Rutgers University Press.

Vattimo, G. and Welsch, W. (1998) (eds) *Medien-Welten Wirklichkeiten*, Munich.

Virilio, P. (1986) *Speed and Politics*, New York: Semiotext(e).

Virilio, P. (1991) *The Aesthetics of Disappearance*, New York: Semiotext(e).

Williams, J. (1998) 'Comic Books: A Tool of Subversion?' in S. Anderson and G. Howard (eds) *Interrogating Popular Culture*, Guilderland, NY: Harrow and Heston.

Young, A. (2004) *Judging the Image*, London: Routledge.

Chapter 2

Crime, punishment and the force of photographic spectacle

Phil Carney

> [...] the picture of a crime presented in the right stage conditions is something infinitely more dangerous to the mind than if the same crime were committed in real life.
>
> Antonin Artaud (1970)

Introduction

When Susan Sontag first visited the Cathedral at Orvieto, she was disappointed. It was not as rich as the images she had seen in the architecture books. Likewise visitors to the Grand Canyon have been known to wonder why it falls short of the astonishing imagery available in the magazines and films. Daniel Boorstin imagined the response of a proud mother who was told that her baby is beautiful: 'Oh that's nothing – you should see his photograph!' Boorstin, the first simulation theorist, was of course bemoaning our unwarranted attachment to the distractions and falsities of the image.

Such a view is conditioned by a long history of Western representation. Social and cultural theorists are accustomed to conceiving of the photograph as a *reproduction*, as an image of something from somewhere else. It is in this way that we risk being seduced by the problem of meaning and representation. We ask 'what does this photograph represent?' or 'what does it mean?', as if photographic practice in all its many social and cultural dimensions is reducible to a small, pale cipher on a surface. Is it any surprise that we might distrust what we see, that we might cede the field to the theorists of textual interpretation, semiotics and psychoanalysis? Here photography must always fail. It is never fully adequate to the object or meaning it seeks to convey. It is never as good as the real thing, or it always hides the real meaning. The photograph falls short, its frame and focus amputate a material or symbolic reality. Jean Baudrillard, perhaps the last high priest of representation, went as far as to argue that the photograph had lost contact with reality altogether. It was just a simulation. Guy Debord and the Situationists urged us to turn away from the empty, illusory image in the spectacle and embrace instead a different politics.

However, another perspective on photography is possible: it *produces* more than it reproduces. It is no longer a deficit but a surplus. It is less a pale symbol and more a social force. What *really happens* occurs in and through the photograph. Understood in this way, we are now obliged to relegate the logic of meaning and simulation to its proper place and appreciate the social practice of photography as *production*. Instead of thinking of the photograph as a deficient image of something else, what if we think of it as a social process of producing images, whether images in the real, or images in fantasy?

One of the intentions of this chapter is to argue the importance of the photograph as a social practice of production, in this case the production of the modern *spectacle*. Photography is a social activity not just in the special events like births, marriages and holidays, but something more everyday in which we both take photographs and perform for the camera. More and more of us carry cameras *all the time* in the form of mobile phones. In another dimension of our everyday life, photography is encountered in newspapers, magazines, on advertising hoardings and product packaging: image practices everywhere. Television, cinema and digital disc, though associated with sound recording and broadcast, are predominantly photographic experiences. In the wide new world of the Internet, the photograph populates virtual space as much as it does our actual space. On television, there are now shows in which control by closed-circuit television is also an opportunity for entertainment in candid camera programmes as well as in the footage of strange happenings and crimes released to the mass media by the authorities. We are looking through a photographic medium to see more photography, and the same happens in cinema or TV drama in which photographs are frequently used as dramatic tools. Every major sporting event now has its photographic apparatus with dozens of camera angles, fixed and mobile. A 'big screen' is now part of large stadium architecture, showing the television view when the direct view is not good enough. Spectators catch themselves on the screen, and thus on television, and the television audience sees their smiles as they see themselves as we see them. Spectatorial performance is part of the event.

Thus, the pluripotent force of the photographic spectacle is everywhere, whether in our personal lives, entertainment, the commodity, the news, the Internet, or, indeed, as a power of control, on CCTV or identity documentation and archives.

Our photographic culture involves us all in the social practices of spectacular production. It inserts us into the powers and desires of the spectacle. In this chapter, I want to examine an important aspect of this force of spectacle through a brief history of its development in modernity, and in particular the spectacle of crime and punishment. I hope to give the reader a sense of the importance of the photographic spectacle and spectatorship to modernity: we now live in a photographic culture in which we are both actors and audience.

From the outset, we should appreciate that the photographic spectacle is no mere image, backdrop, illustration or portrait *of* our lives. It flows through us as a part of our social being. It is not an image of our lives; it is part of our lives. What do we mean by this term 'spectacle'? In one sense, we are talking about the mass media, but here the term spectacle will be used in order to focus on social practice extending well beyond that of communication. In this way, the aim is to show some of the links between mass-mediated practices and performances of everyday life. If, crudely put, the photographic spectacle involves the photograph in mass circulation, then we do not merely gawp at it, we participate in its forces. If we are spectators, we are *active*. We bring to the power of spectacle our own desires, our own social practices and our own practical spectatorship.

In this chapter, we will conduct a small history of spectacle with a set of purposes in mind. The primary aim is to bring out the importance of the photographic spectacle to an understanding of modernity and thus to the project of cultural criminology. In order to understand the dynamics of spectacle, we will emphasize the participatory and active spectator, thus the dependence of spectacle on *festival* in crime and punishment. The spectator brings festive *desire* to the spectacle. Thus, we will also bring out the complex multiplicity of spectacle involving festive loops between image performance and spectators. We will also look at how the circulating photograph can *mark* bodies with the stigma of shame, a force used in the interacting fields of popular entertainment, celebrity and the punishment of criminal bodies. Finally, we will embark on a conceptual and methodological detour in an attempt to deal with a central idea of *spectacular practice* in the context of the problem of method. Throughout, there will be an awareness of the interlinked roles of power and desire in this photographic culture of crime and punishment and hence the importance of a *critical* approach.

How we write about photography, of the photographic enterprise itself, as well as how we interpret it, is a practice that must be cultural, creative and sensitive to the dynamics of the image. Such an approach should also involve an awareness that the lines of force running in and through an image are unruly. They do not follow straight lines. We should therefore be sensitive to the dangers of compressing the photograph and its social forces into simplistic, linear and logical narratives. When we describe a painting, for example, there is no 'beginning' or 'end', there is no straight line through the picture. Even more so for the photograph, because what we see in front of our eyes is never reducible to a set of linear principles, nor can it ever pretend to be 'objective'. In this chapter, I will attempt to build a 'picture' of the photographic spectacle and its practices in the arena of crime and punishment.

Focus

Predation, punishment and paparazzi: a small history of modern spectacle

The birth of our modernity is associated with the rise of a public or mass culture of spectatorship. In our growing cities, consumerism expanded alongside a keen desire to participate in collective forms of viewing pleasure. The apparent chaos of the new urban crowd in the nineteenth century belied the establishment of an organized *audience* (Schwartz, 1998) and the construction of public fields in which spectacle was seen (Clark, 1985). These fields of vision included the written and illustrated news, shopping avenues, arcades and department stores, the display of commodities, the new theatres, cafés and restaurants, parks and museums, novel forms of entertainment such as the panorama, diorama and the wax-work display, and the rapidly growing practices of commercial tourism (see also Hayward [2004] for a cultural criminological discussion of how some of these processes impacted on the urban experience).

Schwartz argues that the attitude of the *flâneur* – a concept emerging from Walter Benjamin's study of Baudelaire, wherein he describes a certain, leisured, mobile individual who delights in the sights of the modern city from a certain anonymous, detached, though far from hidden position – characterizes the spectator in this period. Whether as tourist or *flâneur*, the modern spectator is a physically active, mobile figure who is part of the urban spectacle. Amid this spectacle, and contributing to its forms and forces, there arises the circulating photograph, ushering in a new image world. The urban crowd mixed in architectural space but also in the new spaces opened up by the photographic world.

After its invention in 1839, photography soon became, in Benjamin's words, an 'art of the fairground'. Indeed the name most associated with its invention in France, Louis-Jacques-Mandé Daguerre, had been a showman working on the popular technologies of theatrical spectacle and the new diorama (Gernsheim and Gernsheim, 1968). At the same time as Daguerre's innovation was announced in France, Fox Talbot in Britain invented the negative-positive process which allowed for the potentially infinite reproduction of the photograph and its circulation in mass markets. Photography moved in two directions at once: first, towards the astonishingly real, and, second, through the manipulation of image development, towards the fantastic (Kracauer, 1960). Both of these practices would contribute to the fascination and surprise of the photographic spectacle, the former in news, documentary and portraiture, the latter in cinema, advertising and packaging.

In this new spectacle, the burgeoning middle classes not only collected images of the rich and famous, of politicians and royalty, prominent business figures, scientists and entertainers, but also thronged to have photographs taken of themselves, thus gradually learning to perform in and through the image. At the same time, imperial science acquired a taste for anthropologically exotic figures, whilst domestic governments sought to capture portraits of criminals. Both entered the general circulation of photographic images. If the spectacle of public punishment had rapidly declined in the early nineteenth century, the new spectacle was to open up different forms of spectatorship of crime and punishment. Thus, the photographers who were hired to take images of the arrested in order to trace recidivism amidst the crowd of faces in the ever-expanding prison found that they could supplement their income by selling the images to interested consumers.

Paris, 'the capital of the nineteenth century', witnessed new desires for the real – simulated or otherwise – such as those of the waxwork museum and the Paris morgue (Schwartz, 1998). Opening in 1882, the Musée Grevin's display of waxworks of the famous and infamous was an immediate popular attraction. Prominent among the waxwork tableaux were celebrated crimes, feeding a hunger for the kind of sensation now also found in the popular newspapers. In 1864, the police opened the Paris morgue to the public in the hope that they might aid the identification of dead bodies found in the streets and waterways. Of course, most were driven by curiosity rather than any realistic chance of helping the authorities, making the morgue a great popular attraction. Along with the waxwork museum and the newspapers, the morgue betokened a growing passion to see criminal traces and events in a theatre of the real.

With new technology and increasing levels of literacy, the mass-circulated newspaper became progressively more profitable from the mid-nineteenth century onwards. Its daily news developed an interest in what the French called *faits divers*, the variety of strange, unusual and fearful events in everyday life. In this spectatorial relationship with the news, images of crime added to the thrills. With the spread of photography, audiences were aware that illustrations no longer depended on the imagination of the engraver but on the startling reality of photographic production.

Amid this passionate reality of the image, Moreau-Christophe, the French Inspector General of Prisons writing in 1854, saw the photograph as a technology fit to replace the brand (Phéline, 1985). He perceived its value in identifying recidivists but the comparison to the brand was more than just fanciful. Declining rapidly at the beginning of the nineteenth century (along with other forms of spectacular punitive practice), branding for particular crimes had been both a punitive practice and a means of identification. It combined the pain of hot iron on flesh, the scar of shame and the mark of crime. Moreau-Christophe's nomination of the photograph as successor to the brand was prophetic. Not only did prisoners fear the power of the camera, it *marked* their bodies with a stigma that was more than just symbolic; for in the developing culture of photographic circulation, the spectacle of the 'brand' was extended and intensified. If Moreau-Christophe had thought of simple identification in the imagery of the brand, he also, wittingly or unwittingly, captured the power of the circulating photograph to stigmatize the body of the criminal in front of a mass audience. It was in this way that modernity used the photographic archive not only to arrest, control and identify (Tagg, 1988; Sekula, 1989), but also to stigmatize through display in the photographic spectacle. Our own age of 'naming and shaming' in and through the image was born at this moment.

Meanwhile photography was also recruited by a typological science of criminal bodies. Supported by an atlas of photographs, Cesare Lombroso's theories of the visible criminal type built, first, on older associations between character and facial physiognomy and, second, on the use of the anthropological photograph in the scientific study of other races in the colonies (Edwards, 1992). His criminal anthropology resonated with the power-driven construction of primitives in the far-off lands of the new imperialism. Lombroso's dangerous 'criminal classes' were a race apart. Such forms of power-knowledge were, at the same time, a spectacle in museums, travelling exhibitions, illustrations in the press and public discussion (Morrison, 2004a). As the century closed, photographs of Lombroso's staring criminals, accompanied by the fantastic fictions of degeneration, were circulating in an international physiognomonic spectacle.

Inspired by the images of colonial anthropology, Alphonse Bertillon in Paris sought to turn his photography into a systematic science of identification. With the photograph in mind, he had observed with interest the 1871 uprising and defeat of the Communards in Paris during the Franco-Prussian war. Rather naively, as it turned out, but no doubt driven by the new sense of photographic festival, the rebels at the barricades had proudly posed for many collective and individual portraits. In the counter-insurgent terror that followed the collapse of the revolution, the streets of Paris ran red with the blood of thousands of suspected revolutionaries summarily shot by the authorities. Amidst the intelligence collected by the restored administration were the photographs, now turned from a portraiture of pride into an instrument of ruthless revenge. Bertillon watched and learned.

Initially using photography as part of the systematic measurement of criminal bodies, he soon turned to the problem of individual identification, developing the canonical mug shot familiar to us today as the double photograph combining full-face and profile shots of the head and shoulders. A patchy and unsystematic

Figure 2.1 Group of soldiers in front of a barricade (Eugène Fabius, 1871).

Figure 2.2 Communards in their coffins (A.-A.-E. Disdéri (attributed), 1871). The image of dead communards has been attributed to André-Adolphe-Eugène Disdéri (1818–1889), one of the great entrepreneurs of the mid-century *carte-de-visite* craze. Perhaps he, more than anyone else, persuaded Parisians to pose in front of the camera to obtain cheap photo-portraits (the size of a visiting card) to place in their egalitarian albums, side by side with the famous of their day. No doubt, such a culture influenced the photographic festival in the revolutionary carnival of the Commune. Disdéri was around to capture the bloody consequences.

practice of prison portraiture was transformed into a regularized policing technology of identification and control that would progressively expand in the course of the twentieth century. Today we know that a mug shot in the spectacle is no mere instrument of identification. It also involves the capture of a suspect, the enactment of a power of arrest and, in its release to the mass media, not only an indication of policing power in general but also, as Moreau-Christophe might have hoped, its capacity to brand a detained body with shame.

Michel Foucault (1981) famously argued in *Discipline and Punish* that the beginning of modernity marked the transition from a society of spectacle to one of surveillance. Much criticized in this regard, he was, in fact, addressing the thesis of Debord's *The Society of Spectacle* (1994) [1967], whose unitary notion of power ignored the expansion of disciplinary and surveillant techniques. Elsewhere, much more like Nietzsche (1967) in *The Genealogy of Morals*, Foucault (2000) spoke of an array of punitive tactics, classifiable into four main types: exile, compensation, marking and confinement. They were all found in the premodern 'classical' period and, though confinement is the 'privileged' form in our own time, he by no means excluded, despite the rhetoric of *Discipline and*

Punish, the other kinds of tactic. Marking could 'expose, mark, wound, amputate, make a scar, stamp a sign on the face or the shoulder, impose an artificial and visible handicap, torture' in a process that would 'seize hold of the body and inscribe upon it the marks of power'. We have seen that photographs of criminals, whether as types or individuals, were sought after commodities in the image spectacle, and it was precisely by dint of this that mug shots released into circulation could act as a new form of brand or mark, a mode of punitive exposure in the image.

At the end of the nineteenth century, the British popular press was revolutionized by Harmsworth's *Daily Mail*, aimed at the rapidly expanding lower middle class. Reaching a circulation of a million within five years of its launch in 1896, it sought to distance itself from the crude sensation of the 'yellow press', but it nonetheless revelled in its duty to report crime. Harmsworth had urged his journalists to 'get me a murder a day' (Williams, 1998). As the nineteenth turned into the twentieth century, half-tone technology allowed photographs to be directly

0,90€
le Parisien Edition de Paris
CAPTURÉ
SADDAM HUSSEIN.
12 PAGES SPECIALES

Figure 2.3 *'Capturé' Le Parisien* (December 15, 2003). Saddam Hussein was captured by coalition forces and photographed for the world. This front page tells us about his detention and also performs his photographic capture in a clinical scene of humiliation.

reproduced in newspapers and magazines, a process that would feed and further stimulate the spectatorial appetite for crime and punishment.

The period between 1890 and 1914 witnessed the invention of cinema, the early appearance of photographs reproduced in mass-market publications, the expansion of the postcard industry and the proliferation of popular snapshot photography, the latter enabled by the mass production of cheaper, more portable cameras and an accompanying photo-processing industry. In this photographic culture, there was a close relationship between popular photography and popular spectatorship: many spectators of cinema, for example, were increasingly aware, directly or indirectly, of how pictures were taken. The aftermath of the First World War saw not only the golden age of cinema but also serious investment by the publication houses in the half-tone process, with an ensuing expansion of news, documentary and fashion photo-magazines. In this period, further technological development brought smaller and lighter professional cameras together with faster films and lenses, enabling more candid, spontaneous forms of photo-reportage. In the US, a covert photograph of Ruth Snyder in her execution chair appeared in *The New York Daily News* in 1928 and an avid public drove its circulation up by 750,000 (Valier, 2004).

The interwar period was also associated with extraordinary technological innovations in radio broadcasting and 'talkies'. In this photographic culture, festival mixed with spectacle. While a new mass audience may have sat passively in the dark of the movie theatres, their appetites fed the production of magazines and newspapers and drove the cinema fantasy and fame machine. An *active* relationship with the image was also more clearly expressed in postcards and expanding snapshot photography.

Nevertheless, it was also in this interwar crucible of spectacle that fascism was forged, deploying all the new technologies of sound and light, including newsreel and photographic stills in mass circulation newspapers. As with all modern spectacle, there was also a festive dynamic. Building on Browning's important study of Reserve Police Battalion 101 (2001) (one of the WW2 Nazi death squads in Poland), Wayne Morrison (2004b) has shown how these 'ordinary men' used their own festive form of photography. Like tourists on holiday, and without a trace of the kind of frenzied evil that we seem to require in order to understand genocide, they smiled as they casually posed by their frightened and humiliated victims. Thus, they anticipated in many ways, first, the attitudes of the soldiers who used photogenic torture in the Abu Ghraib prison in Baghdad and, second, the structural relationship between the apparent informalities of festival and the organized formalities of political and martial spectacle (see also Hamm, 2007).

In the course of the forties, a jobbing news photographer in New York, Arthur Fellig, illicitly tuned into police radio frequencies and often arrived at the scenes of crimes before the police themselves. Capturing photographs of casual murders and mob assassination, as well as motor accidents and fires, he developed his naturalistic images in the boot of his car and delivered them to surprised but grateful editors in time for the morning editions. Attributing to him an almost supernatural power to sniff out death and disaster, the press and police wondered if he used a Ouija board. In any case, a nickname, 'Weegee', stuck.

Weegee not only fed the profits of the tabloids but also helped establish a special relationship between the police, the spectacular image and an avid viewing public. Good crime images, then as now, were a valuable source of police PR. However, Weegee's photography also enacted a new practice of the image. With its use of the terms 'shot' or 'capture', for example, photography is replete with metaphors of hunting and seizure, and Sontag (1979) sees this violence as inherent to its operation. Here, the image hunter roams in a kind of wild, natural world. Weegee was perhaps the first photographer to stalk and ensnare his prey with stealth and speed, a practice that would be highly influential in the coming decades.

After the Second World War, television, like the magazine, inserted a powerful public form of imagery into the midst of private domestic space. Among the novelties of the mass consumer society were the famous bodies of the film, pop and fashion industries, relayed in photographic posters, packaging, advertising, magazines and news, and nourished by demand from a new cohort of young consumers. Youth culture arrived in and contributed to the consumer world, a culture combining an insolence, opposition and transgression that was commercialized and fed in loops through photographic and phonographic space. As the images of famous film stars and popular musicians further penetrated domestic space, photographic exaltation found itself side-by-side with intimate proximity. This photographic combination of fame and possessive familiarity, also producing the dialectic of spectacular distance and emotional closeness, would become an important characteristic of celebrity. Anyone surprised (or appalled) by the mass outpouring of emotion following the violent death of Princess Diana should re-examine her life in the photograph. In the spectacle, she combined the 'girl-next-door' with Disney princess, the touching of the sick with red-carpet posing, real intimacy with fantastic exaltation. Hers was a life and a death also crucially marked by an ambivalent relationship to the image, and thus to the audience, which she both courted and fled, with the predatory paparazzi playing a central role on our behalf.

For Marshall McLuhan (1964), writing in the early days of postwar photographic celebrity, the photograph commodified the bodies of the famous, multiplying them into 'mass-produced merchandise'. Indeed, in *Understanding Media*, he went as far as to call the photograph 'the Brothel-Without-Walls'. For McLuhan the photographic image of fame delivered darker desires. The expansion of celebrity into new fields after the Second World War gave this meretricious commodification another twist in the birth of the paparazzi. Until this point, the images of the stars were confined to staged film stills or portrait-studio publicity, though from time to time the stars might pose in the street for a polite photographer. Nevertheless, in an age of declining deference, photographic familiarity and the urgent desire to possess the latest commodities, photographic politesse would be left behind. The paparazzo – a predator capturing candid and *natural* images of the famous, where the spectator rather than the star now commanded the photograph – was another factor in the construction of the celebrity image. Such photography – where an attempt is made by the consumer to wrest power away from the famous person, when celebrity is literally *consumed* – inevitably also provoked and captured scenes of embarrassment, shame or humiliation in which adulation and *schadenfreude* mixed in equal measure. The Brothel-Without-Walls became a kind of cage in which the occupant was painfully prodded for the delectation of the spectator. Indeed, it is in this punitive arena where the paparazzi and the police join hands in the capture of the celebrity mug shot.

Artists since Andy Warhol, who scandalously painted the mug shots of 'Most Wanted Men' in 1964, have commented on the relationship between celebrity and desire in the criminal identification photograph. What happens when a criminal becomes infamous through a mug shot? Marcus Harvey's monumental painting of the Myra Hindley mug shot – shown in 1997 at the appropriately named *Sensation* exhibition of paintings from the Saatchi collection – excited a storm of controversy.

KATE AND DOHERTY IN MOORS MURDERERS SHOCK

Moss is Myra!

BY ROBBIE COLLIN

THESE twisted images of troubled supermodel Kate Moss and her on-off junkie boyfriend Pete Doherty as the Moors Murderers have sparked fury.

The faces of Kate, 32, and Pete, 27, were superimposed on to mug shots of child killers Myra Hindley and Ian Brady by Neil Hepburn.

Graphic designer Neil said: "The point was that Kate and Pete were in a downward spiral and public opinion of them was so low they might as well have been child killers."

Irate fans of Babyshambles singer Pete branded the work—going on show at London's Institute of Contemporary Arts—an "insult" to their hero.

MODEL LOOKS: Kate is made to appear like Hindley

EVIL: Killers Hindley and Brady

BABY FACED: Pete is superimposed on Brady mugshot

Figure 2.4 *News of the World* (May 7, 2006, featuring the work of viral artist Neil Hepburn aka Beau Bo D'Or). When photographs of Kate Moss and Pete Doherty using cocaine were first published and used to vilify them in the press in 2005, the viral artist Neil Hepburn produced a work entitled Cliché 49, amalgamating their photographic images with the child killers Hindley and Brady and posted it on the web site B3TA.com. His intention was to comment on the way in which the media had turned them into folk devils, lending them a notoriety akin to the infamous murderers. Later this image was used to publicize an exhibition at the Institute of Contemporary Arts in 2006, and when it was picked up by the popular newspapers it became yet another shocking story. Russell Young used Hepburn's work and produced a Warholesque screen print that provoked a similar scandal in January 2008.

Figure 2.5 Russell Young, *Kate Moss* and *Pete Doherty*, based on Hepburn's work (Screen print, 2007). 'Nowadays if you're a crook you're still considered up-there. You can write books, go on TV, give interviews—you're a big celebrity and nobody even looks down on you because you're a crook. You're still up there. This is because more than anything people just want stars' (Andy Warhol, 1975).

It is only a small step from these practices to an array of late-modern entertainments including so-called reality television, game shows featuring shame and suffering (Hallsworth, 2009), and 'happy slapping' mobile photography distributed on the Internet, where a warped version of Warhol's prediction comes true and everyone may at last have their fifteen minutes in a cruel festival (see also Ferrell, Hayward and Young, 2008: 9). Paparazzi are not so much the parasites as the inaugurators of this age.

Recalling Nietzsche's (1967) characterization of punishment as essentially 'festive', these entertainment values invest our fascination with crime and desires for punishment. We have seen that the photographic spectacle is also a festival and that this has taken an increasingly predatory and punitive turn in the postwar period. Indeed, it has been suggested that our recent 'punitive turn' is making more use of visual punishment (Pratt *et al.*, 2005). Perhaps the rise of paparazzi culture demonstrates that this is not so much a return to less civilized times but a march forward into the modernity of the photographic image.

Having conducted our short history of the modern photographic spectacle, we now embark on a double detour: first through the concept of spectacular practice and, second, through a set of methodological reflections. Along the way, we will gather together a set of critical tools.

Spectacular practices

The word spectacle might conjure up an elevated screen or stage commanding a quiet, perhaps even docile audience, with a clear line of demarcation between what is performed and the mass of spectators, between activity on the stage and passivity in the auditorium. Indeed, this conception finds particular critical expression in the influential work of Adorno and Horkheimer (1979) as well as Debord (1994) [1967], where the deceived or distracted audience of mass-mediated entertainment is rendered inert in its passive consumption of the products of a monopolistic culture industry. However, without losing its critical thrust, the term spectacle is used in a less monolithic way in recent literature (e.g. Kellner, 2003; Giroux, 2006), and in the field of media studies where the audience is now regarded as much more *active* in its relationship to mass culture (e.g. Abercrombie and Longhurst, 1998). Pop and fashion culture, for example, is increasingly theorized as something to be used and transformed as material in the performance of everyday leisure activities, which, in turn, is fed back into wider society (e.g. Willis, 1990). In this case, audiences not only exercise agency and entrain desire in the way that they receive the performances of culture, but they also actively transform them in their own performances of everyday life. For example, photographic performance plays a central role in so-called 'gangsta rap' in which the complex loops that connect the phenomena of the street with those in the mass media cannot be reduced to the dynamic of 'active' media and 'passive' audience (Ferrell, Hayward and Young, 2008). Another example is the complex loop of football 'hooliganism' running between the news spectacle (as well as celebratory pulp literature) and its subjects who are also a key component of its audience. Such loops may now function as much in virtual as actual space (see Zaitch and de Leeuw, this volume). Even the everyday news of crime and punishment feeds into culture in a way that involves an active audience commenting, conversing, debating, fearing, loathing and desiring. We view images of crime with an eye prepared to judge, but also one that actively consumes and transforms the products of crime infotainment. To posit an active audience is not, however, to forget power. This time, however, the desiring audience is not a passive victim of power but is actively complicit, whether wittingly or unwittingly, in its operation.

Thus, the photographic spectacle is a form of social practice or performance which we should approach in a way that takes seriously *both* the macrosociological *and* microsociological levels. It is a multiplicity that produces flows of forces working in the registers of the cultural, the social, the inter-individual and the unconscious. When the word spectacle is used here, it also embraces those important *festive* dynamics in which the audience is both an active receiver of spectacle and, at the same time, engages in social practices that feed back into its forces of performance. That said, we cannot reduce these social practices to individual performance, even if this also undoubtedly plays its role. Nor, from a political viewpoint, should we use this model as an excuse for imagining that festivity is a micropolitical phenomenon reducible to individual, conscious, liberal agency, negotiation or simple counter-hegemony. Instead, a fully critical approach to the spectacle-festival must also realize that the festive audience of modernity may act as a crowd pulsing with barely conscious desires.

In such way this chapter takes a visual cultural rather than a media studies perspective. Media studies and the use of the term 'mass media' often examines the continuities between media and communications in the practice of sending and receiving messages (evident in the histories of, for example, Williams, 1998; Winston, 1998; Briggs and Burke, 2002). Here, I am more interested in the continuities between the cultural phenomena of the spectacle and the mass media. In this way, *practice and performance* rather than *messages* take centre stage. Hence, the photograph is regarded here not so much as a communications technology but as both scene and means of performance and social practice.

The photographic spectacle is part of that aspect of the mass media which is *practical* or *performative* rather than *communicative*. Most, if not all, photographic images we encounter are performances or, to put it another way, forms of social practice, including, in special cases, the sending of messages. If we recall the great photographic events of our time, we are witnessing forms of practice or performance. Many of these events might not have occurred without the presence of cameras: they are *photographic* performances. Beginning with Boorstin (1963) and argued more recently by Baudrillard (e.g. 1983), there is an unfortunate tendency to regard events performed for the camera as 'unreal' or 'simulated' in some way. Boorstin called an event that would not have happened but for the presence of the camera a 'pseudo-event', while Baudrillard felt that the world of the photographic spectacle was detached from the real. Both took an approach dominated by the logic of representation or meaning. Both also chose to ignore the reality of social practice in the photographic spectacle.

In short, it matters less what the photographic spectacle 'means', what it 'represents', what it symbolizes, and more what it *does* in the real. To illustrate this, we might choose imagery from the recent global 'war on terror', such as the spectacle of 11 September 2001, or the chain reaction of photographic events it set in train; for example, the punitive performance at Camp X-Ray, Guantánamo Bay or the moment of 'Shock and Awe' in the bombing of Baghdad; the photogenic torture at Abu Ghraib, or the photographed and photographic *capture* of Saddam Hussein. All these events possessed an important feature performed *in and by* the photograph, occasions in which photography played a central role, not merely because it captured an image of an important event, but because the photograph was itself *part* of the event.

Methodological reflections

It is strange to think that some might strive for an objective 'methodology' of the photograph or of photographic spectacle. Perhaps it betokens a nihilistic hankering for the hygiene of white coats and the cold distance of clipboards in a world devoid of value. If it is more plausible to maintain such pretence of disinterest when peering at a distant star, it is entirely implausible when we, as both cultural products and producers, seek to investigate cultural production. We bring to any cultural inquiry a culturally inflected propensity to interact with the material of study: culture as part of culture. Moreover, culture enters the critical: in the service of which sort of struggle, with what kinds of pleasure, with which desires, do we conduct our research? Value, creativity, polemic and interpretive policy all have an important role to play in the response to images.

Method must also be contingent, sensitive to circumstance and cannot follow rigid, preconceived dictates (Phillips, 1973). Method must always be a creative enterprise; indeed, we might go as far as striving towards creativity and play as desirable in themselves. It is well known that even as 'rational' and 'empirical' a field of study as the natural sciences tends to make its important discoveries by creative leaps of a playful imagination rather than following the iron rules of orthodox logic and method. Though I am not advocating an entirely free play of interpretation, it is in the service of a broader wisdom that we should still take a cue from Feyerabend who pushes the idea of play and creativity to the limit, *encouraging* rather than discouraging a *proliferating* creativity (Feyerabend, 1970).

Thus, to summarize the theoretical thrust of this 'method': photographic spectacle is also a *festival*, and is not merely the illustrative backcloth on the stage of our culture, but part of its material, everyday reality. Not reducible to a representation, the photograph is part of the very stuff of our social life: it *presents* more than it represents, *produces* more than it reproduces and *performs* more than it signifies. In this way, the photographic spectacle cannot be reduced to code, symbol, illustration, wallpaper, scenographic backdrop, distraction, illusion, hallucination or simulation. It is not primarily a semiotic spectacle. It is not a static picture, but a dynamic power. As a social force, the photograph performs in a field where the material realities of cultural practices in the field of power and desire are at stake.

With its commitment to understanding the roles of emotion, seduction and desire, its resistance to despotic positivism, its commitment to creativity and the ludic, and its approach to the critical analysis of present-day cultural production in all its complexity, cultural criminology is well positioned to take up the implications of this perspective. In its desire *not* to reduce the world to a truth of objective and rational schemata, cultural criminology has the best chance of appreciating this social reality – both inside and outside the image – in transgression, violence, crime, control and punishment (Ferrrell, 2008; Ferrell, Hayward and Young, 2008).

Furthermore what we see in all but the most confected, highly coded photographs 'has occurred only once' (Barthes, 1981), it is a singularity, a particularity, a single event that is too unruly for codes or laws. Could there ever be a 'method' of the single event? Of course, in social research we must take account of the historical, social and cultural contexts of the image event. Nevertheless, this does not bring us any closer to a regulated science. The historical and social context of the photographic event is also a singularity, and thus, following the language of Dilthey, it must be treated idiographically on its own terms. This, as we have seen, still involves us as cultural products, critically interacting with cultural production.

I have tried to emphasize the role of the photographic spectacle in social practice and performance, rather than as a realm of representation, true or false. In his aphorisms on Feuerbach, Marx (1975) criticized the philosopher for dwelling on the correct interpretation of a symbolic world rather than focusing on social practice. In other words, he counselled the reader to appreciate the world less as a realm of representation and more as an arena of social practice. Quite simply he argued that 'all social life is essentially practical'. It is this radical pragmatism of Marx's *On Feuerbach* that should form the focus of our 'methodological' approach to the photographic spectacle. Of course *part of* the social practice of the photographic spectacle is, at certain key moments, a practice of representation where the critical theorist is obliged to *read* codes and symbols. However, this must not be done at the expense of a critical awareness of the way its power often *exceeds* the representational regime.

Conclusion

From its very beginnings modern spectatorship has been active, mobile and hungry to see, and, as the scaffold and other public punishments declined, a new theatre of crime and punishment took their place in the expanding image cultures of the nineteenth-century spectacle. A photographic culture soon developed and was accelerated in the twentieth century as various forms and forces interacted: at the same time as spectators consumed the images of cinema, magazines, newspapers and television, they produced images in a growing snapshot society. After the Second World War, a new kind of photographer, the paparazzo, initiated an age of more active festive cruelty in the image. A predator in the shade and an agent of newspapers and magazines, the paparazzo is also the agent of our desires. It is in this festive theatre of crime and punishment – from which carnival is liable to break out at any time (Presdee, 2000) – that the values of entertainment, vengeful 'naming and shaming' by the authorities, 'happy slapping' and the paparazzi all interact promiscuously. In mass circulation, the photograph applies a mark to the body that shames, humiliates *and* fascinates, whether in the course of police and judicial proceedings or for the purposes of entertainment. Here we return to the original meaning of the word stigma, a brand on the body in a field of vision: a scar more than a symbol.

To emphasize the performative force of the photograph and its festive dynamics of desire is also to engage with power, something of particular importance in the present-day theatre of crime and punishment. It is one of the purposes of this chapter to emphasize the role of social practice as urged by Marx in his reflections on Feuerbach. In highlighting photographic culture as social practice, we are thus obliged to take up, in the most general terms, a *critical* position where we make judgements on the exercise of power, the production of power relations and the play of forces that affect our conduct, including barely conscious forces of desire.

In this story of the eye drawn into a flux of power and desire, we might decide, for example, to undertake a fully cultural critique of fascism, taking account of the various forces of desire in the fetishism of populist authoritarianism, militarism and war. This is not merely incidental to the aims of this chapter but really rather central since, as in Bertold Brecht's play *The Resistible Rise of Arturo Ui* (where the central character was a burlesque amalgam of Al Capone and Adolf Hitler), fascism is a potent mixture of politics becoming gangsterism, and gangsterism becoming politics, both enjoying a relationship with spectacle. As a form of organized political criminality, fascism was at the forefront of 1930s modernity in its appeal to power and desire in the developing mass media. The womb of fascism is still with us today in the photographic spectacle, whether it manifests itself in the habits and tics of consumerism, the sound and light of war, the ceremonials of national and international politics or the many arenas and theatres of transgression, crime and punishment.

As a toxic miasma of war, security and risk management envelops our politics, a kind of fascism or microfascism flows through the late-modern theatres of cruelty scattered across the glittering neverlands of consumerism. It is the task of cultural criminology to take a critical stance and enable practices of resistance amid the flux of power and desire in these arenas. Here, we should seek to understand, play with and resist the forces that bring together the agents of control and commodification with the wills, wants and wishes at the heart of the spectacle of crime and punishment.

Acknowledgements

Thanks to Keith Hayward for his invaluable comments and eagle-eyed editing, to Neil Hepburn and Russell Young for the use of their art, to the McCormick Library of Special Collections, Northwestern University Library for the barricade photograph, and to the *News of the World* for the clipping.

References

Abercombie, N. and Longhurst, B. (1998) *Audiences: A Sociological Theory of Performance and Imagination*, London: Sage.

Adorno, T. and Horkheimer, M. (1979) 'The Culture Industry: Enlightenment as Mass Deception', in *Dialectic of Enlightenment*, London: Verso.

Artaud, A. (1970) 'Theatre and the Plague', in *The Theatre and its Double*, London: Calderand Boyars.

Barthes, R. (1981) *Camera Lucida: Reflections on Photography*, London: Jonathan Cape.

Baudrillard, J. (1983) *Simulations*, New York: Semiotext(e).

Benjamin, W. (1985) [1931] 'A Small History of Photography', in *One Way Street and other Writings*, London: Verso.

Boorstin, D. (1963) *The Image* or *What Happened to the American Dream*, Harmondsworth: Pelican.

Briggs, A. and Burke, P. (2002) *A Social History of the Media: From Gutenberg to the Internet*, Cambridge: Polity.

Browning, C.R. (2001) *Ordinary Men: Reserve Police Batallion 101 and the Final Solution in Poland*, London: Penguin.

Clark, T.J. (1985) *The Painting of Modern Life: Paris in the Art of Manet and his Followers*, London: Thames and Hudson.

Debord, G. (1994) [1967] *The Society of the Spectacle* (trans. D. Nicholson-Smith) New York: Zone.

Edwards, E. (ed.) (1992) *Anthropology and Photography: 1860–1920*, New Haven and London: Yale University Press and The Royal Anthropological Institute.

Ferrell, J. (2008) *Paper given at* 'Crime, Culture and Conflict' *Conference*, London South Bank University, 17 March.

Ferrell, J., Hayward, K., Morrison, W. and Presdee, M. (eds) (2004) *Cultural Criminology Unleashed*, London: Glasshouse.

Ferrell, J., Hayward, K. and Young, J. (2008) *Cultural Criminology: An Invitation*, London: Sage.

Feyerabend, P.K. (1970) 'Against Method: Outline of an Anarchistic Theory of Knowledge', *Minnesota Studies in the Philosophy of Science*, 4: 17–130.

Foucault, M. (1981) *Discipline and Punish: The Birth of the Prison* (trans. Alan Sheridan), London: Penguin.

Foucault, M. (2000) 'The Punitive Society', in *Ethics: Truth and Subjectivity* (*Essential Works of Foucault 1954–1984 Volume One*), London: Penguin.

Gernsheim, H. and Gernsheim, A. (1968) *L.J.M. Daguerre: The History of the Diorama and the Daguerrotype*, 2nd edn., New York: Dover.

Giroux, H.A. (2006) *Beyond the Spectacle of Terrorism: Global Uncertainty and the Challenge of the New Media*, Boulder, Colorado: Paradigm.

Hallsworth, S. (2009) It's Good to Watch: Degradation TV (forthcoming).

Hamm, M. (2007) '"High Crimes and Misdeameanours": George Bush and the Sins of Abu Ghraib', *Crime, Media, Culture*, 3: 259–84.

Hayward, K.J. (2004) *City Limits: Crime, Consumer Culture and the Urban Experience*, London: Cavendish.

Kellner, D. (2003) *Media Spectacle*, London: Routledge.

Kracauer, S. (1960) *Theory of Film: The Redemption of Physical Reality*, Oxford: Oxford University Press.

Marx, K. (1975) 'On Feuerbach', in *Early Writings* (trans. R. Livingstone and G. Benton), Harmondsworth and London: Penguin and New Left Review.

McLuhan, M. (1964) *Understanding Media: The Extensions of Man*. London: Routledge and Kegan Paul.

Morrison, W. (2004a) 'Lombroso and the Birth of Criminological Positivism', in J. Ferrell, K. Hayward, W. Morrison and M. Presdee (eds) (2004).

Morrison, W. (2004b) 'Everyday Photography Capturing Genocide', *Theoretical Criminology*, 8(3): 341–58.

Nietzsche, F. (1967) *On the Genealogy of Morals* (trans. Walter Kaufmann and R. J. Hollingdale) and *Ecce Homo* (trans. Walter Kaufmann), New York: Random House.

Phéline, C. (1985) 'Portraits en règle' in *Identités: de Disderi au photomaton*, Centre National de la Photographie & Editions du Chène.

Phillips, D.L. (1973) *Abandoning Method*, San Francisco: Jossey Bass.

Pratt, J. *et al.* (eds) (2005) *The New Punitiveness: Trends, Theories, Perspectives*, Cullompton: Willan.

Presdee, M. (2000) *Cultural Criminology and the Carnival of Crime*. London: Routledge.

Schwartz, V.R. (1998) *Spectacular Realities: Early Mass Culture in Fin-de-Siècle Paris*, Berkeley and Los Angeles: University of California Press.

Sekula, A. (1989) 'The Body and the Archive', in R. Bolton (ed.) *The Contest of Meaning*. Cambridge, Massachussetts: MIT Press.

Sontag, S. (1979) *On Photography*, London: Penguin.

Tagg, J. (1988) *The Burden of Representation: Essays on Photographies and Histories*, Amherst: University of Massachusetts.

Valier, C. (2004) *Crime and Punishment in Contemporary Culture*, London: Routledge.

Warhol, A. (1975) *The Philosophy of Andy Warhol: From A to B and Back Again*, New York: Harcourt Brace Jovanovich.

Williams, K. (1998) *Get Me a Murder a Day! A History of Mass Communication in Britain*, London: Arnold.

Willis, P. (1990) *Common Culture: Symbolic Work at Play in the Everyday Cultures of the Young*, Milton Keynes: Open University Press.

Winston, B. (1998) *Media Technology and Society, A History: From the Telegraph to the Internet*, London: Routledge.

Chapter 3

The decisive moment

Documentary photography and cultural criminology

Jeff Ferrell and Cécile Van de Voorde

> One must always take photos with the greatest respect for the subject and for oneself.
>
> Henri Cartier-Bresson

Introduction

Of late, criminology has rediscovered the photograph. Many criminologists now include photographic representation in their analytic purview, and following the lead of the new journal *Crime, Media, Culture*, even the most staid of orthodox criminology journals are now beginning to incorporate photographic illustrations among their pages.

This is of course an entirely appropriate – not to mention long overdue – response to a late modern world in which imagery and representation suffuse the practices of crime and crime control. Yet, it is also cause for concern. Importing photographs into a discipline defined by words and numbers may create a certain decorative appeal, but of itself it does nothing to address the taken-for-granted dominance of those very words and numbers. In fact, as we see time and again, many contemporary criminologists seem to believe that by calculating photographic frequency or measuring photographic size they can wrestle the image into analytic submission, and so conquer its visual obfuscation and opaqueness. Other criminologists readily relegate photographs to textual illustration, in the process creating a sort of visual ghetto where the dominance of the text likewise remains unchallenged.

Put simply, orthodox criminology and its social scientific underpinnings offer little in the way of a foundation for the photograph. No matter how many photographs are analyzed, no matter how many included, the dualistic hierarchy of content over form generally remains in place and with it the parallel dualism that divorces 'real' crime and crime control from their 'unreal' image. As criminologists increasingly turn to the photograph, then, we must find a different way – a way to engage the image on its own terms. Just as we should understand that photographs operate within particular social contexts and embody particular constellations of cultural meaning, we should explore ways of engaging such photographs with honesty and sophistication and of immersing ourselves in the processes by which photographs come into being.

Current work in and around cultural criminology has certainly begun this reorientation to the image. Philip Jones and Claire Wardle (2008), Eugene McLaughlin and Chris Greer (2008) and other scholars have recently explored the ways in which the print media constructs the meaning of criminality through the selection and specific placement of photographs for publication. Meticulously analyzing the torture photographs of Abu Ghraib, Mark Hamm (2007) has shown that the photos themselves can be interrogated for evidence of torture's political lineage. Utilizing 'as data for cultural criminology an album of photographs taken by German soldiers and policemen involved in the Holocaust', Wayne Morrison (2004: 341) has likewise explored the interplay of 'genocidal tourism' and war crime. Stephen Lyng and David Courtney have analyzed photographer Taryn Simon's representations of the wrongly convicted (Courtney and Lyng, 2007); surely shattering any remaining shards of the fraudulent 'broken windows' theory of crime, Greg Snyder (2008) has carefully photographed and documented the convergence of illegal graffiti and high-end commerce. Heitor Alvelos (2005), Ken Tunnell (2006) and others have begun to publish visual essays in which their own photographs embody criminological analysis and critique; Michelle Brown (2006), Alison Young (2004), Richard Rodriguez (2003), Claire Valier (Valier and Lippens, 2005) and others have begun to theorize the image in the context of crime and transgression.

If cultural criminology is in this way coming to be associated with a certain visual trajectory, it is already even more closely identified with another: the resurgence of ethnographic field research. As embodied in the work of Jeff Ferrell (1996, 2001, 2006), Mark Hamm (2002), Ferrell and Hamm (1998), and other cultural criminologists, ethnography has been revitalized within cultural criminology as a humanistic counterpoint to the arid data sets of orthodox criminology. Requiring months or years of submersion in illicit worlds, this sort of committed field research is designed to find a deep understanding of those under study, a sort of criminological *verstehen* (Ferrell, 1997), and so to grasp the *meaning* of crime and transgression for those who undertake it (or seek to prevent it). In this sense, good ethnography, as conceptualized and undertaken by cultural criminologists, is inevitably and intentionally *political* as well, at times granting agency and voice to those otherwise excluded from public debate, at other times exposing the contradictions that those in power work to mask.

Generally, these two dimensions of cultural criminology – its engagement with representation and the photographic image and its commitment to in-depth ethnographic research – are seen as alternative strategies within the larger cultural criminological project of critical inquiry into the contested meaning of crime. But what if the two converged? As we go about visual analysis, an ethnographic sensibility could nicely attune us to the nuances of the photographic world and to the complex human process by which visual productions are invested with cultural and political significance. As we go about ethnography, a sensitivity to photographic dynamics could (and should) help focus our field research on the myriad visual representations that increasingly animate everyday life and everyday crime. And if in exploring this convergence of the photographic and the ethnographic we were to look back as well as look forward, we could find yet another reason to embrace this convergence: it has productively been underway for decades.

Focus

The photodocumentary tradition

Traditionally, photography as social documentary has taken two major forms: photojournalism and war photography. The assumed goal in each has been to provide truthful, candid photography – visual narratives reporting on social reality. The photojournalistic style originated with the reporting of news from European battlefields in the nineteenth century. In 1855, British photographer Roger Fenton pioneered the use of documentary photography during the Crimean War, effectively becoming the first official war photographer when his depictions of soldiers were used to complement battlefield sketches. Likewise, the American Civil War was famously documented by U.S. photographer Mathew Brady, who is often lauded as the father of photojournalism.

As photojournalism (*reportage*) became a staple of newspaper and magazine reporting, the golden age of photojournalism (1930s–1950s) exposed the public to the works of influential photographers like W. Eugene Smith, Margaret Bourke-White and Robert Capa. Known for his near-limitless temporal and moral commitment to the subjects of his photographs, Smith described his approach as 'photographic penetration deriving from study and awareness and participation' (in Miller, 1997: 150). French photographer Henri Cartier-Bresson also gained great fame during this period, to the extent that he is now generally credited with being the progenitor of modern photojournalism. Cartier-Bresson worked to master candid *in situ* photography and his emphasis on capturing the 'decisive moment' (*images à la sauvette*, 'images on the run') remains an inspiration for documentary photographers today.

Yet, this 'golden age' was also marked by patterns of sensationalized crime coverage and photographic profiteering. Most infamously, Arthur Fellig (*a.k.a.* Weegee) used on-the-spot black-and-white photography to document street crime in New York City, sometimes resorting to questionable tactics in order to find and photograph crime scenes before the police could arrive. 'If I had a picture of two handcuffed criminals being booked', he once said, 'I would cut the picture in half and get five bucks for each.' *Naked City* (1945/2002), his first collection of these controversial photographs, inspired Jules Dassin's 1948 film *The Naked City,* and Weegee's dubious practices notwithstanding, the book is today regarded as a fine art masterpiece (see relatedly Hannigan, 1999).

The US Farm Security Administration (FSA, 1935–1942) spawned another moment in the evolution of photojournalism. Part of President Franklin D.

Roosevelt's New Deal, the FSA was designed to fight rural poverty and highlight the urgency of rehabilitating rural areas. Roy E. Stryker, an American economist and photographer, was in charge of the FSA Information Division (Historical Section) and, as such, was responsible for a massive photodocumentary project that eventually produced nearly 80,000 images of the Great Depression through the lenses of Dorothea Lange, Walker Evans, Russell Lee, Gordon Parks, Arthur Rothstein and others. A number of these photographs – perhaps most famously Lange's 'Migrant Mother' – have endured as emblematic representations of the Great Depression and the suffering it engendered.

World War II documentary photography is mostly associated with the work of Robert Capa, though W. Eugene Smith and others also created memorably 'in-the-moment' images of the war. As a combat photographer, Capa covered several conflicts – including the Spanish Civil War, where he produced a famous and controversial image of a soldier at the instant of being killed by a rifle shot (see Miller, 1997: 27–9 for a review of the debates surrounding this picture) – but he remains best known for his work in the 1940s. He is especially celebrated for the dozen photographs of the second assault wave on Omaha Beach on D-Day in June 1944. 'If your pictures aren't good enough, you're not close enough', Capa once declared – poignant words indeed from a man who risked his life to document warfare and eventually lost it, camera in hand, while trying to get closer to troops on an Indochinese battlefield.

Robert Capa is also well known for cofounding the international photographic cooperative Magnum Photos with Henri Cartier-Bresson, David 'Chim' Seymour and George Roger in 1947. As Cartier-Bresson (in Miller, 1999: 15) explained, 'Magnum is a community of thought, a shared human quality, a curiosity about what is going on in the world, a respect for what is going on and a desire to transcribe it visually.' Today Magnum photographers continue to document world events and their participants, and the Magnum Photos library constitutes a living archive of the past sixty years, with roughly one million photographs in the physical library and 350,000 online images. In many ways keepers of the photodocumentary tradition, Magnum and its photographers like to point out that when one thinks of an iconic image, the likelihood is it came from Magnum.

Today both photojournalism and documentary photography are widely recognized as legitimate tools for the representation of events and people, and in many cases as art forms in themselves. And the tradition continues to evolve. James Nachtwey (1999) today produces startling war photography; Sebastião Salgado (2001, 2005) is developing an astounding body of black-and-white photographs documenting developing countries and pressing social issues. Camilo José Vergara (1995) has produced some 9,000 images of urban space over an eighteen-year period, so as to create 'pictorial networks' of urban change. Heitor Alvelos (2004) has likewise engaged in a complex, long-term photographic study of urban graffiti, documenting shifting patterns in the dissemination of criminal and commercial images. The historical foundation for much contemporary photography, the photojournalistic/documentary photography tradition continues to inform the world of the image – and continues to offer critical insights into the methods by which the image is produced and given meaning.

Methodological reflections

The dialectics of the decisive moment

The photodocumentary tradition provides an invaluable intellectual and experiential foundation on which to build a photographically attuned cultural criminology. Anticipating cultural criminology's ethnographic sensibility as well as its attentiveness to the image, this tradition offers a framework for critical engagement with the photograph, and for human engagement with the situations out of which photographs emerge. Indulging in a bit of *post hoc* history, we might even say that photographers like W. Eugene Smith and Robert Capa were doing cultural criminology long before cultural criminology existed – that is, that they were immersing themselves in the nuances of everyday transgression, and communicating the vivid symbolism they found and invented there, all in the interest of activism and critique. But lest we reify the work of photodocumentarians as some sort of permanent visual template for cultural criminology, we would do well to remember that this work is most certainly *not the answer* to contemporary issues and images of crime, control and culture. It's really more a set of dialectical *questions*, a series of *creative tensions* that, in animating the history of photodocumentary practices, can usefully come to animate cultural criminology's visual work as well. Among these many tensions, four in particular highlight issues essential to cultural criminology's engagement with the image.

Objectivity/subjectivity

At its most basic, the photodocumentary tradition embodies a tension that has long bedeviled criminology and other 'social sciences': that between objective inquiry and subjective analysis. In fact, photodocumentary work forces this tension to the front, and in more than one dimension. On the one hand, unlike commercial photographers and others, documentary photographers do not seem to stage photographs or resort to special photographic tricks and effects. Instead, they *document* the external events they encounter – and moreover, they do so not with imperfect personal memory, but with a *camera*, a machine designed to capture the visual reality of an event and to commit it to film (or now, digital memory). Yet, on the other hand, documentary photographers quite intentionally put themselves in the middle of the most politically and morally charged of events – Walker Evans (1989) in 1930s revolutionary Cuba, W. Eugene Smith (1998) amidst the tragic aftermath of corporate criminality, Magnum photographers in the middle of one war and another – and then use their photographic skills to interpret and communicate these events, and so to force the viewers of their photographs into visual confrontations with horror, violence, injustice and death.

If ever there were a dialectical tension between the objective and the subjective, between careful documentation and crafted emotion, it is in W. Eugene Smith's photos of corporate crime victims, Robert Capa's images of wartime violence or the FSA photographers' photos of Depression-era suffering.

If we are to explore and learn from this tension, we will do well to first note its technical underpinnings. In a sense, technically, photographs provide a point-by-point visual correspondence to the subject photographed (though the subject is generally reduced in size, made two-dimensional and sometimes made colourless). As Susan Sontag (1977: 53) notes in *On Photography,* 'unlike the fine-art objects of pre-democratic eras, photographs don't seem deeply beholden to the intention of an artist. Rather, they owe their existence to a loose cooperation (quasi-magical, quasi-accidental) between photographer and subject – mediated by an ever simpler and more automated machine … In the fairy tale of photography the magic box insures veracity and banishes error, compensates for inexperience, and rewards innocence'. Indeed, technically, a good photograph can operate as a stunningly objective reproduction of an external reality, capturing the finest of nuances and the most subtle of textures.

Yet, even at this technical level, this reproduction is far from simple; surely only nonphotographers can imagine that a photograph represents an inevitably objective account of the reality it reproduces. At the decisive moment of the shutter's click, the photographer must choose angles, f-stops and distance. Later, decisions must be made about processing, cropping and presentation. In fact, many of the most iconic of documentary photographs – Dorothea Lang's downcast 'Migrant Mother' of the Great Depression, W. Eugene Smith's Pieta-like mother gently bathing a child horribly deformed by corporate poisoning – are in fact carefully cropped and reprocessed versions of the original photographic images (Hill, 1998). Despite its stature, Lange's 'Migrant Mother' has even come to be criticized for a lack of 'truthfulness', after the discovery of negatives and contact sheets showing that the photograph was posed and cropped to convey a specific message. And for Lange's 'Migrant Mother', Smith's mother and child, and many other documentary photos, of course, this is precisely the next dimension of the objective/subjective tension: the message. After all, it is not only the photo itself that embodies the photographer's perspective; it is the chosen subject, the morally charged setting and the critical account the photographer wishes to communicate.

As intractable as it may seem, this tension resolves into an essential insight for cultural criminologists, ethnographers and others concerned with the human image: the documentary photograph is neither the objective reproduction of an external reality nor a subjective construction of the photographer, but rather a visual documentation of the *relationship* between photographer, photographic subject, and the larger orbits of meaning they both occupy. The reality that such a photograph captures is not that of the people in front of the lens, nor that of the photographer, but of the *shared cultural meanings* created between photographer and those photographed in a particular context. In this sense, a good documentary photograph is both objective and subjective – and profoundly *intersubjective*. 'Leaving aside planned fabrications', Collier (2001: 35) argues, 'it may be said that photographs … are, ultimately, complex reflections of a relationship between maker and subject in which both play roles in shaping their character and content'. As we will note subsequently, this relationship can be seen in the content of the photograph – and it can also be seen in the photograph's composition and style, as photographers work to represent their subjects and their relationships with them through these more formal elements as well.

Attentiveness/analysis

A parallel tension in photodocumentary work plays out between the demand for careful attentiveness to the photographic subject and the agenda of broader critical analysis that has regularly animated the efforts of documentary photographers.

The photography of Walker Evans – especially that which he produced in conjunction with the writer James Agee for the book *Let Us Now Praise Famous Men* – occupies one side of this dialectic. Setting out to document the lives of Southern US sharecroppers during the Great Depression, Agee and Evans (1960: xiv–xv) saw themselves as undertaking 'an independent inquiry … [in which] the immediate instruments are two: the motionless camera, and the printed word. The governing instrument – which is also one of the centers of the subject – is individual, anti-authoritative human consciousness.' Agee and Evans (1960: xv) adamantly argued that they were not interested in producing art or politics – or a book, for that matter – but rather 'an effort in human actuality', and so they created text and photos that documented the lives of sharecroppers in intricate detail. So successful were they in this attempt to 'live inside the subject', as Evans (Agee and Evans, 1960: xi) put it, that the book is now considered a classic of phenomenological inquiry – that is, of meticulous commitment to the phenomenon under study, rather than to any external agenda.

From the other side of this dialectic, consider again W. Eugene Smith's photographs of corporate criminality and its aftermath – and his agenda in producing them. Smith shot these photos in and around Minamata, a Japanese fishing village whose inhabitants had been poisoned, deformed and killed by the Chiso Corporation's pervasive discharging of toxic mercury. Smith went to Minamata precisely to promote the villagers' cause and to reveal the company's guilt – and despite being beaten almost blind by company thugs, he managed to produce a series of searingly effective photographs: photographs of filthy industrial waste and arrogant company officials, of protesting villagers and their deformed children. 'Each time I pressed the shutter', Smith once said, 'it was a shouted condemnation….' (Miller, 1997: 140; see Smith, 1998: 302–12)

Quite a dialectic indeed – on the one side, the phenomenologist focused only on the precise particulars of the photographic subject, on the other, the partisan inflamed by a passion for photographic exposé and moral condemnation. In reality, though, each of these orientations requires something of the other – and Walker

Evans, W. Eugene Smith and other documentary photographers have long explored this very tension and the human insights it can provide.

Agee and Evans' project of documenting the lives of sharecroppers, for example, was in many ways as morally charged as was Smith's photographic indictment of corporate crime. They characterized their work as an effort at the 'recording, communication, *analysis*, and *defense*' of those they studied, and all 'in the service of an anger and of a love and of an indiscernible truth' (Agee and Evans, 1960: xiv, 9, emphasis added). For them, to pay close and respectful attention to those they studied was also to declare a certain *affiliation* with them, and so to defend them against those who would degrade or dismiss them. Carefully recording the lives of those forced to the social margins, they quite intentionally invested those lives with dignity and visibility; through this process they in turn offered moral condemnation for those too privileged to pay such attention (including, by the way, those who would encounter the text and photos only as momentary diversion). Even the book's title was meant as 'a deception' (Agee and Evans, 1960: xiv, 405), an ironic commentary comparing the usual adulation afforded the powerful with the anonymity afforded those 'which have no memorial; who perished, as though they had never been'.

Moreover, as Agee and Evans made explicit, they could not in reality 'live inside the subject' and document it at the same time; after all, a written description is not the thing described, a photograph not the person photographed and a book not the world it narrates. Instead, they were left to create an elegantly *aesthetic representation* of a marginalized group generally excluded from such representation; that is, they were left to craft words and images that, in their tone and style, could attune others to the texture of their subjects' everyday lives. This, they well knew, was an inevitable act of cultural translation in the interest of creative communication, an act that both affirmed and violated their commitment to the phenomenon under study.

By the same token, W. Eugene Smith's political commitments were in many ways indistinguishable from his personal commitment to those he photographed. To produce his Minamata photos, Smith lived for three years in the village, conducting research, assisting the villagers and 'existing on $50 a week and a diet of home-grown vegetables, rice and whiskey' (Miller, 1997: 156). Agee and Evans, it can be noted in comparison, lived among the sharecropper families they studied for four weeks. Earlier in his career, Smith had likewise been sent on a brief assignment to produce photographs of the city of Pittsburgh – and ended up spending four years on the project, along the way impoverishing himself, ruining his family and endangering his mental and physical health. Taking Benzedrine so as to work around the clock, Smith shot more than 13,000 photos in an attempt to capture the city's unnoticed nuances. Here again, though, attentiveness was also critical analysis; Smith meant this deep phenomenology of Pittsburgh to undermine the shallow boosterism of his original assignment and to exact 'revenge against the commercial system' (Trachtenburg, 1998: 174) that reduced photographers to paid image producers.

This subtle dialectic of attentiveness and critical analysis seems essential to the continued development of cultural criminology and its visual orientation. Lacking moral and political focus, even the most detailed of ethnographic work into culture and crime will produce little more than a scattergun chronicle of one situation or another; absent the understanding that the researcher inevitably transforms the situation by recording it, such work will perpetuate an unfortunate sort of naïve objectivity as well. Yet, moral and political analysis in cultural criminology cannot stand alone, either; divorced from the particulars of social life, disembedded from the nuances of everyday struggles, such analysis becomes abstract and ill-defined, more an imposition on those we study than a commitment to them. Like the documentary photographers, we must find ways to produce images of crime and culture that embody both – both little moments of human pathos and larger patterns of social harm.

Image/text

Given the logocentrism of mainstream criminology and other 'social sciences', a consideration of image, text and their appropriate interplay is especially critical if cultural criminology is to position itself as an alternative, visually-attuned criminology. As we have already suggested, mainstream criminology generally does photographic images a double disservice in relation to text – first by relegating them to textual illustration and second by doing so with little or no awareness of the assumptions underlying this relegation. As a consequence, as we have shown elsewhere (Ferrell *et al.*, 2008), images of crime are often utilized only for their visual appeal, and worse, utilized in a way that perpetuates stereotypical misunderstandings of crime and justice rather than confronting them.

Unsurprisingly, documentary photographers have more than once confronted the problematic image/text dialectic that criminologists generally ignore – but, as before, have produced from this confrontation not so much clear answers as various creative tensions. The work of Walker Evans is again instructive. In *Let Us Now Praise Famous Men*, Agee and Evans (1960: xiv–xv) take pains to point out that 'the photographs are not illustrative. They, and the text, are coequal, mutually independent, and fully collaborative' – though they worry nonetheless that 'by their fewness' the photographs may be seen as subordinate by readers of the book. As if to guard against this, they group the photos exclusively in the front of the book – preceding even the title page and table of contents – with the 400 or so pages of Agee's text following. Another of Evans' projects reproduced this approach and reversed it. Asked to 'illustrate' a book on 1930s Cuba and its political upheavals (Beals, 1933), Evans agreed only on condition that he retain the right to 'choose the photographs for publication, to establish the sequence, and to collect them at the end of the book so that they appear as an independent entity and not as illustration for the text' (Evans, 1989; Mora, 1989: 9).

Of course, this is no solution to the problem of image and text; it is just a particular sort of disjointed tension. The segregation of photographic images from text certainly serves to wall off the possibility of textual dominance and to deny assumptions that the images function only as textual illustration. Yet, when image and text are meant as complementary forms within a larger project – as in both of Evans' book projects – this 'separate but equal' strategy seems in some ways an odd solution. Structurally divorced from one another, image and text struggle to find affiliation absent the power of immediate juxtaposition – and the reader/viewer is left to toggle, mentally if not physically, between a bank of images here and a swath of text there. Compounded further by the demands of publishers, the limits of paper quality or presentation technology, and other complications, this image/text interplay admits of no easy solution. Cultural criminologists are little help, either, with some of their works dispersing images throughout text (Presdee, 2000; Ferrell, 2001, 2006), and others grouping images between large sections of text (Ferrell, 1996; Hayward, 2004).

This problem of appropriate image/text dynamics can be at least partially addressed by considering the *purpose* of images vis-à-vis text and text vis-à-vis images. The first we have already addressed: The importance of images is such that they must serve a purpose vis-à-vis text that transcends simple illustration. The second – the purpose of text in relation to images – has been explored by Roland Barthes, Susan Sontag and others. In his seminal essay *Rhetoric of the Image*, Barthes (1978: 36) argues that 'the viewer of the image receives at one and the same time the perceptual message and the cultural message', thus illustrating the communicative power of mass images and the need, at times, for textual explication of their cultural norms and perceptual qualities. Barthes' *Camera Lucida* (1981) and Susan Sontag's *On Photography* (1977) further suggest a visual semiotics attuned to the layering of meaning, with *denotation* focusing on what or who is depicted and *connotation* emphasizing the various ideas and values that are expressed through the content and structure of representation.

In this context, Barthes (1978) distinguishes, for example, between *anchorage* and *delay*. In Barthes' terms, 'anchorage' suggests the use of text to fix the otherwise layered and uncertain meanings of the image. Here the text directs the viewer of the image, offering an interpretative guide for identifying and understanding its content. Of course, this dynamic in many ways re-establishes textual dominance of the image, not by relegating the image to textual illustration, but by confining its meaning within the explanatory power of the text. Alternatively, 'relay' suggests an interplay whereby text and image each complement the other – that is, serve to illustrate and illuminate the other – as fragments of a larger narrative. In this sense, both image and text become something more in the presence of the other, amplifying and deepening the layered meanings available within each medium, in the service of integrated communication (on this point in relation to the production of tabloid newspaper front pages see Carney, this volume). This sense of 'relay' does not provide the final answer to the question of image and text – but it does suggest for cultural criminology that the photographic penetration of criminology's logocentrism can in fact produce more powerful images and text alike.

Immersion/immediacy

Henri Cartier-Bresson's notion of the 'decisive moment' – the documentary photographer's ability to capture an image, on-the-spot and in the instant – stands as a definitive concept in photodocumentary work. Yet, Cartier-Bresson meant to suggest far more than simply the quick click of the shutter; for him, the decisive moment signified 'the simultaneous recognition, in a fraction of a second, of the significance of an event as well as a precise organization of forms which give that event its proper expression' (Cartier-Bresson in Miller, 1997: 102). In the immediacy of the decisive moment, then, a merging of form and content, with the resultant photograph embodying both the photographer's understanding of an event's social significance and the photographer's ability to capture and communicate that significance formally.

Now a half century old, Cartier-Bresson's concept of the decisive moment today seems more appropriate than ever – and a particularly important concept for cultural criminology as it goes about critically confronting the contemporary world of late modernity. The rhythms of this late modern world are frequently those of liquidity (Bauman, 2000) and speed (Virilio, 1986), its culture a fast-twitch flow of instant information, shifting populations and emergent meaning. In this world, traditionally stable structures of economy, law and crime are increasingly undermined by all manner of precarious contingencies – and knowledge of these structures and contingencies often comes as much from visual documentation as from textual account. Encountering this world, photographers – and criminologists – must be ready for the fleeting if decisive moment, ready to record the dynamics of power and transgression in the immediacy of a situation or event. Police brutality, street protest, political scandal, ethnic violence – all can be caught and communicated if we are attuned to the decisive moments in which they crystallize. Here, even, is a new sort of sensibility that reimagines cultural criminology's twin foci on visual communication and ethnography: a sense of *instant ethnography* (Ferrell *et al.*, 2008: 179–82), where depth of understanding develops not from long-term involvement but from the immediacy of short-term awareness.

And yet, if Cartier-Bresson's notion of the decisive moment suggests this sort of immediacy, it suggests something of traditional ethnography's long-term immersion as well. Recall that Cartier-Bresson demands, in the decisive moment, the recognition of an event's 'significance' as well as an ability to capture that event in those visual forms that give it its 'proper expression'. But of course understanding the social significance of an exploding street protest or a guard's sudden attack on a prisoner cannot happen only in that moment; it requires prior familiarization, immersion and investigation. Likewise, the photographer's 'proper' formal decision can only be made within an understanding of this same significance. Producing documentary photographs of a prison scene, should we shoot the prison guard's face in shadow, or the prisoner's? When we photograph street protesters, should we include the local police in the background, or the foreground or not at all? As Cartier-Bresson makes clear, these questions cannot be answered on purely aesthetic or technical grounds; they can only be answered through intimate knowledge of the social dynamics that such formal considerations are meant to capture and communicate. Deep knowledge of the prison and its (in)human dynamics will suggest whether shadow or light better animates the photograph; close knowledge of the protesters and their grievances will position the photographer so as to put the protesters and the police in the right place. As with W. Eugene Smith's years in Pittsburgh or Minimata, as with Robert Capa's years in the Spanish Civil War or Indochina, the decisive moment emerges from the countless moments of cultural immersion and human commitment that have preceded it.

Conclusion

The decisive moment is now

In terms of history and culture, the decisive moment – for cultural criminology, for documentary photography, for the development of critical visual analysis – is now. Today we occupy a world so suffused with image and representation, so thoroughly awash in visual information, that it overwhelms even the steadiest of gazes. In this world, existing tensions between objectivity and subjectivity, between attentiveness and analysis, between image and text, are only amplified and exacerbated. Now the everyday use of mobile phone cameras and video phones is such that school kids, bus passengers and street gang members regularly come to operate, if for a moment, as news photographers and visual provocateurs. Now, through photo sharing technology like Flickr.com and Picasa, amateur photographers post and share images in such numbers that, collectively, they create a sweeping, polymorphous archive of everyday life. Now, as Jean Baudrillard (2006: 87) has said, 'there is no longer the need for "embedded" [war] journalists because soldiers themselves are immersed in the image – thanks to digital technology, the images are definitively integrated into the war' – and the goal of the wars they fight is less military victory than symbolic erasure. Now all those that criminology defines as its subject matter – criminals, police officers and law makers – produce, deploy and consume the image as part of their everyday endeavours. In this world, there is no escape from the image, no escape from its implications, no possibility of divorcing crime and crime control from visual representation. The decisive visual moment has arrived, it forms flickering before us, its significance assured.

Yet, the image's increasing saturation of social life has hardly been accompanied by an increase in the general *understanding* of the image and its consequences; just as the distance between the image and the events it represents has collapsed, so has the critical distance separating the image from reflection on its meaning. The very availability of the image inhibits its understanding; the flashes from a hundred mobile phone cameras illuminating a late-night club, the shutters of a hundred high-end cameras clicking at a police chief's news conference, are today cause not for critical inquiry but a reassuring sense of normalcy. Meanwhile, in mainstream academic criminology, the venues are not clubs and press conferences but textbooks, journal articles and electronic lecture presentations – images, images everywhere, but seldom a drop of critical analysis. The monograph's cover photograph, bought from a stock image bank, offers all the emotional depth of a survey research question; the staged textbook photo of 'juvenile delinquency' or 'domestic violence' recalls the stale stench of a laboratory experiment – yet, few criminologists look beyond the photographic decoration to inquire into its meaning and circumstances.

In this sense, we would suggest that now is not only the decisive moment, but the decisive *crisis* – the crisis of a mainstream criminology ill-equipped to critically engage with the image-saturated worlds of crime and control. With its attentiveness to meaning and representation, cultural criminology on the other hand is well-positioned to address this crisis – and with its existing strengths in visual analysis and ethnographic methods, it is particularly well positioned to draw on the insights offered by the long history of documentary photography. Still, as we have emphasized throughout this chapter, the photodocumentary tradition is most useful not as a template, but as a series of sensitivities to essential tensions that inform any serious engagement with the image. And even these tensions must be reimagined under present conditions. Researchers and activists with access to emerging digital technology now create and share extensive photographic archives, in the process developing powerful photodocumentary accounts that can subvert officially sanctioned images. As independent documentary filmmakers like David Redmon, Ashley Sabin and Bill Daniel are showing, in-depth filmic accounts of social control, social harm and resistance are likewise now being created by those who are outsiders to political and economic power, but insiders in the world of do-it-yourself image-making technology (Daniel, 2005; Sabin and Redmon, 2007; see also Hoffman and Brown, this volume).

In fact, moving beyond orthodox criminology by revisiting and reimagining the photodocumentary tradition suggests a final tension, and one entirely appropriate to the iconoclastic style of cultural criminology: We might best learn the promise of documentary photography if we embrace it as an adventure in *unlearning*. The more we learn from the photodocumentary tradition, the more we unlearn the stifling imperatives of conventional research design, unlearn conventional images of criminals and control agents, unlearn an orthodox criminology choking on its own words. Moments of intellectual estrangement are, after all, moments of anomic insight – moments in which we can battle what Barthes (1979: 16) calls the 'sedimentation' of knowledge with *sapientia*: 'no power, a little knowledge, a little wisdom, and as much flavour as possible'. As visual sociologist Emmanuel David (2007: 251) says, photographic work in this subversive context can operate as a significant form of 'visual resistance', not only to the powerful and their carefully calculated imagery, but also to 'the milieu of social researchers who choose not to look at the world'.

Recognizing the significance of this decisive moment, catching something of its animating tensions, cultural criminology can only gain from formulating its proper expression.

Figures 3.1, 3.2 Decisive Moments. Photographs by Hughes Leglise-Bataille, by permission.

Figure 3.3 A Decisive Moment. Photographs by Hughes Leglise-Bataille, by permission.

References

Agee, J. and Evans, W. (1960) *Let Us Now Praise Famous Men*, New York: Ballantine.

Alvelos, H. (2004) 'The Desert of Imagination in the City of Signs', in J. Ferrell, *et al.* (eds) *Cultural Criminology Unleashed*, London: GlassHouse, pages 181–91.

Alvelos, H. (2005) 'The Glamour of Grime', *Crime, Media, Culture*, 1(2): 215–17.

Barthes, R. (1978) *Image-Music-Text,* New York: Hill & Wang.

Barthes, R. (1979) Lecture in Inauguration of the Chair of Literary Semiology, Collège de France, 7 January 1977. *October* 8: 3–16.

Barthes, R. (1981) *Camera Lucida,* New York: Hill & Wang.

Baudrillard, J. (2006) 'War Porn', *Journal of Visual Culture,* 5(1): 86–88.

Bauman, Z. (2000) *Liquid Modernity,* Cambridge: Polity.

Beals, C. (1933) *The Crime of Cuba,* Philadelphia: Lippincott.

Brown, M. (2006) 'The Aesthetics of Crime', in B. Arrigo and C. Williams, (eds) *Philosophy, Crime, and Criminology,* Urbana, IL: University of Illinois Press, pages 223–56.

Collier, M. (2001) 'Approaches to Analysis in Visual Anthropology', in T. V. Leeuwen and C. Jewitt (eds) *Handbook of Visual Analysis,* London: Sage.

Courtney, D. and Lyng, S. (2007) 'Taryn Simons and The Innocence Project', *Crime, Media, Culture,* 3(2): 175–91.

Daniel, B. (2005) *Who Is Bozo Texino?* [film].

David, E. (2007) 'Signs of Resistance', in G. Stanczak (ed.) *Visual Research Methods,* Los Angeles: Sage, pages 225–54.

Evans, W. (1989) *Walker Evans: Havana 1933,* New York: Pantheon.
Ferrell, J. (1996) *Crimes of Style,* Boston: Northeastern University Press.
Ferrell, J. (1997) 'Criminological *Verstehen*: Inside the Immediacy of Crime', *Justice Quarterly,* 14(1): 3–23.
Ferrell, J. (2001) *Tearing Down the Streets,* New York: St. Martin's/Palgrave.
Ferrell, J. (2006) *Empire of Scrounge,* New York: New York University Press.
Ferrell, J. and Hamm, M. (eds) (1998) *Ethnography at the Edge,* Boston: Northeastern.
Ferrell, J., Hayward, K. and Young, J. (2008) *Cultural Criminology: An Invitation,* London: Sage.
Hamm, M. (2002) *In Bad Company,* Boston: Northeastern.
Hamm, M. (2007) '"High Crimes and Misdemeanors": George W. Bush and the Sins of Abu Ghraib', *Crime, Media, Culture,* 3(3): 259–84.
Hannigan, W. (1999) *New York Noir,* New York: Rizzoli.
Hayward, K. (2004) *City Limits: Crime, Consumer Culture and the Urban Experience,* London: Cavendish/Glasshouse.
Hill, J. (1998) 'W. Eugene Smith: His Techniques and Process', in W. E. Smith, *W. Eugene Smith: Photographs 1934–1975,* New York: Harry Abrams, pages 336–43.
Jones, P. and Wardle, C. (2008). '"No Emotion, No Sympathy": The Visual Construction of Maxine Carr', *Crime, Media, Culture,* 4(1): 53–71.
McLaughlin, E. and Greer, C. (2008) 'Reporting Murder', Paper presented at the Crime, Culture and Conflict Conference, London, England, March.
Miller, R. (1999) *Magnum: Fifty Years at the Front Line of History – The Story of the Legendary Photo Agency*, New York: Grove.
Mora, G. (1989) 'Havana, 1933: A Seminal Work', in W. Evans. (ed.) *Walker Evans: Havana 1933,* New York: Pantheon, pages 8–23.
Morrison, W. (2004) '"Reflections with Memories": Everyday Photography Capturing Genocide', *Theoretical Criminology,* 8(3): 341–58.
Nachtwey, J. (1999) *Inferno,* London: Phaidon Press.
Presdee, M. (2000) *Cultural Criminology and the Carnival of Crime,* London: Routledge.
Rodriguez, R.T. (2003) 'On the Subject of Gang Photography', in L. Kontos, D. Brotherton and L. Barrios (eds) *Gangs and Society: Alternative Perspectives,* New York: Columbia University Press, pages 255–82.
Sabin, A. and Redmon, D. (2007) *Kamp Katrina,* Carnivalesque [film].
Salgado, S. (2001) *The Impact of War on Children,* Hampshire, England: Palgrave Macmillan.
Salgado, S. (2005) *Migrations,* New York: Aperture.
Smith, W.E. (1998) *W. Eugene Smith: Photographs 1934–1975,* New York: Harry Abrams.
Snyder, G. (2008) *Graffiti Lives,* New York: New York University Press.
Sontag, S. (1977) *On Photography,* New York: Picador.
Sontag, S. (2004) *Regarding the Pain of Others,* New York: Picador.
Trachtenberg, A. (1998) 'W. Eugene Smith's Pittsburgh: Rumours of a City', in W. E Smith (ed.) *W. Eugene Smith: Photographs 1934–1975,* New York: Harry Abrams, pages 174–82.
Tunnell, K. (2006) 'Socially Disorganized Rural Communities', *Crime, Media, Culture,* 2(3): 332–37.
Valier, C. and Lippens, R. (2005) 'Moving Images, Ethics and Justice', *Punishment and Society*, 6(3): 319–33.

Vergara, C.J. (1995) *The New American Ghetto,* New Brunswick, NJ: Rutgers University Press.

Virilio, P. (1986) *Speed and Politics,* New York: Semiotext(e).

Weegee (1945/2002) *Naked City,* Cambridge, MA: Da Capo Press.

Young, A. (2004) *Judging the Image,* London: Routledge.

Chapter 4

Hindley's ghost

The visual construction of Maxine Carr

Philip J. Jones and Claire Wardle

Introduction

In August 2002, two schoolgirls, Jessica Chapman and Holly Wells were abducted and murdered by their school caretaker in the small town of Soham in rural England. Ian Huntley was found guilty and sentenced to life imprisonment in December 2003. His girlfriend Maxine Carr was charged with two counts of assisting an offender. She was cleared of these offences but was found guilty of conspiring to pervert the course of justice, for which she received a sentence of three and a half years. She was released on licence in May 2004 and in February 2005, Carr was granted indefinite anonymity by the high court. Only three other individuals in the UK have ever been the recipient of such an order: Mary Bell,[1] Robert Thompson and Jon Venables[2]. Significantly, Maxine Carr is the only one not to have committed a murder.

Public hatred for Carr has been both extreme and transparent. The decision to enforce her anonymity order was taken because of concerns that there was 'a real and significant risk of injury or … worse … killing, if the injunction [was] not granted' (Edward Fitzgerald QC, quoted in the *Guardian*, 25 February, 2005: 6). Though the crimes of Ian Huntley were despicable in the extreme, Carr's crime – that of perverting the course of justice – would not usually merit such fierce public feeling. Carr's lawyer, Mr Fitzgerald QC certainly believed the media had been instrumental in causing the public's extreme reaction to his client, stating at the injunction hearing that, 'the tone and content of much of what has been published does increase the risk both of physical attack and of harassment', citing evidence of remarks in Internet chat rooms which 'linked to particular unfounded

1 In 1968, eleven-year-old Mary Bell was convicted of the manslaughter of four-year-old Martin Brown and three-year-old Brian Howe. A high court decision in 2003 provided life-long anonymity for both Mary Bell, now 46 and for her eighteen-year-old daughter.

2 In 1993, two-year-old Jamie Bulger was abducted from a Merseyside shopping centre by ten-year-olds Robert Thompson and Jon Venables. The schoolboys were later convicted of the toddler's murder and sentenced to eight years in prison (later increased to ten).

allegations that have been made in the press' (Dyer, *Guardian*, 25 February, 2005: 6).

Article 6 of the European Convention of Human Rights guarantees every defendant the right to a fair trial, and this article has been incorporated into English Law by the Human Rights Act of 1988, complementing the presumption of innocence which has been part of English Common Law for many decades. Article 6 stipulates that those charged with any criminal offence 'shall be presumed innocent until proved guilty according to law'. It is this principle which underpins the 1981 Contempt of Court Act, designed to prevent trial by media. The unenviable position in which Carr finds herself begs the question: how could any contemporaneous trial reportage be so damaging as to warrant a *Contra-Mundum* injunction of indefinite anonymity without once being held in contempt?

This chapter explores the role of the media in constructing Carr as Huntley's accomplice, thereby creating the false impression that the crime of which she was convicted was equal to his. We focus on the visual coverage of the Soham murder trial in the centre-right national press, exploring the ways in which Carr was visually constructed in comparison to Huntley. We are not arguing that it was newspaper coverage alone which caused such high levels of public hatred, and certainly it needs to be acknowledged that there were a series of interwoven factors which culminated in the coverage Carr received: her gender, her class, the severity of Huntley's crime and the context of a desperately competitive newspaper market which was well aware of the ability of this particular crime story to sell newspapers. Her gender was a particularly powerful factor as the idea that a woman could be in any way involved in harming a child remains incomprehensible to most. Stereotypical notions of women as exclusively nurturing make certain of this. Women who have been involved in serious crimes are dismissed as insane, possessed or lovesick, acting solely to impress a lover. Much could be written about the significant role played by Maxine Carr's gender in terms of the public's negative view of her. This chapter, however, deals with the role played by the media in constructing Carr's public image, reflecting on the way in which gender intersected with the type of coverage she received.

Whereas processing text requires time and dedicated mental consideration, a visual, or collection of visuals can be read instantaneously, allowing the viewer to draw immediate conclusions. However, these conclusions, though seemingly logical in construction can often be entirely false. While acknowledging that it may not appear worthwhile to demonstrate yet again that coverage of the Soham trial was far from satisfactory, we focus here on a commonly overlooked aspect of media coverage: the formatting of newspaper pages, *particularly the combination of visuals and headline text*. Allowing ambiguous imagery to become a factor for claims of contemptuous coverage would be very difficult, but the way newspapers are able to use visuals to tell misleading stories has often been overlooked, both in terms of legal affairs, but also as a central area of interest within journalism studies.

There were two ways in which the newspapers we studied portrayed Carr: firstly, by drawing on stereotypical depictions of female criminals, particularly using Myra Hindley[3] as their 'template' (Kitzinger, 2000); and secondly, by juxtaposing newspaper images which encouraged a dominant reading of Carr's guilt as Huntley's accomplice. Throughout the coverage we analysed, Carr was portrayed alongside Huntley, with the same level of interest. Just as the newspapers visually examined his life story, his motivations, and his lifestyle, the same questions were visually asked of Carr, positioning her on an equal footing with Huntley. The visual images 'told' a very different story to the accompanying newspaper articles, whose detailed texts spelled out the differences in their crimes. Significantly, there were no such qualifications in their visual representation, with Carr in many cases featuring more frequently than Huntley.

Given the rubric of this volume, and especially the ongoing struggle over the 'power of the image' that animates cultural criminology, it is important to note that Maxine Carr's indefinite anonymity order directly affected how this research has been published. In order for us to share our findings, it was clear that we would need to include a number of reproductions of the kind of images these newspapers used. Reprinting newspaper images requires copyright permission; this is usually a straightforward process. However, in this case, none of the newspapers we contacted granted us the permissions required. Rather ironically, we have been told that this is due to the newspapers *upholding* Carr's anonymity order. As a direct result of this embargo, this chapter cannot reproduce any of the images that we suggest added to the public's loathing of Maxine Carr. We have therefore been denied the opportunity of using these images to support our argument that their prior use facilitated the granting of an indefinite anonymity order – *because of that same order.* When we pointed out that all of the images we wanted to include have already been freely available in the public domain, and in no way compromised Carr's current anonymity status, we were told again that the embargo covered all images regardless of the date of publication. Furthermore, we have been instructed that any artistic impressions or line drawings of the layouts concerned would not be permitted. Any reproduction, whether photographic, artistic or schematic is an infringement of copyright law. It seems then, that the vicious newspaper coverage we are describing here has led, not only to Maxine Carr's current public personae, but also to a mechanism through which the newspapers responsible are now protected from criticism. Because of these complications, the following analysis relies heavily on descriptive portrayals of the newspaper layouts and headlines in this sample.

3 Myra Hindley, alongside her boyfriend Ian Brady, was convicted of the abduction, abuse and murder of three children in Britain in the mid-1960s. They were known as the Moors Murderers as the children's bodies were found on the Yorkshire Moors. Because of the notoriety of the crimes, in 1990, the Home Secretary ruled that both Hindley and Brady should never be released from prison. Hindley died in prison in 2002.

Focus

The power and influence of press photography

The influence press photographs have had in the public's understanding of violent crime is not well understood. Their power may lie in an ability to function on two levels simultaneously (Sekula, 1974; Barthes, 1977; Tagg, 1988; Zelizer, 1995, 1998). On the one hand, photographs work denotatively, 'naturally' displaying real-life events. On the other hand, images work connotatively, drawing on broad symbolic systems, visually representing much larger hidden codes of meaning. In *Image, Music, Text*, Roland Barthes (1977) explored how myth affects the connotative/denotative interpretations of the photograph. He stated that all of the imitative arts, such as drawing or painting, contain two systems of meaning: (a) their denotative meaning, which Barthes defined as 'the analogue itself'; the actual 'thing' that is being imitated; and (b) the connotative message, defined as 'the manner in which the society ... communicates what it thinks of [the object]' made up from stock stories, stereotypes or genres (Barthes, 1977: 17). However, the press photograph seems at first glance to be unique in that it has a certain denotative meaning, but is devoid of any connotative system; it simply 'is' the thing that it portrays.

Hall (1981: 227) reiterated Barthes theory that the photograph signifies through 'the lexicon of expressive features distributed throughout the culture of which the reader is a member'. These codes depend for their decipherment upon the reader's ability to 'resolve a set of gestural, non-linguistic features ... into a specific expressive configuration' (ibid). Once interpreted, the photograph becomes a sign of these same interpretations. It becomes what Hall calls the 'index of an ideological theme' (ibid: 238). A photograph imbued and read within the dominant ideology will itself become expressive of those ideas; will solidify them, then seem to connote them inherently.

Hall argues that the dominant ideology of a society is that which seems pedestrian in nature; '[w]e have seen it before, a thousand different signs and messages seem to signify the same ideological meaning' (ibid: 239). In representing the world, news photographs become something different; they become part of the 'great storehouse' of information; another brick in the wall of representation and a tool to make us interpret the world in a particular way. Like Barthes, Hall argues that this ideological function has become naturalized; that the 'image loses its motivation and appears naturally to have selected itself' (ibid: 247).

Accepting this to be the case, how do readers process a 'naturally selected' photograph, when it appears alongside text? While there has been research which suggests visual accompaniments encourage more readers to focus on an article and facilitate information recall (Thorson, 1995), and other research has deconstructed the way in which different visual features: headline size, number, size and colour of photographs, position of captions on the page influences the way in which readers receive information (Kress and Van Leeuwen, 1996), the relationship between words and images in news texts has been understudied. Judging from simply the focus of much journalism studies research, the assumption remains that images are regarded as secondary to the texts and considered as having a merely supportive role in terms of emphasising the messages inherent in them. As Zelizer (1998: 2) writes 'we still do not know enough about how images help record public events, about whether and in which ways images function as better vehicles of proof than words, and about which vehicles – word or image – takes precedence in situations of conflict between what the words tell and the pictures show us'.

Content analysis

A content analysis of the relative size, number and content of images in this sample was carried out in order to explore 'how much' coverage Huntley and Carr each received.

In our sample, the image of Huntley appeared 124 times (the *Sun* 76, the *Daily Mail* 33 and the *Times* 15). The image of Carr appeared 104 times (the *Sun* 53, the *Daily Mail* 34 and the *Times* 17), and while the *Sun* included 23 fewer images on Carr than Huntley, the *Daily Mail* and the *Times* included slightly more images of Carr than Huntley. While these figures are surprising, it is in the size of these images that real discrepancies between the amount of newspaper space given to Carr and Huntley are most apparent.

As Table 4.1 illustrates, in total, photographs of Maxine Carr took up more space in the *Daily Mail* and the *Times,* than photographs of Ian Huntley. In the *Sun*, the total size of all photographs of Huntley was 10947 cm^2 compared with 8799 cm^2 for Carr, however, when this figure was divided by the number of individual photographs, an image of Maxine Carr was actually 22 cm^2 larger than that of Ian Huntley. Overall, in the *Sun* and the *Times*, photographs of Carr were on average larger than photographs of Huntley, and in the *Daily Mail,* the difference was only three squared centimetres. The difference in the *Times* was the most striking, with a difference of 46 cm^{2}. Across all three sample newspapers, the average size for a single image of Huntley was 166 cm^2. The average size of a single image of Carr was 187 cm^2. In this sample, images of Carr are therefore on average 21 cm^2 larger than those of Huntley.

Table 4.1 Content analysis: Image size by paper.

	Sun		*Daily Mail*		*Times*	
	Total	*Average*	*Total*	*Average*	*Total*	*Average*
Carr	8,799 cm^2	166 cm^2	5,826 cm^2	171 cm^2	3,842 cm^2	226 cm^2
Huntley	10,947 cm^2	144 cm^2	5,742 cm^2	174 cm^2	2,710 cm^2	180 cm^2

This simple content analysis provides the foundation for our discursive visual analysis. There is no denying visual coverage of Maxine Carr was substantial, with larger, more colourful graphics and in two newspapers, more images of Carr than Huntley. This seems astonishing considering the crimes with which they were individually charged and ultimately sentenced. In the following section, we explore those images further, emphasising the ways in which the images worked alongside one another and were contextualized by the headline. It is clear that newspaper picture editors decided to rely on conventional portrayals of female offenders, emphasising stereotypical ideas positioning female criminality somewhere between lunacy and monstrosity. In addition, page layouts, photographic montages and headlines narrativised the events, placing Maxine Carr in a central role, elevating her actions above those with which she was ultimately charged.

Visual analysis

The archetypal male-female partnership in recent crime history could be argued to be Myra Hindley and boyfriend Ian Brady, who were convicted of a number of child murders between 1963 and 1965. Hindley's infamy far outweighed Brady, a phenomenon explained by research undertaken by Grabe *et al.* (2006) which demonstrates how women who commit crimes which violate gender stereotypes (violent crimes and crimes against children) and women who work alongside a man are given the most vicious treatment of all. Birch (1993: 33) in her exploration of Hindley's representation in *If Looks Could Kill* argues that the 'symbolic weight' she carries, 'far exceeds the crimes of two individuals at a particular place and time'. Hindley has passed smoothly into folklore, her image, iconic now; the dyed blonde hair, the impassive stare, 'what she herself has called "that awful mug shot"[4] connotes 'modern affectless evil in a way that the contemporary photograph of Brady never has' (French, 1996: 38).

The image of Hindley has become entangled with the very worst representations of criminal women. Her position in the cannon of evil is concrete. Her image has become a tool with which we understand and somehow comprehend the incomprehensible. When a man offends he can be sure that his crime will be 'both imaginable and possibly even seen as human,' after all, argues Morrissey (2003), 'male crime in all forms, from fictional to factual, is frequently articulated, debated, portrayed, glorified, even fantasized' (2003: 16; see relatedly Ferrell, Hayward and Young, 2008: 206–10). Conversely, the actions of the female offender connote, what Helena Kennedy has called the 'profound expression of our worst fears about the social fabric falling apart' (quoted in Meyers and Wight, 1996: xiv).

4 On the day Hindley and Brady were convicted, the police photographs from the day of their arrest were printed side by side on the front cover of the *Daily Mirror*. The photograph has become iconic through countless reproductions.

Many images of Carr recalled the 'lunatic' template of female criminality. In one particular image, the comparison is not with Myra Hindley, but with Lady Macbeth. In a double page spread from the *Sun*, the full page headline shrieks 'Carr scrubbed tiles so hard she said paint was coming off' with an accompanying large image of Carr, defiant, cold and outwardly calm (7 November 2003: 6–7). While what we see is Carr, upright, neat and presentable, the image conjured is of a woman dishevelled, on hands and knees desperately stripping paint from blooded walls. The lunatic imagery was underlined by one recurring image of Carr. In the *Daily Mail*, beneath the headline, 'Maxine talked about the girls in the past tense, then laughed', we see Carr smirking, with her tongue pushed out of the side of her month, and curled up at the end. The image suggests that once exposed the mask falls away and we see the real Maxine; a grinning, tongue curling, duplicitous gargoyle who laughs in the face of other's pain. This was a photograph which clearly appealed to photo editors in all three newspapers, as the same image appeared in the other two newspapers on other dates, although they were outside the sample period (*Times*, 25 February 2005, p. 3, *Sun* 15 January 2004).

The most entrenched template for representing female offenders is of the monster (Smart, 1977a, 1977b; Carlen, 1985; Cameron and Fraser, 1987; Birch, 1993; French, 1996; Knelman, 1998; Morrissey, 2003) and the archetypal violent 'monstrous' woman remains Myra Hindley. Maxine Carr did not commit any violent crime, but she suffered guilt through association, not just from Ian Huntley, but also from Myra herself. On 4 December 2003, a full front page spread in the *Sun* showed Carr, in half profile looking to her right staring blankly into space. Though she is facing forward, she does not look directly at the reader, but drops her eyes slightly.

This is an example of a photograph of Carr associated with the iconic 'mug-shot' image of Hindley from 1965. However, for those readers unable to draw that connection, a smaller, updated image of Hindley is printed in the corner of the page. Along this image, a banner headline presented in block capitals, coloured red and outlined in white, screams, 'MYRA MK II'. The *Sun* does not directly compare this fresh faced image of Carr with the terrible, platinum haired, devil eyed Myra that was her own unfortunate emblem, but with the withered, middle-aged and beaten Myra, just months before her death. The effect of this is to imply that as the old evil dies, the new takes its place. It is as if there will always be a Myra; that evil this powerful is somehow immortal. It does not grow out of human nature, but jumps from body to body.

On the 18 October 2003, the *Times* published a double page spread on pages 10–11. In the far top left, a mid to small size reproduction of Huntley appears. The image is in black and white, small and inconsequential. To his right, the main headline reads, '[t]he strange and tangled past of a man who lost his bride to his brother'. Below this an additional headline reads, '[h]e took a girl aged eleven to an orchard and sexually assaulted her. She ran, he gave chase and threatened to kill her if she told'. Surprisingly, however, half of the adjacent page is taken up with Carr's mug shot, in colour, above the headline, '[a] quiet home-loving girl with the fatal knack of falling for the wrong man'. Below this, a second image of the young Carr appears. What is interesting here is the imbalance between image size, quality and number with the content of the stories they complement. Though two headlines here concern Huntley, and Huntley alone, two of the three images seen depict Carr. Over half of the text across these pages is copy concerning Huntley, yet his image, relatively small, black and white, is pushed into the far corner; sidelined by a considerably larger advertisement for PC World. The colour images of Carr, while only accompanying an approximately 1000 word fairly inconsequential biography piece cover four times as many square cm as Huntley's (Huntley image was 234 cm^2, while the two Carr images totalled 852 cm^2).

A double page spread from *the Sun* (8 December, 2003: 8–9) exemplifies these themes. Here, in the top left hand corner a ('non-connected') headline reads: '2 baby murders defy belief – QC'. At the bottom right, the images of Holly and Jessica appear superimposed across a larger image of Huntley. To his right, on the opposing page, an image of Carr holds the infamous card given to her by the two schoolgirls.[5] Below her, a subheading reads 'Holly card was a talisman … you knew she'd died', and to her left, a large headline reads 'you lied and lied'.

The point to be made here concerns the image chosen to represent Huntley; in profile staring directly at the image of Carr. This layout implies narrative progression. The top left hand corner concerns the death of two children. The eye moves instinctively to the small children below (though, it should be said, not those of the previous story). These children having been superimposed upon the image of Huntley, whom we know to be the accused in this case, cements their association. Huntley then looks to Carr. Carr, for her part, stares at the reader; she forms the end of the story. The effect of this narrative play of images represents Huntley as merely a player in a larger story, the dénouement of which still belongs to Carr.

The most striking example of this kind appears in a centre spread from the *Daily Mail* (2 December, 2003: 6–7). Here a headline reads, 'I picked Jessica up, took her downstairs and went back for Holly. I put the bodies in my car and drove.' To the immediate right of this headline we see a large, colour image of Maxine Carr. To her right, in a smaller frame, is the house and car she shared with Huntley, both images superimposed across a picture of the woods where Holly and Jessica were found.

Why, when the headline directly quotes Huntley's court testimony does it appear in conjunction with an image of Carr? A tiny caption to Carr's right reads, 'Maxine Carr … she knew nothing about the deaths of Holly and Jessica.'

5 Before the girls' bodies were found and Huntley and Carr were charged with their respective crimes, both of them had appeared on television talking about the girls. Maxine Carr, who had been a classroom assistant in their school, showed a note to camera which had been written by the girls and given to Carr on the last day of the previous term.

In these tiny words, we hear what was proved; what cannot be held in contempt while the construction of this page *implies* quite the opposite. Whether intentionally or unintentionally, it is Carr, and not Huntley, who plays the larger role. There is no image of Huntley in this set; no headline mention of his name. The only context in which to imbed the first person 'I' of the headline is with reference to Carr: *Carr* picked Jessica up, *Carr* took her downstairs. Behind her, the ditch where *she* hid the bodies, to her right, the house where the deed was committed and outside the infamous red Ford Fiesta, consistently associated with Carr throughout this sample. Again, whether intentionally or unintentionally this layout pictorially represents the major aspects of the story: the crime scene, the transportation, the grave, the confession, each a crucial, unforgettable part of the murder investigation, and each unequivocally aligned, associated and inextricably linked more directly with Carr than with Huntley. Forcing the reader to infer meaning through the lack of any solid context is used repeatedly to hint at ideas and opinions that may be illegal if expressed through text. If expressed through images – image association between image and text – there can be no proof that these messages are anything other than the overtly subjective interpretations of the reader; a result of what was *seen*, rather than what was shown.

In a further example from the *Sun* (5 November, 2005: 8–9) under the standfirst, '[t]he Soham Murder Case: Jury Sworn In', a large headline reads 'NO EMOTION, NO SYMPATHY'. To the left of this headline two equally sized black and white images of Carr and Huntley are positioned above a list of the charges held against them. The two defendants are on an equal level, just as the two girls are, positioned beside one another in their matching red football shirts superimposed across an image of the courtroom. Once again, due to the lack of context within the headline, the reader must ask 'who' is being described; who has 'no emotion, no sympathy'? Subconscious association pulls the images of Carr and Huntley across to fill this contextual gap. An impression of the defendant's characters has been manufactured through association. Associated with the sentence, 'no emotion, no sympathy', they are represented as a particular *type* of person; a person, in short, much more like a murderer than the rest of us. In fact, this headline refers to Mr Justice Moses' warning to the jury; telling them that they must not 'fall prey to emotion or sympathy' and try the defendants only according to the evidence.

The power of this kind of signification lies in its ability to push the reader to a particular conclusion without their knowledge; to persuade the reader that this or that message was not constructed by the newspaper, but was gleaned and interpreted in their own unique way through instinct. These images promote the impression that the associations contained are 'plain to see' or 'common-sense'; that it is the reader who gleans, interprets and eventually creates meaning. In reality, the reader is guided at every turn into thinking a specific way, conforming to a specific set of values and accepting some things as 'truth' and others as 'lies', all the time believing that these values come from within.

Discussion

The main objective of the 1981 Contempt of Court Act is to avoid trial by media. For journalists, the most important part of the 1981 Contempt of Court Act is set out in sections 1 and 2; The Strict Liability Rule and its limitations. In cases where legislation calls for strict liability, the prosecution has *no need to prove intent*; that the act was committed is enough to secure a conviction. In contempt of court hearings, strict liability guarantees that 'where a publication creates a *substantial risk of serious prejudice* to proceedings... it will be no defence that such an affect was not intended' (Crone, 2002:142). Of specific relevance is that, under the 1981 act, any reportage that portrays a defendant as 'the *type* of person who would commit the crime with which he is charged or which suggests that he should not be believed is likely to attract a charge of contempt [our italics]' (Crone, 2002: 148).

This last point is crucial, because as the aforementioned analysis has demonstrated, Carr and Huntley are equally represented as *exactly the type* of monsters to have committed such crimes. However, this kind of prejudicial contemporaneous reportage did not bring a halt to proceedings, because those opinions deemed contemptuous by this study were communicated via indirect means; through the vagaries of metaphorical signification rather than plain text. It must also be stated that the current climate of heightened emotion regarding child safety and the massive public outcry in reaction to previous murders against children meant it would have been almost impossible for a judge to allow the case to collapse (Critcher, 2002; Kitzinger, 2004; Wardle 2006, 2007).

Newspaper image discourse is becoming increasingly complex in its construction. The use of the 'naturally' denotative and therefore 'objective' nature of the press photograph acts as a mask for political/ideological bias, not just in the reporting of crime, but in newspaper discourse more generally. The very systems used to promote a particular agenda are also those which protect from reproach. How can it be the newspaper's fault if a particular opinion was gleaned from a particular picture, even when cropped, juxtaposed with others, juxtaposed with text, denied context and repeated relentlessly?

Zelizer (1998) has argued that the collective memory has no beginning, no end, is unpredictable and completely irrational (p.4). Nowhere is this more startlingly exemplified than in the formation of the eternal female criminal; she is the weak, the strong; the dolt, the manipulator; the leader, the follower; the prisoner, the jailor; the nun and the whore, she can be all of these things, and all of them at once. Carr can be the monstrous demon who 'told [Huntley] to burn the bodies', she can be 'the misfit who lied for her lover'; she can be the lost child in search of a father while still scrubbing blood from the tiles. They can all exist together in the same representation, unquestioned and unchallenged. She *told* him to do it; he *made her* do it; *they did it together!* The connotative significance of any image of female criminality does not spring unaided from the page, but is injected through the passage of history. As Grabe *et al.* (2006) demonstrated, the power of the Bonnie and Clyde myth in newspaper reporting remains a persuasive one. Even in this case, where Carr and Huntley did not act together, the press constructed them as equals. The mythical narrative of partners committing a crime together 'doub[les] the potential for journalistic titillation' (Grabe *et al.*, 2006: 159). The accepted gender stereotypes can be enforced: the testosterone driven male and the passive women committing a crime, because she is 'blinded by love' and unable to challenge her partner's dominance. However, for the press, romantic mythical explanations are not acceptable when a woman violates the nurturing, nonviolent 'norms' associated with her gender. In Carr's case, even the appearance of being involved in a violent crime towards children ensured her fate.

This study has attempted to show the 'power' images in news can have on representation. Its aim was, in part, to explore how techniques of image construction, juxtaposition and manipulation can force specific inferences while apparently maintaining ideals of journalistic 'objectivity'. We have argued that with regards to the media representation of Maxine Carr during the Soham murder trial the result was one approaching total annihilation. That this reportage was in contempt of court seems unequivocal. It is the manner in which contempt emerged that is interesting. Here, it is almost metaphorical contempt, implicit and subpsychological. This is no less damaging, in fact, as we have already argued, due to its 'naturalised', masked connotative signification, it may be more damaging. However, whether coverage is overt or implicit Strict Liability states that prosecution in contempt cases do not need to prove intent. Whether inference in this case *forced* a particular ideology or not is utterly irrelevant; it is the effect, not the intent that matters.

The strict demands of any legal document, means it is unlikely that the subjective realm of newspaper visuals will ever be considered for judgement through the Contempt of Court Act. However, in our opinion, perceptions of Maxine Carr and her role in the murders of the two children were significantly influenced by the visual coverage in the press.

Methodological reflections

This study includes a quantitative content analysis combined with a qualitative visual analysis to examine the visual press coverage of Maxine Carr in the Soham murder trial. Three British newspapers were chosen to form the basis for this analysis: a 'traditional broadsheet' the *Times*, a 'middle-market' newspaper, the *Daily Mail* and a tabloid, the *Sun*. All newspapers are published nationally on a daily basis. Each also has its equivalent Sunday edition; the *News of the World*, *Mail on Sunday* and *Sunday Times*, however, these papers were excluded, to prevent repetitious coverage. Creating a sample from the ten British daily newspapers is always challenging, because of the different format types and ideological positions. In this particular study, we decided to include different examples of format type, keeping the ideological position of the newspapers as similar as possible, by choosing three centre-right newspapers. Using the newspaper database Lexis/Nexis, the search term 'Huntley OR Carr AND Soham' between 1 November 2003 and 31 December 2003 was used to create a database of all articles referencing the trial. This sample period was chosen to coincide with the trial which began on the 3 November and ended on the 17 December 2003. The additional seventeen days served as a 'buffer' to catch any prior build-up or subsequent comment. In total, 371 newspaper articles met the search criteria (78 in the *Daily Mail*, 170 in the *Sun* and 123 in the *Times*). Using the information provided by the database, the original articles and their accompanying images were located.

Individual images were coded according to their content, and the number of depictions of each character was calculated. All images of Huntley and Carr, separately, together or with additional individuals were coded. If Huntley appeared alone then this constituted one image of Huntley, however, if Huntley appeared with Carr (in the same image, photographed together) this constituted one image of Huntley and one image of Carr. In addition, each overall image was measured (irrespective of the number of individual image elements contained). Cut out images, or images of undefined, spherical or haphazard framing were measured from their widest and tallest points. Overlapping, superimposed or compound images were treated separately and measured accordingly. In total, there were 228 individual images of the two offenders.

This study uses the system of image signification theorized by Lev Kuleshov during the 1920s. Kuleshov began experimenting with raw film stock in order to determine the general rules which governed film communication. He took unedited footage of the expressionless face of one of the popular actors at the time and inter-cut it with three highly emotive images; a bowl of soup, a dead woman and a child. When the film was shown to a randomly selected audience they reported 'seeing' the actor's expression change, in relation to the inter-cut images, to whatever emotion was deemed appropriate. Kuleshov concluded that the image has two inherent signifying values: '[t]hat which it possesses itself, and that which it acquires when placed in relation to others' (Cook, 1990).

Kuleshov, however, was working with the signifying properties of film, whereas Newspaper discourse contains another important factor, text. The image analysis undertaken here takes as its basis three given assumptions; (a) that meaning (in terms of the use of images) in newspaper discourse is constructed through the image itself (its contents, framing, colour, quality and composition), (b) its relation to other images and (c) their relation to the headline text.

We deliberately omitted the article text from this study, believing that headlines interplay more directly with images, contextualising them within the newspaper layout; helping to form impressions or opinions more immediately. Article text, being smaller, longer and more openly narrativised is not so quickly assimilated. This is not to say that the text does not have an effect upon the reception of images, but to state that this effect is not instantaneous; it must first be read, digested and internalized.

These basic laws of connotation described by Kuleshov are used here alongside the representative codes theorized by Huxford (2001). Huxford argues that the photograph has long been upheld as the epitome of 'objectivity', not least because of its claims to purely denotative significance, but also due to its reliance on context to make meaning. Over the years, journalists have found other ways of injecting more than simple referential meanings into their publications (2001: 45). These new meanings, he says, go beyond the referential by 'underpinning or contradicting the photographs' indexical features' while still being received as objective by the reader (p.45). Huxford classifies three methods of this type of signification; two form the basis of our analysis: temporal and metaphorical signification. Temporal signification utilizes different sequences of photographs or differing shaped or cropped images to imply the passage of time. Metaphorical signification concerns the creation of visual metaphors through image juxtaposition. The result can imply relations between events and individuals that have no bearing in reality. Given cultural criminology's ongoing interest in visual representation and media analysis, the combination of quantitative and qualitative textual analysis can produce some powerful results, both in terms of uncovering the systematic 'patterns' of crime coverage, but also exploring what those patterns represent, through in-depth qualitative analysis.

Conclusion

In November 1968, Raymond Morris was convicted of the murder of Christine Darby in August 1967. He was interviewed in the first week after her murder, as his car met the description of a key eyewitness and two times subsequently. Although convinced of his guilt, the police were unable to charge him as his wife consistently provided an alibi for him. In November 1967, after five hours of police questioning she broke down and admitted she had lied. She was not charged with any crime. While the case did receive a certain level of publicity, Carole Morris received no press criticism, with one of the only vaguely critical articles being an op-ed piece in the *Daily Mail* asking whether it was right for women to 'stand by their man'. The similarities between the actions of Maxine Carr and Carole Morris are striking, as are the differences in their treatment by the criminal justice system, the press and the public.

Our analysis has explored how these connotations are understood through the use of Carr's image, the juxtaposition of this image with others and the relation these images have to the headline text. The importance of Huxford's work is to underline the fact that 'in seeking to supply 'visual evidence', journalists routinely create, through symbolism, photographic validation that they do not possess' (2001: 65). These codes often go unnoticed on the page; their constructed nature assimilated into notions of common sense (2001: 67). It is this, coupled with stereotypical notions of female criminality that have underlined the representation of Maxine Carr. The fact that she has been granted an indefinite anonymity order, considering the crime she committed, should result in a serious consideration of the way the press covers individuals related to crimes which engender such passionate and emotional reactions.

Furthermore, in view of the difficulties encountered in reproducing our original image sample, does the question now need to be asked: In what position are academics who are critical of print journalism's use of the image now left, when we are prevented from utilizing examples taken from the public domain? Carr's indefinite anonymity order was granted to protect her from the violent reprisals of the general public. Could it be that some newspapers are now using it for quite a different purpose? In this case, the damage has been done, and Carr has gone to ground. Now, thanks in part to what we consider prejudicial and perhaps even contemptuous reportage, our hands are tied. Without recourse to examples, what future is left for criticism?

References

Barthes, R. (1972 [1957]) *Mythologies,* London: Vintage.

Barthes, R. (1977) *Image/Music/Text,* London: Fontana.

Birch, H. (1993) 'If Looks Could Kill: Myra Hindley and the Iconography of Evil', in Birch, H. (ed.) *Moving Targets: Women, Murder and Representation,* London: Virago Press, pages 32–62.

Cameron, D. and Frazer, E. (1987) *The Lust to Kill: A Feminist Investigation of Sexual Murder,* Cambridge: Polity Press.

Carlen, P. (1985) 'Introduction', in Carlen, P. (ed.) *Criminal Women: Autobiographical Accounts,* London: Polity Press.

Cook, D.A. (1990) *A History of Narrative Film. Second Edition*, London: W. W. Norton & Company.

Critcher, C. (2002) 'Media, Government and Moral Panic: Paedophilia in the British Press 2000–1', *Journalism Studies*, 3(4): 521–35.

Crone, T. (2002) *Law and the Media: An Everyday Guide for Professionals*, 4th edn, Oxford: Focal Press.

Domke, D., Perlmutter, D. and Spratt, M. (2001) 'The Prime of Our Times? An Examination of the "Power" of Visual Images', *Journalism*, 3(2), 131–59.

Dyer, C. (2005) 'Maxine Carr Wins Anonymity for Life', *The Guardian*, 25 February 2005: 6.

Dyer, R. (1993) *The Matter of Images: Essays on Representation*, London: Routledge.

Ferrell, J., Hayward, K.J. and Young, J. (2008) *Cultural Criminology: An Invitation*, London: Sage.

French, S. (1996) 'Partners in Crime: Defending the Female of the Species', in Meyers, A. and Wight, S. (eds) *No Angels: Women Who Commit Violence*, San Francisco, California: Pandora Press.

Grabe, M.E., Trager, K.D., Lear, M. and Rauch, J. (2006) 'Gender in Crime News: A Case Study Test of the Chivalry Hypothesis', *Mass Communication and Society*, 9(2): 137–63.

Hall, S. (1981) 'The Determinations of News Photographs', in Cohen, S. and Young, J. (eds) *The Manufacture of News: Deviance, Social Problems and the Mass Media,* London: Constable, pages 226–43.

Huxford, J. (2001) 'Beyond the Referential: Uses of Visual Symbolism in the Press', *Journalism: Theory, Practice and Criticism*, 2(1): 45–71.
Kitzinger, J. (2000) 'Media Templates: Patterns of Association and the (Re)Construction of Meaning over Time', *Media, Culture and Society*, 22(1): 64–84.
Kitzinger, J. (2004) *Framing Abuse: Media Influence and Public Understandings of Sexual Violence Against Children*, London: Pluto Press.
Knelman, J. (1998) *Twisting in the Wind: The Murderess and the English Press*, Toronto: University of Toronto Press.
Kress, G. and Van Leeuwen, T. (1996) *Reading Images: The Grammar of Visual Design*, London: Routledge.
Meyers, A. and Wight, S. (1996) 'Introduction', in Meyers, A. and Wight, S. (eds) *No Angels: Women Who Commit Violence*, San Francisco, California: Pandora Press.
Morris, S. (2003) 'Papers could face prosecution over reporting of case', *The Guardian*, 18 December 2003: 6.
Morrissey, B. (2003) *When Women Kill: Questions of Agency and Subjectivity*, New York: Pandora.
No Author Listed (2003) 'Media warned by Soham trial judge', Story from MediaGuardian. co.uk: http://media.guardian.co.uk/print/0,3858,4790740-105414,00.html. [Accessed 02 May 2005].
Press Association, (2003) 'Media warned by Soham trial judge', MediaGuardian.co.uk: http://media.guardian.co.uk/print/0,3858,4790740-105414,00.html. [Accessed 02 May 2005].
Sekula, A. (1974) 'On the Invention of Photographic Meaning', in *Photography Against The Grain*, Rpt. Halifax: Press of The Nova Scotia College of Art And Design, 1984.
Smart, C. (1977a) 'Classical Studies of Female Criminality', in *Women, Crime and Criminology: A Feminist Critique*, London: Routledge and Kegan Paul.
Smart, C. (1977b) 'The Treatment of Female Offenders', in *Women, Crime and Criminology: A Feminist Critique*, London: Routledge and Kegan Paul.
Tagg, J. (1988) *The Burden of Representation: Essays on Photography and History*, New York: Macmillan.
Thorson, E. (1995) The Impact of Hillary Photos on Newspaper Readers, *News Photographer*, 50: 7–9.
Wardle, C. (2006) 'It Could Be You: The Move Towards "Personal" and "Societal" Narratives in Newspaper Coverage of Child Murder, 1930–2000', *Journalism Studies*, 7(4): 515–33.
Wardle, C. (2007) 'Monsters and Angels: Visual Press Coverage of Child Murders in the US and UK, 1930–1990', *Journalism*, 8(4): (forthcoming).
Winter, J. (2002) 'The Truth Will Out? The Role of Judicial Advocacy and Gender in Verdict Construction', *Social and Legal Studies*, 11(3), London: Sage.
X, A Woman Formally Known as Mary Bell v. O'Brien [2003] EWHC 1101 (Fam) E.M.L.R. 37
Zelizer, B. (1995) 'Words Against Images: Positioning Newswork in the Age of Photography', in Hardt, H. and Brennen, B. (eds) *Newsworkers: Towards A History of the Rank And File*, Minneapolis: University of Minnesota Press.
Zelizer, B. (1998) *Remembering To Forget: Holocaust Memory Through The Camera's Eye*, Chicago: University of Chicago Press.

Chapter 5

Screening crime

Cultural criminology goes to the movies

Majid Yar

Introduction

Insofar as cultural criminology is concerned with the multiple intersections between crime, deviance, control and symbolic representation, then the study of film would appear to be a necessary element of any such project. As Ferrell (1999: 395–6) proposes, cultural criminology 'references the increasing analytic attention that many criminologists now give to popular culture constructions, and especially mass media constructions, of crime and crime control'. As such, it consolidates 'the emergence of this general area of media and cultural inquiry as a relatively distinct domain within criminology' (ibid: 396). Of central importance here are the ways in which collective, socially shared understandings of crime and deviance, justice and punishment, are generated and sustained through the practices of mediated meaning-construction and textual reading. This orientation has inspired a wide range of media-oriented criminological scholarship, examining variously newspaper coverage of crime and crime control; televised representations of crime, criminality and policing; and images of crime in popular music, comic books, video games, the Internet and other contemporary media channels. The starting point for this chapter is the understanding that the cinematic construction of crime (in its manifold dimensions) should comprise a central part of this wider project.

It has been suggested that the moving image (and hence the 'movie') was the quintessential and dominant cultural form of the twentieth century. Shared meanings, social changes and challenges, narrations of human drama and social reality, utopian dreams and dystopian nightmares, our fears and fantasies, have been *projected* (both literally and metaphorically) through the lens of cinematic technology. Since its inception, issues of crime, order, law, conflict, deviance and punishment have figured centrally within the medium. However, as O'Brien *et al.* (2005a: 17) note, the intersections between crime and its popular representation have until recently remained somewhat marginal within criminological inquiry, the lion's share of attention being directed towards various historical, statistical, theoretical (and to a lesser degree ethnographic) studies of criminal behaviour and its consequences. Within the criminological study of media representations, film has itself been something of a poor relation, lagging well behind studies of factual reportage through newspapers and television [see, for example, Cohen and Young, 1973; Ericson *et al.,* 1991; Soothill and Walby, 1991; Wykes, 2000; Chibnall (ed.), 2001]. The reasons behind this neglect are a matter for speculation; perhaps the fictional character of crime films, as opposed to the ostensibly factual basis of news reportage, has led criminologists to dismiss movies as having only a tangential connection to those all-important interactions between crime, media and society. This marginalization of film, however, is I would suggest difficult to sustain. Firstly, we can note that there is no *a priori* basis to assume that fictional representations will play a lesser role in articulating and shaping social sensibilities where it comes to crime and criminality. Secondly, the very distinction between the 'factual' and 'fictional' is itself somewhat suspect on epistemological grounds. After all, decades of concerted effort within media and cultural studies has striven to demonstrate the manifold ways in which 'factuality' is itself a complex construct that achieves the appearance of truthfulness only through the mobilization of genre codes and elaborate representational techniques. Thirdly, film has long been 'parasitic' upon historical personalities and factual events in organising its narratives (consider the multiple cinematic efforts reconstructing the activities of Jack the Ripper, Dr Crippen and Ted Bundy, as well as the myriad crime films prefaced by well-known phrases such as 'Based on a True Story' or 'Based Upon Real Events'). Indeed, a closer inspection of news reporting provides ample evidence that the tropes and codes of cinema have overwhelmed factual representation, undermining once and for all any clear-cut fact-fiction distinction (we now live in a mediated world in which fictional representations mirror factual reporting, and factual reporting looks live a fictional movie). For all of these reasons, crime films are a worthy object of criminological analysis for those aiming to uncover the 'media loops' (Manning, 1998) through which we experience crime and come to know it, reflect upon it and react to it. Fortunately, the bourgeoning interest in cultural criminology has helped film analysis move from the disregarded margins to a more central and legitimate place within the discipline over the last decade (for some notable contributions, see, for example, Allen *et al.,* 1998; Rafter, 2000, 2006; O'Sullivan, 2001; Wilson and O'Sullivan, 2004; O'Brien *et al.,* 2005a, 2005b, Tzanelli *et al.,* 2005).

Focus

The symbolic constitution of crime in crime films

This chapter will map out a number of distinctive approaches, or styles of analysis, that can be used to understand the place of crime films in the symbolic constitution of crime. Each of these approaches, inevitably, draws upon somewhat different epistemological, methodological and/or theoretical presuppositions. These underpinnings will be drawn out, and the kinds of substantive analysis enabled by the different perspectives will be illustrated using examples of popular crime movies.

Counting criminal representations: the content analysis approach

Content Analysis (henceforth CA) is amongst the most established techniques for exploring mass media representations. It is distinguished by the attempt to forgo subjective interpretation of textual meaning in favour of a supposedly 'objective' approach that aims to enumerate the presence or absence of particular words, phrases or images within a medium or across different media (Hansen *et al.*, 1998; Roberts, 2001). Hence, CA makes resort to counts of *frequency* or *incidence* – how many times does a particular representation occur? How does the pattern of incidence vary across different media channels? What are the trends over time? Proceeding in this way, CA research typically studies large sets of data, for example, all outlets in a medium at a given point in time, or a cross-section of outlets over a span of time.

Long a favoured method for studying the content of factual media such as newspapers and television reporting, CA has been recently adopted by criminologists as a tool for examining crime films. A prime example is the study undertaken by Allen *et al.* (1998) that examined the representations of crime in British films between 1945 and 1991 (see also Reiner, 2002). The authors justify the use of CA by pointing out that debates about media representations of crime and their effects often proceed on a speculative basis without any firm factual basis e.g. claims are made either asserting (or refuting) a link between film content and actual criminal behaviour, but without any solid evidentiary basis about what precisely is being represented, how often, and how these representations vary over time. Hence a much-repeated claim such as 'the rise in violent crime has been caused by public exposure to ever more frequent images of violence in crime films' can be neither proven nor disproven unless we know whether or not such images have in fact become a more frequently occurring feature in films.

Allen *et al.* (1998: 58–9) examined the detailed synopses of a sample of all those crime films (some 15,000 in total) released in the UK in the post WWII era until 1991. They define a movie as a 'crime film' if '(1) the central focus of the narrative is the commission and/or the investigation of a crime and/or (2) the principal protagonist is either an offender or a professional working in the criminal justice system'. They found that the proportion of all films that could be defined as primarily 'crime films' remained relatively constant over the period as a whole, at around 20 per cent (although there were inevitably some fluctuations on year-to-year basis). A further 20 per cent of films (again remaining fairly constant) were found to contain some significant crime content, but did not take crime as their primary focus (ibid.: 60–1). This finding is in itself interesting, as it puts pay to claims that we are increasingly 'saturated' by crime images in popular film, a claim that is often used by cultural conservatives to help explain the sharp postwar rise in recorded crime. However, in addition, the authors examined the representational content of a sample of the most successful films (determined by box office position). They found that some 48 per cent of crime films dealt with homicide, an emphasis out of all proportion with the extremely small contribution of homicide to the overall figures of actual crimes committed during the period under examination. Moreover, they claim to have found that over time the representation of violence in such films grew increasingly graphic, that the victims of crimes were represented as increasingly traumatized, and that the law-and-order protagonists were increasingly shown resorting to vigilante tactics that were justified by the extreme threat of crime and disorder (ibid: 65–9). A similar study by Shipley and Cavender (2001) examined the violent images in crime films over a four-decade period. They also come to the conclusion that the representation of 'violence, graphic violence, and death increases across the four decades' (Shipley and Cavender, 2001: 1). Such findings suggest a significant shift in the representational content of crime films, shifts that may be connected to wider social and political changes taking place over the postwar period.

Despite the obvious appeal of the CA approach to crime films, the method has drawn sustained methodological criticism. Not least, it has been argued that counting frequency or incidence of representations does little to help us understand the *meanings* of those representations (Leiss *et al.*, 1990). We might now know that 48 per cent of postwar crime films centre on homicide, but this fact tells us little about how homicide is constructed by either the producers of the films or interpreted by their audience. From the standpoint of cultural criminology, imposing upon the domain of culture the epistemological and methodological prescriptions of 'scientific' analysis serves merely to rob subjective sense-making activity of its essence. The CA approach *reifies* cultural codes into objective artefacts that can be grouped, classified and counted. As such, it moves away from the heart of sociological *verstehen*, which holds that meaning does not exist 'thing-like' 'out there', but is actively produced through ongoing creative interpretations by social subjects (for an explicit critique of 'scientific' criminology from the perspective of cultural criminology see, for example, Young, 2004). What a representation *means* can only be appreciated by exploring what it means to real (as opposed to hypothetical) people – there is no meaning, no symbolic construction, apart from that generated by audiences and viewers, speakers and listeners, through the act of communicative engagement.

For this reason, CA is increasingly supplemented by qualitative research that attempts to uncover audience understandings of cinematic narratives and images. Thus, Allen *et al.* chose to supplement their content analysis of crime films with focus group discussions with viewers. However, this supplementary introduction of a qualitative dimension to CA research does not necessarily fully overcome its limitations. Most important here is the fact that behind the seemingly objective classification, categorization and counting involved, researchers' own subjective understandings and decisions will play a key role in framing the analysis. It is a matter of subjective judgement as to what gets classified as a 'crime film' or as 'crime content'; moreover, there is no objective basis for distinguishing between lesser or greater degrees of 'violence', 'trauma' and so on. While CA uses quantitative methods to create an aura of objectivity, it can nonetheless be seen as fundamentally dependent upon the meaningful interpretations that researchers place upon what they view, which in turn may be at odds with the kinds of understandings that audiences themselves may bring to bear upon those same representations [as Ferrell (1999: 400) notes, 'the researcher, and the researcher's own situated experiences' cannot be separated from 'the collective construction of crime's reality'].

In the shadow of Marx: crime films as ideology

In marked contrast to the supposed descriptive neutrality of content analysis, the Marxian tradition has inspired a much more politicized approach to reading crime films. For Marxists, cultural products embody a set of 'truths' and values that serve to legitimate and thus reproduce the power of dominant class interests. Ideology thus assumes a functional role in preserving a false understanding of society (including the responsibility for social inequalities, problems and injustices), an understanding that the critic attempts to expose. Such a view lead some neo-Marxists, such as Adorno and Horkheimer (1997), to dismiss popular culture as irretrievably corrupted by the interests of capitalism and its ruling class (see also Adorno, 2001). Others, like Althusser (1994) view mass media, along with other key institutions, as 'ideological apparatuses' that support the capitalist state by producing conformity through the versions of reality that they propagate. A more nuanced approach, however, emerges in the Gramscian tradition, wherein the production of political authority (or *hegemony*) is viewed as a contested terrain; alongside those images, narratives and texts that encode dominant interests, there will also exist counter-hegemonic understandings that offer critical and alternative understandings of society. This approach has been applied to popular films by the likes of Kellner and Ryan (1988), who argue that recent Hollywood movies give voice to competing constituencies within American political culture. Thus, for example, the 1980s saw films such as *Rambo* (1982) and *Top Gun* (1986) that legitimated Reagan's hawkish militarism, yet the same period also produced movies such as *Platoon* (1986), *Missing* (1982) and *Salvador* (1986) that explicitly critique American militarism and its human and moral consequences. In this way, popular films can be seen as a contested terrain in which conservative, liberal and radical voices propose different viewpoints on issues of morality, justice, order, fairness, violence and retribution.

The Marxian model of cultural analysis has been applied to crime films most clearly in the work of Rafter (2000, 2006). Rafter sets out by framing film as a medium for ideology, understood as 'the myths that a society lives by, as if these myths referred to some natural, unproblematic "reality"' (Kaplan, cited in Rafter, 2001: 8). She goes on to distinguish between what she calls 'traditional' and 'critical' crime films (a distinction that maps closely onto Kellner and Ryan's conservative-liberal/radical classification). 'Traditional' crime films will send reassuring messages about the heroism and fundamental decency of law-enforcers, the wickedness of offenders and the inevitability of a just and justified punishment for evildoers. Such movies adopt a clear-cut distinction between the 'normal' law-abiding majority and the 'abnormal' or deviant minority who transgress society's clearly demarcated norms and values. Moreover, where they offer some causal hypothesis (an answer to the question of why people offend) these tend to be individualized, thereby bracketing-off wider social processes that might in fact play a key role in the genesis of crime. In this way, they reinforce the authority of existing legal institutions and normative codes and deflect attention away from any critical questioning of the sectional interests that the law serves or the ways in which crime is linked to prejudices and inequalities. Examples of such 'traditional' films might include cop movies such as *The Untouchables* (1987) (heroic and incorruptible officers bring Al Capone to justice), courtroom dramas such as *12 Angry Men* (1957) (justice triumphs through the jury system) and serial killer chillers such as *Silence of the Lambs* (1991) (the criminal as amoral psychopath who must be stopped at all costs). Conversely, the less numerous instances of 'critical' crime films subvert clear-cut distinctions between good and evil, maintain a dark and pessimistic vision of social conflict and insist 'on the impossibility of heroism and the inevitability of injustice' (ibid: 12). Instances of such films include *The Bad Lieutenant* (1992) (there *are* no good cops), *Dead Man Walking* (1995) (the futility of the death penalty and its inability to secure a just outcome) and *Mystic River* (2003) (the inextricable entwining of guilt and innocence, such that we can no longer clearly demarcate offenders and victims).

The Marxian approach provides the critical analyst of crime films with a powerful tool for exposing the ways in which popular representations embody dominant narratives of law and order and in doing so help to maintain existing systems of power and powerlessness, inclusion and exclusion, normalization and stigmatization. It can be viewed as a valuable contribution to cultural criminology, especially insofar as it makes space for appreciating the cultural and political *background* against which the work of meaning production takes place. For example O'Brien (2005: 608–9) notes the disjunction between, on the one hand, the microsociological focus of ethnographically oriented cultural criminology (especially from the US), and on the other the enduring influence of British cultural Marxism in research originating from the UK [examples of the former ethnographic approach include Ferrell (1996, 2002, 2006) and Lyng (ed.) (2004), while the latter approach is exemplified by the likes of Young (1999), Presdee (2000), Hayward (2004) and Hall and Winlow (2006)]. What the former lacks, and a Marxist understanding of ideology can inject, is a sensitivity to the ways in which individual or local constructions of meaning are shaped by macro-level political frameworks, processes and interests. Thus, the meanings of crime films can be appreciated as articulations of wider dominant ideological frameworks shaped by class structure and capitalist relations of domination.

However, analysing crime films (and films more generally) in this manner invites also some pertinent criticisms. Firstly, the Marxian model can be said to adopt an overly monolithic conception of ideology, such that the meaning content of particular texts embodies a clear and distinctive commitment to upholding dominant class and other interests. In other words, films are either 'traditional' (and hegemonic) or 'critical' (and counter-hegemonic). This leaves little room to explore the ambiguities and tensions that might permeate any given text, the complex coexistence of meanings that give voice to *both* socially conservative *and* critical viewpoints. Secondly, the Marxian model assumes that textual and representational meaning is something that is structurally 'built into' communication; all the analyst has to do is uncover those meanings. This leaves little room for appreciating the role played by audiences (viewers and readers) in actively constructing the meanings of film, a process that may lead different viewers to derive very different messages from the same text.

Postmodern pluralism: the semiotic free-for-all in crime films

The critique of Marxian analysis noted in the foregoing section has been most clearly articulated by the postmodern perspectives on culture that emerged in the 1970s and 1980s. While postmodernism is a notoriously difficult concept to define, we can for present purposes understand it as a perspective that disputes claims that it is possible to have a clear-cut and objective understanding of society and its workings, of culture and its meanings, and of the difference between truth and falsehood, fact and fiction. In terms of film analysis (and the analysis of other cultural artefacts), postmodernism stresses the inherent indeterminacy of meaning, the fragmented, multiple and often contradictory nature of representation. Postmodernism turns its critical lens on Marxist accounts, arguing that it is not possible to talk anymore in terms of any dominant ideology that permeates popular culture. Such postmodern sensibilities have, as Ferrell (1999) notes, made their presence felt within cultural criminology, with a new enthusiasm for 'deconstructing' textual meaning within popular media representations of crime (see, for example, Young, 1996). Two broad arguments are proposed in support of such a claim. Firstly, it is claimed that the social basis of any dominant ideology no longer exists, as structures of class (and their associated interests) have irretrievably fragmented through the process of social change. Social structures have become so fluid as to undermine the existence of stable social constituencies whose shared interests could provide the basis of any widespread ideology. What we have instead is a multiplicity of transitory voices that reflect the shifting and unstable character of contemporary society (for an elaboration of this position see for example Collins, 1989). Secondly, it is argued that Marxists (and other so-called 'modernists') misunderstand the fundamental basis of human communication. Modernists assume (wrongly) that the meaning of representation is clear-cut and objective, such that we can determine with confidence what a text means, what it says, and how it is to be understood. In contrast, postmodernism holds that meaning is inherently indeterminate, such that it is not possible to attribute a definitive meaning content to any representation. Language (be it verbal, written or visual) is so 'slippery' that any given text will be received and understood in variable and unpredictable ways. Consequently, we cannot legitimately claim that a film, for example, represents crime is this or that way. What it means will vary from moment to moment, reading to reading and from viewer to viewer. This being the case, it becomes impossible to attribute any ideological message to a film. The best that we can do is to attend to this variability and flow in meaning, the very *absence* of clear messages within the text. Methodologically, postmodernism has done much to reorient film analysis way from uncovering textual meanings as such, and towards the ways in which viewers produce their own versions of cinematic 'truth' through the creative appropriation of signs (see, for example, Jenkins, 1992; for a specifically criminological take see also Milovanovic and Henry, 1999). If a film can mean 'anything' (depending on the viewer) then it means *nothing in particular*, it becomes a 'blank slate' upon which can be written just about any meaning whatsoever. From this viewpoint, the attempt to divide crime films between, say, 'traditional' and 'critical' becomes highly problematic. If we consider a film such as *12 Angry Men* (1957), which Rafter classifies as a 'traditional' film defending dominant conceptions of justice, we see that its meaning may be much more complex and indeterminate than at first meets the eye. The movie deals with the deliberations of the jurors in the trial of a young Latino who is accused of murdering his father. All of the jurors bar one are ready to hand down a guilty verdict. 'Juror No. 8' (played by Henry Fonda) refuses to agree with the others, thereby forcing the jury into a protracted examination and weighing up of the evidence. Consequently, serious doubts about the accused man's guilt emerge, and he is ultimately acquitted. On one reading, this narrative vindicates the jury system, showing that individual integrity and the good sense of 'ordinary Americans' can be trusted to deliver justice. However, it can equally easily be read as a damning indictment of the racial prejudices that permeate American society, and of an error-prone system that is only rescued in this instance by the contingent presence of a single juror who is atypical in his willingness to reflect on the facts of the case. Thus, depending upon the reading position adopted by the viewer, the very same cinematic text offers of potentially divergent and contradictory meanings. It is this inherent ambiguity of meaning that renders problematic any straightforward categorization of crime films' content in terms of ideologically conformist and/or subversive messages.

A further significant feature of the postmodern approach concerns the cultural credibility of 'truth claims'. Jean-Francois Lyotard (1984) famously argued that the modern era had been characterized by a belief in over-arching ideas and ideals, such as the possibility of scientific knowledge, progress and justice (what he calls 'meta narratives' or 'grand narratives'). With the transition to postmodernity, however, there is widespread scepticism (or 'incredulity') about such narratives. This shift is reflected in the content of popular culture, which adopts an increasingly 'ironic' stance towards such ideas, actively subverting their credibility through reflexive interrogation and parody. From a postmodern reading, crime films increasingly 'play' with notions of justice and fairness, guilt and innocence, pain and pleasure and good and evil. Prime examples include films such as Quentin Tarantino's *Reservoir Dogs* (1992) and *Pulp Fiction* (1994) and the Tarantino-Robert Rodriguez collaboration *From Dusk Till Dawn* (1996). In *Reservoir Dogs*, scenes of graphic violence and torture are subverted, as the perpetrator dances and sings along with a musical sound track while assaulting his victim. In *Pulp Fiction*, the apparent 'heroes' are a pair of brutal hitmen who quip their way through a narrative of bloodletting and death with comic exchanges about Burger King, the edibility of various animals and sundry other prosaic matters. Violence, death, comedy, music, dance and pastiche combine in a manner that makes it well nigh impossible to read any clear ideological and moral message from the film. *From Dusk Till Dawn* takes this subversion in a somewhat different direction by derailing the genre conventions that make it possible for audiences to read the text as a 'crime film'. The movie starts as a seemingly conventional tale of two bank-robbing brothers who make their escape by kidnapping a family and forcing them to drive across the US-Mexican border. However, half way through, the film sabotages its own generic framework by abruptly switching genre, transmuting into a comic horror tale about vampires. Other crime films that can also be situated within a postmodern frame include *Natural Born Killers* (1994), *Fargo* (1996) and *Sin City* (2005). What such films share is a refusal to conform to any 'realistic' representation of crime and its consequences, opting instead to engage in knowing reference to previous films and existing conventions, merrily mixing, matching and juxtaposing them in a playful and ironic way (for more detailed discussion of the defining elements of postmodern aesthetics and culture see Denzin, 1991; Hutcheon, 2004). For postmodernists the emergence and popularity of such films is symptomatic of a more general social and cultural shift in which clear ideological and moral messages no longer dominate popular representations.

Methodological reflections

In the preceding sections, we have seen that there are a number of distinctive approaches available for the criminologically oriented analysis of films. While content analysis adopts a formal and quantitative strategy for mapping textual content, both ideology theory and postmodernism focus more upon the meaning of narratives, images and characters. However, these latter perspectives diverge significantly, insofar as ideology approaches aim to uncover the dominant and prescribed understandings that serve to reproduce power relations, while postmodernists focus upon the diversity and indeterminacy of meaning, stressing the impossibility of deriving any coherent ideology from films. In this final section, I will outline a more 'synthetic' approach that mediates between ideology critique and postmodern sensibilities. As such, I suggest that it offers the most fruitful avenue for developing a full-fledged cultural criminology of film, combining close textual reading of individual 'sites' of meaning production with an appreciation of the wider social and political contexts that shape cultural frameworks.

Between ideology and contingency: a synthetic and critical framework for crime film analysis

Recent work developed by O'Brien *et al.* (2005a, 2005b) and Tzanelli *et al.* (2005) has already done much to outline such an orientation. These authors support Marxist claims that crime films (and popular culture more generally) *do* play a significant role in constructing a 'criminological common sense' that is bound-up with existing institutional practices and political relations (what they dub 'popular imaginaries' of crime). However, they argue that such imaginaries cannot and should not be reduced to any monolithic ideology that is strategically constructed by powerful social actors. In other words, 'crime film does not "partake" in a conspiracy of the state apparatus against the public' (O'Brien *et al.*, 2005a: 17). Rather, crime films not only draw upon the sensibilities and meaning systems of culture, but also inflect and shape them in sometimes new and unexpected ways (Tzanelli *et al.*, 2005: 99). Moreover, any given text can carry contesting visions of crime and order – not so much (as postmodernists argue) because of any inherent instability of meaning as due to the fact that cultural artefacts will refract the wider tensions and divisions with the society that they represent (see also Nellis, 1988 and O'Sullivan, 2001). In other words, crime films become sites within which the meanings of crime and criminality are simultaneously articulated, explored and negotiated. Rather than attempting to classify particular films as *either* conservative-traditional *or* liberal-critical, we should instead unpack the dissonance within any given film text as a reflection of the ambivalent meanings of crime that circulate in society as a whole.

The aforementioned approach can be exemplified through the analysis of a number of recent popular Hollywood crime movies. Particularly useful is Tzanelli *et al.*'s (2005) examination of Steven Spielberg's *Catch Me If You Can* (2003). This film is a somewhat fictionalized version of real-life conman Frank Abagnale Junior's autobiography of the same title (Abagnale, 2003). At one level, the film can be seen to reproduce and recuperate an interlocking system of 'conventional' beliefs about the causes and consequences of crime and the roots of desistance. For example, the film links young Frank's initial foray into confidence crime as a teenager to familial factors. Firstly, Frank (played by Leonardo Di Caprio) models himself upon his father (Frank Senior, played by Christopher Walken), a small businessman who makes a habit of 'sharp practice' and 'bending the rules' when it works to his advantage. Young Frank stands in awe of his father and seeks in some way, shape or form to emulate him, an endeavour that Frank Senior appears to heartily approve of. Hence, the movie reiterates a criminological 'common sense' that sees parental role models as key factors in an individual's paths to delinquency or conformity. Secondly, Frank Junior's full-blown investment in a criminal career occurs only after his parents' traumatic divorce, following his mother's infidelity with a family friend. Again, this narrative move mirrors commonplace understandings of crime and delinquency as causally connected to 'broken families', and thus partakes of socially conservative worldview that favours the nuclear family structure as the instrument *par excellence* of social control over children. The film's representation of desistance can be read as equally conformist. Throughout the movie, Frank is doggedly pursued by FBI agent Hanratty (played by Hollywood 'everyman' and 'good guy' Tom Hanks). Through the pursuit the pair form an increasingly intimate bond, with Agent Hanratty coming to replace Frank Senior as the 'father figure' to whom the young man looks for validation and guidance (while Hanratty, conversely, finds in Frank a replacement for the child he has lost through divorce). The film ends with Frank's rehabilitation, as he takes his place beside Hanratty helping the FBI *catch* confidence criminals, while his new 'law abiding father' looks on with a benevolent authority, viewing with satisfaction the successful product of his 'tough love' strategy.

All of the foregoing, taken together, suggest that the film might unequivocally be positioned as an instance of what Rafter calls 'traditional' crime film. However, Tzanelli *et al.* go on to point out that coexistent with its conservative elements and implicit understandings, is another level of meaning that film simultaneously subverts its apparent 'crime is pathology' and 'crime doesn't pay' motifs. This is most clearly communicated at the *affective* level through a constant demonstration of the obvious *pleasures* of lawbreaking [what Katz (1990) famously dubbed the 'seductions of crime']. This subversive element is clearly acknowledged by Speilberg himself, who responds to an interview question about the appeal of conmen thus: 'we all sometimes fantasize about, gee, could I do that? We don't really want to become those people but we kind of admire their nerve' (Spielberg, 2002). Our admiration for, and seduction by, Frank's exploits functions on (at least) two levels. Firstly, there is the apparent pleasure of the 'con game' itself, in which the 'artist' shows his superiority over the 'marks', 'mugs' or 'punters' by misleading and manipulating them effortlessly. As such, he becomes the epitome of the 'self made man' beloved of the 'American Dream', a figure who makes remakes himself out of the resources of his own ingenuity, creativity and daring. Secondly, there is a range of material and sensual rewards of criminal endeavour. In the course of the film, Frank goes from penury to lavish living, surrounded with the trappings of success such as fast cars, beautiful apartments, travel to exotic locales and sexual dalliances with gorgeous young women. In one particularly telling scene, Franks enjoys a night of passionate lovemaking with a high-class 'call girl', only to con her by paying for her (very expensive) services with a counterfeit cheque. This manoeuvre appeals in particular to a dominant male sexual imaginary in which women are the 'prizes' of success, commodities to be consumed and enjoyed. As such, Frank offers a position into which the (male) viewer can willingly transpose himself, vicariously partaking of the delights that are usually offered only to the 'lucky few'.

The foregoing reading must be understood in its appropriate theoretical context. The authors do not suggest that the contrasting meanings of the film were a matter of conscious premeditation on the part of its creators. No one sat down with the explicit intent of making a movie that expressed the ambivalent meanings of criminal endeavour. Nor was it, on the other hand, simply a matter of accident that these layers or levels of meaning came to imbue the cinematic text. Rather, it was the unconscious reflection of a deep-seated feature of our common cultural dispositions, one in which we simultaneously hold normatively conflicting views of crime as both 'evil' *and* 'heroic', as both repulsive *and* seductive. It is through a nuanced and appropriately sensitive reading that the complexity of cultural meanings inherent in crime films can be brought to our conscious attention.

Conclusion

This chapter has sought to present an overview of the main theoretical and methodological perspectives through which cultural analysts approach crime films, and sought to situate these in relation to the cultural aims and orientations of cultural criminology. In terms of method, there is in fact space for the coexistence of different investigative strategies. For example, a quantitatively oriented content analysis of a genre can provide a valuable counterpart to a more intensively qualitative reading of particular films. However, at the level of theory, a more decisive choice needs to be made. Different perspectives recommend analysis based upon diverging assumptions about the place of culture in society as such. Marxist and related ideology theories look to films and other cultural products as the fairly unequivocal manifestations of worldviews favourable to dominant classes and structural relations of power. Postmodernists, in sharps contrast, claim that finding coherent and clear structures of meaning in film texts is well nigh impossible, as there is an inherent instability in the process of communication and interpretation, a kind of 'shifting sand' which does not allow us to discern a stable set of codes, ideas or beliefs from any given movie. Instead, the best we can do is to show the multiplicity of meanings that can be read into the very same text from different reading positions. While both of the foregoing theories offer something of value to the criminological analyst of film, their very tendency to gravitate to opposite poles limits their usefulness (meaning is *either* monolithic and overarching *or* irretrievably fragmented and indeterminate). As an alternative, I have advocated the kind of synthetic approach developed by Tzanelli, O'Brien and myself over recent years. I exemplified this position through an (necessarily brief) account of Tzanelli *et al.*'s (2004) reading of *Catch Me If You Can*. In this article and elsewhere, these authors have attempted to illuminate a range of criminologically pertinent issues through the analysis of film (such as cultural understandings of gender and crime, 'race' and crime, gang conflict, political violence and the contemporary intersections between celebrity and criminality). The advantage of this reading strategy, I have suggested, is that it enables us to appreciate the richness and diversity of film texts, while simultaneously discerning the ways in which they play a role in the wider politics of law, order and punishment. Within the wider project of cultural criminology, such an approach offers the ability to uncover the complex mediation and construction of crime and criminality in its sociopolitical context, linking symbolic framings to the broader currents of sensibility with which they constantly interact.

Acknowledgements

I would like to express my heartfelt thanks to Martin O'Brien and Rodanthi Tzanelli, with whom I have enjoyed the good fortune to work on the analysis of crime films over recent years. Their insights and understandings have been central in shaping my own, and I draw liberally here on some of the coauthored work that we have produced. Nevertheless, they cannot be responsible for any lacunae or lapses in the present piece, nor for my own interpretation or framing of our collaborative endeavours. Where I have put my own idiosyncratic slant on our collective work, I hope they will forgive the expression of any ideas and views with which they may not wholeheartedly agree.

References

Abagnale, F. (2003) *Catch Me If You Can: The True Story of a Real Fake,* Edinburgh: Mainstream Publishing.

Adorno, T. and Horkheimer, M. (1997) *Dialectic of Enlightenment,* London: Verso.

Adorno, T. (2001) *The Culture Industry,* London: Routledge.

Allen, J., Livingstone, S. and Reiner, R. (1998) 'True Lies: Changing Images of Crime in British Postwar Cinema', *European Journal of Communication*, 13(1): 53–75.

Althusser, L. (1994) 'Ideology and Ideological State Apparatuses (notes towards an Investigation', in S. Zizek (ed.) *Mapping Ideology*, London: Verso.

Chibnall, S. (ed.) (2001) *Law-and-Order News: An Analysis of Crime Reporting in the British Press,* London: Routledge.

Cohen, S. and Young, J. (1973) *Manufacture of News: Deviance, Social Problems and the Mass Media,* London: John Constable.

Collins, J. (1989) *Uncommon Cultures: Popular Culture and Postmodernism,* London and New York: Routledge.

Denzin, N. (1991) *Images of Postmodern Society: Social Theory and Contemporary Cinema,* London: Sage.

Ericson, R.V., Barnek, P.M. and Chan, J.B.L. (1991) *Representing Order: Crime, Law and Justice in the News Media,* Buckingham: Open University Press.

Ferrell, J. (1996) *Crimes of Style: Urban Graffiti and the Politics of Criminality,* Boston: North Eastern University.

Ferrell, J. (1999) 'Cultural Criminology', *Annual Review of Sociology*, 25: 395–418.

Ferrell, J. (2002) *Tearing Down the Streets: Adventures in Urban Anarchy,* London: Palgrave Macmillan.

Ferrell, J. (2006) *Empire of Scrounge: Inside the Urban Underground of Dumpster Diving, Trash Picking, and Street Scavenging,* New York: New York University Press.

Hall, S. and Winlow, S. (2006) *Violent Night: Urban Leisure and Contemporary Culture,* Oxford: Berg.

Hansen, A., Cottle, S., Negrine, R. and Newbold, C. (1998) *Mass Communication Research Methods,* Houndmills: Macmillan.

Hayward, K.J. (2004) *City Limits: Crime, Consumer Culture and the Urban Experience,* London: Routledge Cavendish.

Hutcheon, L. (2004) *A Poetics of Postmodernism: History, Theory, Fiction,* London: Routledge.

Jenkins, H. (1992) *Textual Poachers: Television Fans and Participatory Culture,* London: Routledge.

Katz, J. (1990) *Seductions of Crime: Moral and Sensual Attractions in Doing Evil,* New York: Basic Books.

Kellner, D. and Ryan, M. (1988) *Camera Politica: The Politics and Ideology of Contemporary Hollywood Film,* Bloomington: Indiana University Press.

Leiss, W., Kline, S. and Jhally, S. (1990) *Advertising as Social Communication,* London: Routledge.

Lyng, S. (ed.) (2004) *Edgework: The Sociology of Risk-Taking,* New York: Routledge.

Lyotard, J-F. (1984) *The Postmodern Condition: A Report on Knowledge,* Manchester: Manchester University Press.

Manning, P.K. (1998) 'Media Loops', in F. Bailey and D. Hale (eds) *Popular Culture, Crime and Justice,* Belmont CA: Wadsworth.

Milovanovic, D. and Henry, S. (1999) 'Introduction: Postmodernism and Constitutive Theory', in S. Henry and D. Milovanovic (eds) *Constitutive Criminology at Work: Applications to Crime and Justice,* Albany NY: SUNY Press.

Nellis, M. (1988) 'British Prison Movies: The Case of "Now Barabbas"', *Howard Journal of Criminal Justice*, 27(1): 2–31.

O'Brien, M. (2005) 'What is *Cultural* About Cultural Criminology?', *British Journal of Criminology*, 45: 599–612.

O'Brien, M., Tzanelli, R., Penna, S. and Yar, M. (2005a) '"The Spectacle of Fearsome Acts": Crime in the Melting P(l)ot in *Gangs of New York*', *Critical Criminology*, 13: 17–35.

O'Brien, M., Tzanelli, R., Penna, S. and Yar, M. (2005b) 'Kill n' Tell, and All That Jazz: The Seductions of Crime in Chicago', *Crime Media Culture*, 1(3): 243–61.

O'Sullivan, S. (2001) 'Representations of Prison in Nineties Hollywood Cinema: From *Con Air* to *The Shawshank Redemption*', *The Howard Journal of Criminal Justice*, 40(4): 317–34.

Presdee, M. (2000) *Cultural Criminology and the Carnival of Crime,* London: Routledge.

Rafter, N. (2000) *Shots in the Mirror: Crime Films and Society,* New York: Oxford University Press.

Rafter, N. (2006) *Shots in the Mirror: Crime Films and Society*, 2nd edn, New York: Oxford University Press.

Reiner, R. (2002) 'Media Made Criminality', in M. Maguire, R. Morgan and R. Reiner (eds) *The Oxford Handbook of Criminology*, 3rd edn, Oxford: Oxford University Press.

Roberts, C.W. (2001) 'Content Analysis', in N.J. Smelser and P.B. Baltes (eds) *International Encyclopedia of the Social and Behavioural Sciences*, vol. 4, Oxford: Elsevier.

Shipley, W. and Cavender, G. (2001) 'Murder and Mayhem at the Movies', *Journal of Criminal Justice and Popular Culture*, 9(1): 1–14.

Soothill, K. and Walby, S. (1991) *Sex Crime in the News,* London: Routledge.
Spielberg, S. (2002) *Catch me If You Can*. Dreamworks Studios.
Tzanelli, R., O'Brien, M. and Yar, M. (2005) '"Con Me If You Can": Exploring Crime in the American Cinematic Imagination', *Theoretical Criminology*, 9: 97–117.
Wilson, D. and O'Sullivan, S. (2004) *Images of Incarceration: Representations of Prison in Film and Television Drama,* Winchester: Waterside Press.
Wykes, M. (2000) *News, Crime and Culture,* London: Pluto Press.
Young, A. (1996) *Imagining Crime: Textual Outlaws and Criminal Conversations,* London: Sage.
Young, J. (1999) *The Exclusive Society: Social Exclusion, Crime and Difference in Late Modernity,* London: Sage.
Young, J. (2004) 'Voodoo Criminology and The Numbers Game', in J. Ferrell, K.J. Hayward, W. Morrison and M. Presdee (eds) *Cultural Criminology Unleashed,* London: GlassHouse Press.

Chapter 6

The scene of the crime

Is there such a thing as 'just looking'?

Alison Young

Introduction

Crime compels us as well as repels. One of the achievements of the diverse range of scholarship carried out under the heading of cultural criminology has been to establish that crime is not simply something that the community censures. Bound up with disapprobation and distaste for crime is an intense interest in its forms, motivations and impacts. This doubled relation, oscillating between censure and desire, can be called *fascination*. Cultural criminologists have, for example, investigated the fascination of crime by researching the pleasures of criminal behaviour (most obviously Katz, 1988; Lyng, 2004) and the challenges posed to dominant groups by various subcultural groups (for example, see Miller, 1995; Tunnell, 2004). In this early strand of cultural criminological research, as in interactionism, the emphasis is on the asymmetrical flow of (labelling) power: despite its contention that style has constitutive force not only for criminal subcultures but also for 'the broader social and legal relations in which these subcultures are caught' (Ferrell and Sanders, 1995: 5), this variant of cultural criminology has on the whole tended to focus primarily on an accumulation of criminal subcultures, without placing the subcultural subject within a broader discursive sphere in which images of crime and criminality are produced, mediated and consumed.

However, a further strand of cultural criminological research exists – one which focuses upon what can be called a *criminological aesthetics* (see further Young, 2008) and engages with the ways in which our ambivalence about crime manifests itself in the images we produce of it (see, for example, the work of Young, 1996, 2007; Hutchings, 2001; Valier, 2002; Jewkes, 2004; Lippens, 2004; Phillips and Strobi, 2006; Biber, 2007). Yet, even within this latter strand of research, attention has mainly been focused upon the social or criminological implications of our images of crime; there has been little attempt until recently to analyse the images themselves and the relation between the spectator and the image. Thus, although the question of representation and its interpretation has exercised a range of other disciplines (notably social theory, feminist studies and cultural studies) over the last three decades, criminology has more or less ignored it. Such an omission is strange given that media representations of crime constitute a mainstay of cultural consumption, deriving their popularity, as Richard Sparks puts it, from their capacity to offer 'a set of stories which address certain social anxieties in its audience' and 'render the messy and troubling complexities of law enforcement pleasurable by assigning them to the ancient simplicities of crime and punishment' (1990: 123).

This essay situates itself within criminological aesthetics, and to the enterprise of investigating crime's fascination it contributes an analysis of our particular relationship to the *cinematic* image. More specifically, I seek to discover how law, violence and justice appear and reappear in the image on screen, in order to open up and give access to the *affective* dimension of crime and its structures of identification (I will return to the concept of affect shortly). To that extent, this essay builds on concerns threaded through my previous work on our entanglement in and with the image (for example, see Young, 1996, 2005). But this essay also constitutes a discrete part of a larger project: an analysis of the cinematic image of crime and the relationship of the spectator to the representation of crime, violence and justice on screen (Young, 2009, forthcoming). In this essay, then, and in the larger project, I engage with the practice of looking – *spectatorship* – and its construction of a relation between spectator and image. My aim is to explore the relationship between spectatorship and the representation of law, crime and victimage. My particular interest is in the cinematic scene of violence and the ways in which the spectator's encounter with that scene has implications for the theorization of law, judgment and justice.

Focus

Criminological aesthetics and the affective image

The starting point of a criminological aesthetics is that 'crime's images are structured according to a binary logic of representation. Oppositional terms (man/woman, white/black, rational/irrational, mind/body and so on) are constructed in a system of value which makes one visible and the other invisible' (Young, 1996: 1). The notion of a system of value, structured through the logic of binary oppositions and subject to varying shifts in the social economy of representation, moves the criminological theorizing of culture away from a framework which constructs acts as having symbolic meaning (in an epiphenomenal relation to their literal effects) and individuals as actors arrayed around the social field at a greater or lesser distance from the dominant centre. A criminological aesthetics instead emphasizes practices of *interpretation* over the generation of meaning (which tacitly relies on a conception of truth, authenticity or actuality), processes of *signification* rather than symbolization (which posits a zero sum relation between meaning and image), and *affect* instead of emotion. The imagination of crime is an affective process, which does things to the bodies of individuals (whether criminals, the agents of criminal justice, victims, judges or the cinema audience) as much as it has effects in the evolution of practices of criminal justice or paradigms of criminological thought.

The concept of affect has only recently been given serious attention within criminological scholarship (for example, see Watson, 1999; De Haan and Loader, 2002; Karstedt, 2002; Halsey and Young, 2006; Hickey-Moody and Malins, 2008). Within criminological scholarship, however, there is a tendency for some to conceptualize the term 'affect' as synonymous with emotion. My deployment of the term 'affect' derives instead from the tradition of post-Deleuzean social theory, rather than using it to signal some lost emotional dimension in social signification. Massumi writes that affect is akin to the 'ways in which the body can connect with itself and with the world' (1992: 93), and, as such, has to do with *intensity* rather than identity (which is the touchstone of subcultural criminology's approach). Furthermore: 'In affect, we are never alone. That's because affects … are basically ways of connecting, to others and to other situations … With intensified affect comes … a heightened sense of belonging …' (Massumi, 2002: 214). In the cinematic context, Pisters puts it thus: '[T]he affection-image … works directly on the affective nervous system that has its sensors everywhere in the flesh … Affection, where subject and object … coincide, is the way the subject feels itself "from the inside"' (2003: 70).

Where subcultural criminology builds from its Katz-derived concentration upon emotion to ask of criminal actors 'what does it feel like to commit a crime?', the deployment of affect in this post-Deleuzean sense broadens the interlocutive possibilities to ask questions also of those who name or respond to crime in various ways: what affect arises from an encounter with crime?; what affect arises from an encounter with an image of crime?; how does such an affective encounter relate to the politico-cultural and legal factors which limit what it is possible to say and do about a particular image? It allows questions to be asked of these subjects on the understanding that one is never just 'a criminal', or 'a victim', or 'a police officer', or 'a fan of crime films', so much as sites of potential whose subjectivities are made and remade according to the images ascribed to them. To emphasize affect, then (and to do so in a way which does not see affect as simply 'emotion') is to start from a position which acknowledges that crime connects bodies known and unknown through the proliferation of images. The connection might be a minor or substantial interruption to one's sense of the proper, or a reinforcement of one's view of 'the state of society today' or an experience of the exhilaration of illicit behaviour. Whatever the case, *crime as image connects bodies*.[1]

Although seen for decades as of limited relevance to criminological research, it is increasingly clear that, far from being a minor aspect of the criminological

1 For a detailed discussion of such an approach in the context of graffiti, see Halsey and Young (2006).

enterprise, critical engagement with representations of crime and justice orients us as researchers towards the constitutive relation between subject and discourse.[2] Looking at an image or reading a story requires an acknowledgement on the part of the individual that representation exists in the world, that appearance has a place and a force within society. Criminological aesthetics attends to the matrix of intersections between the spectator, the image and the context of reception, with perhaps the most important factor in any instance being the possibility that the subject – including the legal institution as well as the individual – feels *addressed* by the image and thus bound up in a relation with it.

What does such an approach mean for the project of theorizing the cinematic image of crime? First, it is important to clarify its orientation. The term 'postmodern' is a convenient shorthand term frequently used to categorize much of the criminological research inspired by poststructuralist theorizing. Whether used to condemn or acclaim such research, the appellation is often based on a misunderstanding of the contentions of poststructuralist theory. Thus, for example, researchers who emphasize the flexibility of interpretive processes, and who refer in their research to the writings of thinkers such as Derrida, Lyotard or Foucault, may find themselves characterized as claiming that all is relative, or that no definitive meanings exist, or that any one interpretation is as valid as another. My approach to cinema, which is much indebted to the insights of thinkers such as those mentioned earlier, is not based on any assumption that all meaning is negotiable or relative. Rather, my aim is to highlight the constructed nature of the image and the significance of its address to the spectator. Such an approach holds as central the idea that every cinematic image is constructed around a preferred reading. Of course, the spectator may well interpret the image against the grain of its preferred reading, but, as with any act of resistance or differentiation, such an interpretive gesture operates both to generate a new reading and to affirm the unstated norm.

Second, such an approach is obviously different to that of criminologists or film researchers who generate taxonomies for films, allocating movies to boxes as though meaning was indeed uncontestable (for example, see Kellner and Ryan, 1988, and especially Rafter, 2000, 2006). It is closer in orientation to that taken by Tzanelli *et al.* (2005), who emphasize the different readings that can be generated in response to a filmic text. For those authors, however, the fact that different readings are possible becomes the central teleological point of their filmic analysis, in order to argue that the meaning of the category 'crime' gets articulated and negotiated within film in a manner which reflects the ambivalences about crime in society in general (for more on this, see the essay by Yar in this volume). Rather than seeing the cinematic as a mirror of society, I seek to move away from the opposition between the textual and the social.

---

2 For a succinct account of the historical value for criminology of analyzing the cinematic image, see the essay by Yar in this volume.

My reading of the cinematic image of crime takes seriously the relation that exists between spectator and film: rather than subordinating it to the status of a reflecting device, my analysis instead locates itself in the relation between spectator and image, looking at how the spectator feels connected, at the level of sense, with an event on the screen. The spectator thus can be said *to make sense of the image* – in such an affective relation, meaning is effected. Following the Deleuzean frame adopted in Bennett's theorization of affect in the context of viewing artworks, it can be proposed that a cinematic image is an 'encountered sign': a 'sign that is felt, rather than recognized or perceived through cognition' (2005: 7), in which we find the body of the spectator registering sensations relating to what she/he is seeing without undergoing or having undergone what is depicted and seeing sensation become sense (meaning).

Finally, this approach to film analysis is markedly different to that which dominates the burgeoning parallel field of 'law-and-film' scholarship. Where most writings on film within cultural criminology remain resolutely sociological in orientation, thus far most scholarship within law-and-film studies can be characterized as analogous to that of literary criticism, entangled in questions of narrative.[3] The demands of narrative then tend to colonize the available space of critical thought: law-and-film scholars frequently end up recounting the details of what happened, who did that, what was the consequence, and the density of the cinematic image means that exegesis of a scene's events can prevent consideration of any other aspects of the text. While valuable insights can be generated from analyses of cinematic narratives that concentrate wholly on story and character, such an approach overlooks the fact that *cinematic* representations of law, crime and justice are not the same as those found in other cultural forms (such as a short story, a novel, a painting or a newspaper article).

In sum, then, there is an urgent need for an approach to film analysis, both in cultural criminology and in law-and-film studies, that does not simply relate the depicted events to questions of the social or read how a story 'about' crime unfolds, but which also engages with the *cinematic nature of the medium of film*.[4] To that end, then, my aim is to engage with cinema's unique harnessing of image, sound, affect, memory, plot, episode, character, story and event. Such an approach

3 For example, see Berkowitz (2004) on cinematic images of prosecutors; Chase (2004) on the cinematic depiction of due process; Christie (2004) on the courtroom drama; Clover (1998) on juries and the jury-like role of the audience; Greenfield, Osborn and Robson (2001) on films about lawyers, judges, private eyes and so on; Kamir (2005) on atrocity and the legal process in *Death and the Maiden* and (2006) on issues concerning women and law as represented in various films; MacNeil (2007) on the cinematic representation of a number of jurisprudential paradigms; Rafter (2007) on films about sex crime and (2000, 2006) on films about policing; Sherwin (2000) on public disenchantment with the legal process as manifested in *Cape Fear* and Valverde (2006) on films concerning policing, psychiatry and other issues.

4 Obviously, film studies have long grappled with the nature of the medium, examining issues of suture and the gaze, but within that field, there has been little or no interest in how these affect the representation of violence, law and justice.

restores the overlooked *cinematic* dimension to scholarship on crime and justice in film, and in so doing we can theorize the implications of cinema's affective relationship with the spectator for theories of crime, justice and the image. To that end, my method in what follows can be characterized as *scenographic*, in that it attends to particular key scenes and engages in detail with their construction. The remainder of this chapter pursues a scenographic analysis of two films dealing (to a greater or lesser degree) with sexual violence and justice, *Kill Bill vol.1* and *The Accused*, in order to think through the following issues: first, the affective address of the image to the spectator and second, the intersections of violence, looking and (in)justice.

Methodological reflections

Entering the scene of the crime

We are in a room in a hospital, silent except for two sounds: the regular beep of life-support equipment and the erratic whine of a mosquito. There are four beds in the room, and in each there lies a motionless figure. The mosquito lands; its proboscis is inserted into the skin, which throbs red and painfully. Suddenly the motionless figure jolts awake. Her name is The Bride, and she has been in a coma for four years, after Bill and his Deadly Viper Assassination Squad attempted to kill her on her wedding day. The scene occurs in *Kill Bill (vol.1)* (2003, Quentin Tarantino), a film entirely concerned with revenge murder, as The Bride seeks to murder each member of the assassination squad in turn, including the eponymous Bill (who shot her in the head, rendering her comatose). The scene constitutes an interval before The Bride's search for revenge begins and condenses the film's overall thesis on crime and revenge, justice and injustice. Furthermore, the scene raises questions about the role of the image in the imagination of justice and injustice and about the affective relation between spectator and image.

We hear the sounds of a door slamming in the corridor and a man's whistling. An orderly enters, accompanied by another man. The Bride has lain down, to pretend that she is still unconscious. The two men stand at the foot of the hospital bed, looking at The Bride. Since the camera has taken up the point of view that The Bride would have were her eyes not shut, they are in fact looking direct to camera. The orderly says: 'Price is $75 a pop, my friend. You getting your freak on or what?'. The orderly then makes a speech instructing his companion in 'the rules':

> Rule number 1: no punching. Nurse comes in tomorrow and she's got a shiner or teeth missing, jig's up … Now, are we clear on rule number 1? Rule number 2: no monkey bites or no hickeys; in fact, don't leave no marks of any kind. After that, it's all good, buddy. Now, her plumbing down there don't work no more, so feel free to come in her all you want. Now keep the noise down, try not to make a mess, and I'll be back in twenty… Oh, by the

Figure 6.1 Kill Bill (vol.1) (2003, Dir, Quentin Tarantino).

> way, sometimes this girl's cooch can get drier than a bucket of sand. So if she dry, you just lube up with this [a filthy jar of Vaseline, which he throws to the man] and you're good to go. *Bon appetit*, good buddy.

The importance of this speech lies in its performative qualities: its experiential tone reveals that the orderly is not just pimping The Bride but also that he himself has raped her in the past. The orderly leaves; the other man climbs on to the bed, straddling The Bride's body.

The camera has been pointed squarely at them in medium close-up from its position a few feet from the bed; at this point, however, it abruptly swivels away from the bed towards the other side of the room. When the camera has completed this 180° turn, the man's agonized scream is heard, and the camera abruptly cuts back to the bed. We see, in close up now, The Bride biting the man's lower lip while he screams; her eyes bulge and her expression is one of utter ferocity. As he pulls away from her, his lower lip stretches until it is around four inches in length. Just as it seems it must be about to rip itself off, the camera performs that cut instead, as the screen goes black and the man's scream fades into silence. Almost immediately, however, the image resumes; The Bride is shown pushing the man's now-dead body off the bed; but it appears her legs are paralyzed, for she falls to the floor. The sound of the orderly's whistling is heard, as he returns to the room. Finding a hunting knife in the dead man's possession, she drags herself out of sight, as the orderly opens the door.

The camera lingers on what he sees: the empty, disordered bed, his friend's dead body, water spilled on the floor. A cut to a close up of the corpse is answered by a cut back to the orderly's shocked disbelief; he is shown in medium close up and the camera then pans, in slow motion for the first time in the scene, slowly downwards to show The Bride lying on the floor behind him, the knife clutched in her hand. The arpeggios of the music have been gradually increasing in volume and menace, and as they reach a climax The Bride slashes the orderly's Achilles tendon with the knife. The blade's slicing into the ankle is shown in extreme close-up, (the knife and ankle fill the entire screen), just as The Bride's bite of the lip was, as though acts of violent resistance to sexual violence demand to be shown in the fullest of detail.

The Bride drags the orderly to the doorway and notices his nametag, which states 'BUCK' and a tattoo on his knuckles, 'F-U-C-K'. Their rhyming juxtaposition prompts her to recall the orderly standing, alone, at the foot of her hospital bed, saying, 'I'm from Huntsville, Texas. My name is Buck … and I'm here to fuck'. She slams the door on his head with such force that he is killed. She then takes his car keys and hospital scrubs, and wheels herself to the hospital car park, where she spends the next thirteen hours in his truck regaining the ability to walk.

Cinematic aesthetics: 'just looking' at the scene of the crime?

What can this scene tell us about justice and injustice? Any attempt to answer this question returns us to the question of imagination – the making of images.

In analyzing this scene, my interest lies in the relationship between imagination and the image, between the spectator and the image and between the image and justice. As such, I am preoccupied with looking and its relationship to justice and injustice. In emphasizing looking, I wish to leave behind the simple summarizing of a narrative (which recounts 'what happened' in a scene or a film) and interrogate the medium of cinema in order to engage with *how we look* at what happened. In doing so, the question of imagination is linked to the possibility of justice and injustice.

Consider the response frequently offered when a shop assistant offers help to an individual browsing among the goods on sale: 'no, thanks, I'm just looking'. The subject's relation to the object is minimized, the very idea of looking is evoked as a kind of defence against the imputation of desire for the goods on display, and the potential relationship with the sales assistant can be warded off – all through the notion of 'just looking'. No further response or responsibility is thus required. Such evasiveness should not be permitted in the spectator's relation to the cinematic image. Looking is never 'just looking'. Thanks to the spectator's affective relation with the image, cinematic representations of crime, violence and revenge provide admirable stages for considering whether the image on screen can connect the body of the spectator to the possibilities of judgment and ethics. To put it otherwise, a cinematic aesthetics engages with the question of whether the relation between spectator and cinematic image can ever be constituted as a kind of *just* looking.

The hospital scene from *Kill Bill vol.1* enacts my concerns with the conjunction of looking and justice in a context involving sexual violence. Before returning to that scene, it is worth recalling that that conjunction was famously elaborated in *The Accused* (1988, Jonathan Kaplan), which told the story of the gang rape of a woman, Sarah Tobias, in a bar on a pinball machine by three men in front of a crowd of cheering spectators.[5] The actual rapists plead guilty to a nonsexual offence; and the film's main narrative centres on whether the prosecutor can convict three of the male spectators in the bar of criminal solicitation. The film-makers made the decision not only to film the rapes, but in fact to make the scene long, graphic and brutal. Producer Sherry Lansing stated:

> Once you see this movie, I doubt that you will ever, ever think of rape the same way again. These images will stick in your mind, and you will be more sympathetic the next time you hear of somebody being raped … Until I saw this film, I didn't even know how horrible [rape] is. (quoted in Faludi, 1992: 170)

5 *The Accused* is based on an actual event which involved the rape of a woman on a pool table in a bar called Big Dan's, in New Bedford, Massachusetts. On the New Bedford case, see Bumiller (1991) and Horeck (2004). On the reimagination of the Big Dan's case in *The Accused*, see Horeck (2004) and for an exemplary reading of *The Accused*, see Clover (1992).

Critical responses to this scene have been mixed, but for my purposes here, the significant issue is that such a scene is included at all. Members of the audience therefore watch the rape much as the individuals in the bar watch it. Just as the film's suspense is located in the question of whether the prosecutor can prove that there can be criminal culpability attached to watching a rape, it should be asked whether culpability attaches to the gaze of the cinematic spectator. Does the audience member watch as a witness to a crime, with the capacity to testify as to its brutality, or as a spectator, able to find entertainment in what is depicted?

The intention is no doubt for the audience viewer to watch in a forensic way: appalled and alienated. Various cinematographic techniques are deployed to this end. The scene's lengthy duration is one, as though the discomfort engendered in the spectator from experiencing the scene's continuation beyond the limits of mainstream genre expectations might echo the discomfort experienced by the rape victim.[6] Many shots are included which attempt to convey the victim's point of view, and specifically to depict her suffering, for example, showing the point-of-view Tobias would have had while being held down on the pinball machine. (Note, however, that these are alternated with point-of-view shots of her, from the rapists' position, and shots of the cheering crowd.) In Tobias's point of view shots, vision and sound are distorted, again as if the very cinematography might imitate the rape victim's suffering. And it is clear that Tobias is suffering: she is shown being held down, and her protesting voice is silenced by a hand over her mouth.

The Accused, then, clearly sought to engage the spectator in the scene of sexual violence by depicting it as an event of great brutality. However, of equal importance to the manner of the event's representation is the question of its location within the narrative. Many reviewers wrongly recalled the rape scene as a flashback occurring during Tobias's testimony in the prosecution of the three men for criminal solicitation. It does not: the camera remains in the present tense of the courtroom while Tobias recounts what happened to her. The flashback to the rape occurs when another male bystander gives evidence. Since the medium of cinema inevitably privileges the visual, it must be asked why *The Accused* gives empirical verification to the words of a male bystander rather than to the rape victim. In this way, the visual narration of 'what really happened' is taken away from the woman who experienced it and given to a male character only secondarily involved in the event. Justice in *The Accused* is certainly tied to the image, but in a way that is, literally, mediated, in that the injured woman can achieve justice only through the intercession of two agents: the lawyer who argues the case in court and a male bystander, in whose memory is found the actuality of the victim's rape.

6 Protraction of the scene has become a trope in the cinematic depiction of sexual violence: lengthy rape scenes can also be found in *Once Upon A Time in America* (1984, Sergio Leone) and *Irreversible* (2002, Gaspar Noe).

Kill Bill imagines justice differently. In the hospital scene, when The Bride remembers what has happened to her (rape by Buck and others), this impels her to kill him. *Kill Bill* therefore gives the empirical verification derived from visual rendition to The Bride's memory – we *see* her visualizing what has happened to her; we are not required to watch the scene of the crime in order to *know* that the crime occurred. The film thus invests The Bride's memory with the force of law (and here, I mean not the institutional law found in *The Accused* but rather the force of law as judgment unfettered by institutional processes). It might be argued that *The Accused* has a more direct relationship to questions of justice and injustice (since its events lead to a court case rather than to a bloody murder), but the film's interest in institutional processes occludes the question of justice for the victim of sexual violence. *Kill Bill*, on the other hand, allows the spectator to see sexual violence without contingency; that is, as an event which demands response irrespective of the uncertainties of the legal process.

'Just looking' in *The Accused* concerns only the gaze of the male bystanders (and the film's spectator); the woman's body, experience and subjectivity are of relevance only to the extent to which they have been represented by and to others. This evacuation of the woman's subjective gaze leads the film's spectator to a position in which spectatorship matters only in terms of legal contingency: will the prosecutor succeed in convincing the jury?; will the male bystander give evidence? 'Just looking' in *Kill Bill* leads the protagonist to immediate murder. The gaze in this scene travels from the orderly and his accomplice to the comatose body of The Bride, but it also, crucially, encompasses The Bride's interior, memorial, gaze in her recalling of the event of rape.

The reading of the cinematic image that can be generated through a cinematic aesthetics can include not only what is contained within a scene or film but also what has been left out. Films which deal with sexual violence usually include a scene of rape (as *The Accused* does); *Kill Bill* does not. Instead we hear Buck's instructions to his friend on how to have 'a good time' and see The Bride's memory of Buck standing at the foot of her bed. Does the omission of any explicit depiction of sexual violence make this scene less effective in showing that repeated rape of a comatose woman is reprehensible? The scene hums with dread and horror – and its affective encounter with the spectator is not accomplished by means of any depiction of penetration, degradation or suffering. Rather, the spectator realizes what has been happening to The Bride by means of Buck's performative exhortation to his friend, from the repetitive insistence of the soundtrack, and from the camera angles which provide no shots objectifying The Bride as a victim but which emphasize her point of view both in the present and in the past.

Kill Bill demonstrates, then, that the automatic inclusion of a rape scene in a rape-revenge film is unnecessary. Despite arguing for the pedagogic benefits in the depiction of rape, films such as *The Accused* do worse than take insufficient care in their representation of the event – they perpetuate the notion that rape must be seen before it can be condemned. In this notion resides the assumption that a woman's words, and a woman's memories of sexual injury, cannot be trusted or taken for granted: both the spectator and the law are alike in requiring corroboration of her claim.

Conclusion

That images of law and justice are tied to the image is not a new point to make (although it is always worth reiterating). My aim in this essay has been to emphasize that the ties that bind law and justice to the image should not be taken for granted. The scenographic analyses provided here of key scenes in *Kill Bill vol.1* and *The Accused* demonstrate that every component of a scene (not simply action and character but also crucially music, cinematography, editing, sound and so on) can have affective impact upon the spectator and works towards the textual construction of categories such as 'sexual violence', 'justice' and 'crime'. It matters enormously that *The Accused* included a rape scene and *Kill Bill* did not, and that the rape scene in *The Accused* was placed in a position within the narrative which compounded that film's structural tendency to negate the point of view of the rape victim.

Comparison of scenes from two films such as these reveals not just the substantive differences in their approaches to sexual violence but also that, as scholars of the image and of imagination, we need to acknowledge what Kuhn has called 'the power of the image' (1985) and its links to injustice as much as to justice. The image should always be on trial, as should our spectatorship of it.[7] This has not yet taken place. If the hospital scene from *Kill Bill* were analysed according to the narrative-driven approach which dominates film analysis in criminology and law-and-film studies, the result would read something like this: 'the comatose Bride recovers consciousness and thwarts an attempted rape in the hospital room. She discovers that the orderly has been pimping her body and raping her himself, and kills him'. What is lost in such an action-oriented account? What is lost is *the image* as image and our relation to it. What is lost is the slow-motion close-up of the orderly's ankle as The Bride slashes it, a shot which makes audiences squirm and gasp when they see it. And lost are the moments when the spectator is constructed as looking at or from a particular location, moments which encourage identification and interpellation in the scene – in other words, the *affective processes* through which the image on the screen binds us to itself.

This affective relation should be the starting-point for our interrogation of the cinematic imagination of justice and injustice. It must be a thorough-going interrogation, analyzing the multilayered aspects of every scene by questioning their consequences. Every scene could have been filmed differently. Any image is therefore contingent and metaphorical, standing in for an infinite number of alternative imaginings. It must always be asked: what has been excluded? What is the

7 For an interesting account of the links between spectatorship and justice, see Sklar (1990). For an extended version of my argument about vision, justice and violence, see Young (2009, forthcoming).

effect of that exclusion? Such an analytical approach to the image has the potential to mark out a new terrain of political inquiry for cultural criminology: for underlying this cinematic aesthetics is a conviction that interrogation of imagination and the image can provide a new path towards social change and legal transformation.

References

Bennett, J. (2005) *Empathic Vision: Affect, Trauma and Contemporary Art,* Palo Alto: Stanford University Press.

Berkowitz, R. (2004) 'The Accusers: Law, Justice and the Image of Prosecutors in Hollywood', *Griffith Law Review*, 13(2): 131–52.

Biber, K. (2007) *Captive Images: Race, Crime, Photography,* London: GlassHouse Books.

Buchanan, R. and Johnson, R. (2009) 'Strange Encounters: Exploring Law and Film in the Affective Register', *Studies in Law, Politics and Society,* 46: 33–60.

Bumiller, K. (1991) 'Fallen Angels: The Representation of Violence against Women in Legal Culture', in M. Fineman and N. Thomadsen (eds) *At the Boundaries of Law,* London and New York: Routledge.

Chase, A. (2002) *Movies on Trial: The Legal System on the Silver Screen,* New York: New Press.

Christie, I. (2004) 'Heavenly Justice', in L.J. Moran, E. Sandon, E. Loizidou and I. Christie (eds) *Law's Moving Image,* London: Glasshouse Books.

Clover, C. (1992) *Men, Women and Chainsaws: Gender in the Modern Horror Film,* Princeton, N.J.: Princeton University Press.

Clover, C. (1998) 'Law and the Order of Popular Culture', in A. Sarat and T. Kearns (eds) *Law in the Domain of Culture,* Ann Arbor, MI.: Michigan University Press.

De Haan, W. and Loader, I. (2002) 'On the Emotions of Crime, Punishment and Social Control', *Theoretical Criminology*, 6(3): 243–53.

Faludi, S. (1992) *Backlash: The Undeclared War Against American Women,* New York: Crown.

Ferrell, J. and Sanders, C. (1995) (eds) *Cultural Criminology,* Boston: Northeastern University Press.

Greenfield, S., Osborn, G. and Robson, P. (2001) *Film and the Law,* London: Cavendish.

Halsey, M. and Young A. (2006) '"Our Desires are Ungovernable": Writing Graffiti in Urban Space', *Theoretical Criminology*, 10(3): 275–306.

Hickey-Moody, A. and Malins, P. (eds) (2008) *Deleuzian Encounters: Studies in Contemporary Social Issues,* New York: Palgrave MacMillan.

Horeck, T. (2004) *Public Rape: Representations of Violation in Fiction and Film,* London and New York: Routledge.

Hutchings, P. (2001) *The Criminal Spectre in Law, Literature and Aesthetics: Incriminating Subjects,* London: Routledge.

Jewkes, Y. (2004) *Media and Crime,* London: Sage.

Kamir, O. (2005) 'Cinematic Judgment and Jurisprudence: A Woman's Memory, Recovery and Justice in a Post-Traumatic Society (A Study of Polanski's *Death and the Maiden*)', in A. Sarat, L. Douglas and M.M. Umphrey (eds) *Law on the Screen,* Palo Alta, CA.: Stanford University Press.

Kamir, O. (2006) *Framed: Women in Law and Film,* Durham, NC.: Duke University Press.

Karstedt, S. (2002) 'Emotions and Criminal Justice', *Theoretical Criminology*, 6(3): 299–317.

Katz, J. (1988) *Seductions of Crime: Moral and Sensual Attractions of Doing Evil,* New York: Basic Books.

Kellner, D. and Ryan, M. (1988) *Camera Politica: The Politics and Ideology of Contemporary Hollywood Film,* Bloomington: Indiana University Press.

Kuhn, A. (1985) *The Power of the Image: Essays on Representation and Sexuality,* London: Routledge and Kegan Paul.

Lippens, R. (2004) 'Introduction: Imaginary. Boundary. Justice', in R. Lippens (ed.) *Imaginary Boundaries of Justice,* Oxford: Hart Publishing.

Lyng, S. (ed.) (2004) *Edgework: The Sociology of Risk-Taking,* New York: Routledge.

MacNeil, W.P. (2007) *Lex Populi: The Jurisprudence of Popular Culture,* Palo Alto: Stanford University Press.

Massumi, B. (1992) *A User's Guide to Capitalism and Schizophrenia,* Cambridge, MA.: MIT Press.

Massumi, B. (2002) 'Navigating Movements: A Conversation with Brian Massumi', in M. Zournazi (ed.) *Hope: New Philosophies for Change,* Annandale: Pluto Press.

Miller, J.A. (1995) 'Struggles over the Symbolic: Gang Style and the Meaning of Social Control', in J. Ferrell and C. Sanders (eds) *Cultural Criminology,* Boston: Northeastern University Press.

Phillips, N.D. and Strobi, S. (2006) 'Cultural Criminology and Kryptonite: Apocalyptic and Retributive Constructions of Crime and Justice in Comic Books', *Crime, Media, Culture*, 2(3): 304–31.

Pisters, P. (2003) *The Matrix of Visual Culture: Working with Deleuze in Film Theory,* Palo Alto: Stanford University Press.

Rafter, N. (2000) *Shots in the Mirror: Crime Films and Society,* New York: Oxford University Press.

Rafter, N. (2006) *Shots in the Mirror: Crime Films and Society,* 2nd edn, New York: Oxford University Press.

Rafter, N. (2007) 'Crime, Film and Criminology: Recent Sex-Crime Movies', *Theoretical Criminology*, 11(3): 403–20.

Sherwin, R. (2000) *When Law Goes Pop,* Chicago: Chicago University Press.

Sklar, J. (1990) *The Faces of Injustice,* New Haven, Conn.: Yale University Press.

Sparks, R. (1990) 'Dramatic Power: Television, Images of Crime and Law Enforcement', in C. Sumner (ed.) *Censure, Politics and Criminal Justice,* Milton Keynes: Open University Press.

Tzanelli, R., O'Brien, M. and Yar, M. (2005) '"Con Me If You Can": Exploring Crime in the American Cinematic Imagination', *Theoretical Criminology*, 9: 97–117.

Tunnell, K.D. (2004) 'Cultural Constructions of the Hillbilly Heroin and Crime Problem', in J. Ferrell, K. Hayward, W. Morrison and M. Presdee (eds) *Cultural Criminology Unleashed,* London: GlassHouse Books.

Valier, C. (2002) 'Punishment, Border Crossings and the Powers of Horror', *Theoretical Criminology*, 6(3): 319–37.

Watson, S. (1999) 'Policing the Affective Society: Beyond Governmentality in the Theory of Social Control', *Social and Legal Studies*, 8: 227–51.

Young, A. (1996) *Imagining Crime: Textual Outlaws and Criminal Conversations*, London: Sage.

Young, A. (2005) *Judging the Image: Art, Value, Law*, London: Routledge.

Young, A. (2007) 'Images in the Aftermath of Trauma: Responding to September 11th', *Crime, Media, Culture*, 3(1): 30–48.

Young, A. (2008) 'Culture, Critical Criminology and the Imagination of Crime', in T. Anthony and C. Cunneen (eds) *The Critical Criminology Companion,* Leichhardt, NSW: Hawkins Press.

Young, A. (2009) 'The Scene of the Crime: Judging the Affect of Screen Violence', *Social and Legal Studies*, 18(1): 5–22.

Young, A. (2009, forthcoming) *Visions of Violence: Cinema, Crime, Affect,* London: Routledge.

Chapter 7

Imagining the 'war on terror'

Fiction, film and framing

Alexandra Campbell

Introduction

We are, as Jock Young (2004:13) poignantly remarks, 'confronted at this moment with an orthodox criminology which is denatured and desiccated', a criminology, moreover, that is reductive and uncritical as it treats social categories as variables to be controlled for and 'events' as fixed 'facts' to be explained. Sharply critical of normative methodologies and the underlying belief that 'truth' is to be found in aggregate data, cultural criminology has been vociferous in its articulation that crime and its control should be approached as 'cultural enterprises'.

Understanding that crime occurs – and is made sense of – within a circuit of culture where collective meaning is made and remade, cultural criminology places emphasis on the inextricable dynamic relationship between crime and its representation. In these late modern times when even our deepest sense of self is caught up in an endless circulation of mediated images and narratives, this emphasis is vital, for our individual and collective experience of crime is also caught up in this representational loop. Images of crime saturate the global media-marketplace, mediating our experience of crime, shaping how we comprehend criminal events, and, crucially, how we contend with them. Acutely aware of the capacity of symbolic processes to orientate our experiences of crime, law and order cultural criminology makes clear that attention must be focused on the power-inhered images which construct (rather than benignly reflect) crime.

Indeed images *do* something, and while their effects are not determined – for meaning is neither stable nor final as they are deciphered within polysemic interpretive communities, making meaning volatile – images circulate in and through a matrix of power. Bourdieu (1991) reminds us that meaning is constrained, as political and social authority flow through everyday cultural representation, giving rise to a set of preferred meanings which encourage us to 'see' in very particularized ways. The regulatory and performative capacity of an image and its relationship to power, authority and injustice are central concerns to a cultural criminology which intends to take questions of power and (in)justice seriously. By focusing on cultural imageries, then, an analysis which intervenes in the meaning-making process is possible, providing a starting point for exploring how mediated meaning 'socializes and directs our thinking and actions in a range of hierarchical, complex, nuanced, insidious, gratifying, pleasurable and largely imperceptible ways' (Carter and Weaver, 2003: 167).

As a cultural criminologist interested in a post 9/11 world where the US is engaging in global penal projects such as Guanatanamo Bay and Abu Ghraib (Rose, 2004; Agamben, 2005; Brown, 2008) and in a war which contravenes international legal conventions (Kramer and Michalowski, 2005), I want, in this essay, to showcase the value of interrogating the 'image' with concerns of power and justice in mind, by exploring the regulatory effects of mass-mediated images of terrorism. Indeed, the image of terror provides a crucial starting point in making sense of these increasingly authoritarian times. Scholars across disciplines are already beginning to pay attention to the relationship between terrorism and its representation, appreciating the primacy of representation in shaping reality as visual culture and symbolic processes offer us frames to structure and organize the (unruly) social world. Within media and cultural studies a mushrooming literature has emerged which seeks to make sense of this post 9/11 climate, focusing, in particular, on the mass-mediated social, cultural and political discourses which ceaselessly keep terrorism on the collective consciousness. Jackson's (2005) research, for example, focuses on the public language of 'the war on terrorism', arguing that without this surrounding discourse the actions pursued under the catchphrase's reach would not be tolerated. Drawing attention to the reproduction of myths through the 'terror' narrative across cultural institutions, Jackson spotlights how a set of standing assumptions have emerged which normalize violence, torture and war. The public lexicon, argues Jackson, shapes public perception in regard to the identities and types of people within the discursive frames, affecting psychical and social lives, as a combination of words and images engender anger, sadness, fear and anxiety, creating a 'public emotion' (2005: 22). In a similar way, Lewis (2005) highlights the inextricable relationship between global media and political struggle in the contemporary world, placing emphasis on how current political rhetoric meshes with popular cultural framings; the language of the 'war on terrorism' interplaying with popular fictions of chaos and restored order, violence and resolution.

Both Lewis and Jackson make the script of terrorism the object of inquiry, opening up the opportunity to ask vital questions revolving around the ways in which the script is rolled out, and, importantly, how the attendant meanings are leading to *real world* injustice. Given cultural criminology's trans-disciplinary epistemological framework (Schofield, 2004: 131), it is well situated to engage with this burgeoning literature and to integrate modes of inquiry which enable an untangling of the image and its consequences.

In this essay, I wish to illustrate the value of an approach which, drawing on the insights of cultural and media theorists, makes use of a 'mode of looking' which takes seriously the power of the image. In particular, I focus on cinematic imageries, which are, I would suggest, an important site for exploration for cultural criminologists interested in exploring the intricacies and impacts of symbolic power, for as Nicole Rafter (2007) argues, film is one of the primary sources through which people get their ideas about the nature of crime.

Focus

Hollywood film and the construction of the 'Other'

My focus in this chapter is a case study of the Hollywood film *The Siege*. Drawing on semiotic and textual analysis to deconstruct the image of the 'Muslim-Other'[1], this chapter moves beyond a content-based media analysis, to illustrate how orientalist (Said, 1970) images and narratives of the 'enemy' contribute to a 'terrorism/counter-terrorism' script. I seek to show how such a script, in which extreme (fictional and real-world) extra-legal and violent strategies are made reasonable, is made ever more compelling as the image of the Muslim, whose suffering and humanness is obliterated through representational absences, is reduced to *bare life*; a life that, according to Giorgio Agamben (1995), does not count as life at all.

Culture and the authority of representation

Focusing on the filmic images and narratives which contribute to a particular cultural milieu, is one way into the cultural script; a script that must be attended to if we are to understand what is currently occurring in public life. Indeed, we are at present living at a time when the US and its allies are behaving as 'rogue heroes', increasingly indifferent to the rule of law as they act against labelled 'terrorists' who are construed as terrorist killing machines (Rose, 2004). Under the mantra 'the war on terror' the US's actions appear to be viewed and widely accepted as a means to restore order, with little note to the well-documented suffering of this interminable 'war' felt mostly by Muslims both domestically and internationally (Dixon, 2004). A global campaign of this nature requires political and social consent, and inducing consent requires a lexicon, a public narrative, that manufactures approval (Herman and Chomsky, 2002; Jackson, 2005). Lewis (2005) points out that the lexicon is not entirely new, and that 9/11 and the ensuing responses to it resonated with an imagery already created by Hollywood.

---

1 The concept of the 'Other' is vital to the understanding of identities. We construct the self through our (imagined) difference with 'others', and thus, the Other is someone other or different to oneself. The Other is, then, *constitutive*, for, it makes possible a discrete and separate self. Edward Said makes use of this notion in his research on *Orientalism*, demonstrating how the West's self-identity was predicated on the construction of the East-as-Other as its binary opposite. These othering processes gave rise to a positive, superior Western identity; moreover, the specific images of the East legitimated the West's treatment of the East.

What I want to suggest through this essay is that the image of the Other made this imagery even more compelling; a racist caricature which readily fitted a story in motion. Moreover, because of the semiotic structure of genre films, whose underlying architecture rests on binary oppositions where motifs of good/bad are played out, the frame for interpreting the us/them binary was already in place and helped make the Muslim/Other 'our' natural enemy. Meeuf's (2006) analysis of action films usefully illustrates this point as he demonstrates how melodrama, as a narrative, has been used through US cinema to address challenges to its own conception of itself as morally righteous. The melodrama rehearses motifs of good and bad, emphasizing an essential US sense of goodness; a logic that has dynamically informed US official discourses of terrorism. Indeed, the dominant narrative is augmented by familiar imageries which feature innocent victims of unspeakable violence who are showcased to serve as a moral imperative for the spectacle of retributive violence that follows. This mediated violence, as Lewis (2005: 42) observes:

> confront[s] viewers with a miasma of emotional and psychological effects within a familiar narrative of moral ideological conflict. The viewer, entranced by the horror and excitement of the drama, is inevitably seduced by the possibility of heroic restoration, the conquest of good over evil, order over chaos.

Here, I want to focus on the fictional images of the Muslim-enemy who is situated in dominant narratives as the West's binary adversary, and to suggest that this social construction, which appears to prohibit a narrative which might humanize the Other, bolsters a largely unaccountable political sovereign power – the US administration. By narrating the Muslim Other in particularized ways, a spectral enemy – who remains outside the frame of human – functions as grounds for the sovereignty exercised through real life policy. As a result, violence and inhuman treatment appear as the only intelligible courses of action as representational framings systematically strip this category of people of their humanity, mimicking, and hence helping to support, the US administration's sovereign stripping of the detainees' political status and identity in Guantánamo Bay. The body of the Muslim (made analogous to danger), reduced to bare life through fictional narratives, helping to (re)create a general clause for the real-world detainment, treatment and torture of Muslims; a clause which does not, under these circumstances, need to be in response to a *real or proven danger*, for the dangerousness of the Muslim is already 'known' in the public's imagination.

Cinematic framings: The Siege

Examine the history of cinematic depictions of Arab Muslims, and it is not difficult to discern the recurring trope of uncivilized fundamentalist which connects disparate films. And it is not difficult to discern how the consistency and constancy of the representations have helped to solidify a set of meanings which make the heterogeneity of this identity inconsequential. Jack Shaheen's (2001) systematic analysis of more than 900 films featuring Arabs draws attention to their habitual negative representation as irrational villains, intent on killing Westerners, usually Americans. From the 1920s Sheik movies to the more familiar terrorist film which feature the fundamentalist up against the intrepid American hero, a stream of depictions have created a systematic filmic narrative, which is practically unfailing in its creation of a mass of faceless, human-less people waiting to be killed off by Westerners (including black Westerners) (Said, 1997: xxvii).

Alongside these depictions – and running through many of them – is a motif of paranoia that values 'sacrifice, the cult of the hero, and the doctrine of constant warfare' (Dixon, 2004: 20), which work to emphasize the uniqueness and manifest destiny of Americans to set wrongs right. Deeply embedded in Hollywood films, suggests Landy (2004: 97), is the idea of American exceptionality, which valorizes America's role as policeman of the world, divinely sanctioned through the Hollywood Melodrama of good and evil.

It is within these existing and formulaic frames that the 1998 film, *The Siege*, directed by Edward Zwick, emerged. Denzel Washington stars as Anthony 'Hub' Hubbard, head of the FBI (Federal Bureau of Investigation) terrorism task force, who is in charge of investigating a number of terrorist bombings. Hubbard is partnered with Frank Haddad (Tony Shalhoub), an Arab-American. Elise Kraft (Annette Bening) is an undercover CIA (Central Intelligence Agency) official and Middle East expert who joins Hubbard and Haddad to investigate the terrorist attacks. As they work to uncover the source of the terrorism, the violence escalates and the President sends in General William Devereaux (Bruce Willis) who takes over the city and declares martial law. This state of emergency, with its attendant exercise of sovereign power, leads to the internment of the male Arab-Muslim American population of New York who are presumed to be terrorist suspects.

On the surface, the film appears to critically question the excess of state power illustrated through this suspension of law and the declaration of martial law. In deconstructing *The Siege*, however, it is apparent that despite first impressions this is a cinematic representation which (re)capitulates a set of orientalist meanings, which in familiar ways prohibits a humanizing discourse, placing the Muslim-Other outside the frame of human. The film does examine the problem of balancing 'rights' with security, yet, this question is not explored in relation to the suffering and trauma of an Arab-Muslim people brutalized and traumatized by the exercise of an unaccountable power. Rather, it is framed around abstract notions of 'ideal' Western democracy, which is understood as being under siege, as the spectacle of an enemy (already known in the public's imagination) performing as the general clause for this exploration.

This film is of particular interest since it predates 9/11, and it has been heralded by some as prescient of the 2001 attacks on New York, seemingly adding to the film's authenticity in its treatment of Arab-Muslims. The film also appears to resist demonizing Arab Muslims in a straightforward way. Certainly, it appears to transcend the usual orientalist character binaries of good/evil, civilized/uncivilized, Western/Other habitually cast along racial/ethnic lines. The casting of black actor, Denzel Washington, as the principled FBI officer complicates the racial imagery at play, but, more crucially, the representation of Muslims is problematized by the Arab-American character, Frank Haddad. Indeed the audience is invited to recognize Haddad, to view him within human frames, as his son is indiscriminately interned.

For the audience to identify with Haddad, however, he must be recognizable as a normative human subject. Here, Islam is split into two: the Westernized, fully assimilated Muslim up and against the essentialized, authentic Muslim. The depiction of Haddad is not simply a tokenistic inclusion of a positive ethnic representation, for the representations which constitute this character make Haddad's life, in Agamben's (2005) terms, a *qualified life*. Haddad's life is qualified precisely because he is separated from authentic Islam. A character with an Anglicized name who belongs to a quintessentially American agency, the FBI, who plays football with his son and speaks with ease as an American, betraying no accent or ties to the East, Haddad is untethered from the burdening signifiers of Islam as he is bestowed an American identity. We are invited to recognize Haddad not as Muslim but as Western, as a patriotic citizen of the US. This gesture is critical, for appended to Western identity are a set of signifiers – civilized, brave, compassionate, just and more – and this nullifies Haddad's purported Islamic connections. His characterization fits existing frames of the human; we recognize his name, his speech and his attire, which collectively connote his proximity to 'us'.

While Haddad's life is recognizable to the audience as he enunciates as an American, the most prominent Arab-Muslim featured in the film, Sami Bouajilia, appears in more familiar terms as the Muslim enemy. Bouajilia – a name barely pronounceable let alone recognizable – 'babbling' in an incomprehensible language in a tone often inflected with anger and derangement, is the leader of the terrorist cells which intend to heap as much destruction on innocent Americans as possible. Untrustworthy and fervent, Bouajilia is portrayed leading an anonymous group of fanatics, who we view from afar, through the prism of an alien language and through camera shots which linger on the mostly nameless followers just long enough for the audience to gauge their fundamentalism and dangerousness. Demarcated through generalized and reified symbols of Islam, the Muslim is not rendered through frames which humanize: we are presented with no story of suffering, no biography, no family, no history. Instead, the film's iconography connects in a seamless way Muslim practice and violence. As the audience views the Muslim ablution, the ritual washing of hands before prayer, there is an understanding that what will follow in the next frame is a terrorist act. This sequence requires no in-depth explanation since the body of the Muslim is already culturally coded, established and presumed to be acting in predetermined

Islamic ways. This (re)citation of the Muslim bears the indubitable marks of past representations, which collectively constitute an ahistorical biological body of people, unsullied by reason.

Obfuscating, at times, the orientalist meanings at play in *The Siege*, is a seemingly sympathetic portrayal of the Arab-Americans interned when martial law is declared. We see ordinary Americans protesting against the internment, and in the process we witness and are invited to identify with the free and compassionate spirit of the American citizens who stand up for rights and freedom. On the other hand, we witness the suffering and persecution of the interned from afar. Again, there is no discourse which describes the experience of being taken away without reason and for an indefinite period; there is no frame for viewing the suffering and trauma of interminable detention, no narrative which engenders empathy, and no one recognizably human for us to identify with in order to experience the despair and pain of torture. *The Siege* forecloses the audience's ability to recognize the Muslim as a suffering, vulnerable subject as they are reduced to biological entities programmed to destroy.

This logic is illustrated through the choices which the film presents in terms of dealing with the terrorism question; the quandary so laid out: how to balance the rights of the (American) individual against the rights of society to ensure security of the nation? The question is explored not in relation to *their* humanness, which does not enter the frame, but, rather, it revolves around *our* humanness. The narrative focuses on two possible strategies which are represented through the characters of Hubbard and General Devereaux. Hubbard takes an investigative approach, attempting to take out terrorist cells through surveillance and infiltration. Once these measures appear to fail, General William Devereaux, on orders from the President, imposes martial law on the city of New York. Although these policies appear to stand in opposition in the film, they are in fact analogous; they are both reactive and imply that the solution to terrorism is to be found in defence.

The omnipresent threat of the enemy contributes to a paranoiac culture where violence against the Other is sanctioned at the moment it is deployed. Indeed, aggression is cast as the solution to terrorism, as opposed to its foundation. *The Siege* appears to offer context but it does not, as America's foreign policy is only selectively revealed, effacing the circumstances under which terrorism flourishes. As a consequence, the film solidifies the familiar racist caricature of the Muslim, frozen in time, compelled to violence and destruction by essential forces, never acting in response to policies and actions of the West (Said, 1997). Western identity is cast as Islam's binary opposite, leading to America's sense of itself as an ordained destiny in the world, which justly uses violence and war in order to impede these forces that seek to inhibit the West's progress (ibid).

The state of exemption and bare lives

The meanings contrived through films such as *The Siege* do not remain confined to the world of fiction, of course. Meanings produced through cinematic imageries seep their way into our consciousness, providing a lens or framework for interpreting events and identities, insidiously compelling us to understand the world in particularized ways. While we often feel immune to the meanings created through fictional imagery, as though our consciousness was able to separate 'fact' from 'fiction' in a meaningful way, films help provide a ready, though nonlinear, script to help us make sense of crime and the protagonists involved. This dynamic interplay of mediated meaning and practice means, as Hayward and Young (2004: 259) succinctly declare, that 'the street scripts the screen and the screen scripts the street'. As Mariana Valverde (2006: 59) points out, bound up in this script are also messages about the 'authorities to whom we are supposed to entrust our safety. Messages about authorities and solutions will emerge at the same time', and thus images of law and order, intimately connected to structures of power, shape our experience, not only of crime and disorder but also the resolution of the disorder.

This circular scripting process is evident when we consider the relevance of the meanings (re)created through *The Siege*. The film engenders a way of viewing Muslim and American identities, and, at the time, provides solution to the problem of 'terrorism', assigning authority and righteousness to those solutions. These meanings permeate the broader social and cultural fabric, adding to the repertoire of orientalist meanings which gives rise to a Western identity which is as benevolent as Eastern identity is malevolent (Said, 1970). The wider resonance of these binary meanings is apparent if we consider, even briefly, current political rhetoric. The equivalency made between Muslims and violence – as articulated through *The Siege* – is made clear through Donald Rumsfeld's groundless suppositions that the Muslims detained without charge at Guantanamo Bay 'are committed terrorists', that they are 'among the most dangerous, best-trained, vicious killers on the face of the earth', while his deputy's description of them as 'dangerous people ... a special breed of person', is illustrative of the extent to which these meanings are more extensively understood as essential and unchangeable. Our easy acceptance of these assertions as truisms speaks to the efficaciousness of representations, which collectively have led to a contemporary situation where a group of human beings, completely deprived of their rights and prerogatives (as the Muslims detained in Guantanamo Bay are) is made reasonable; to a situation where no act that 'we' commit against Muslims could appear as a crime.

Indeed, many of the policies enacted to contend with terrorism, make clear that the creation of a binary 'us' and 'them' – whereby the 'them' are understood as essentially outside of the frames of the human, as a 'special breed of person' – has real effects on the people violently subjected to these socially constructed linguistic systems. The detainment of hundreds of Muslims at Guantanamo Bay, for example, who are there without charge and without legal protection as domestic and international law have been suspended, is suggestive of the interrelationship of symbolic and political power.

Agamben's (1995, 2005) theorizations of the 'state of exception' and *homo sacer* usefully explicate the workings of state power when legal structure is

Figure 7.1 The 'state of emergency' with its attendant exercise of sovereign power in *The Siege*.

suspended, but, crucially, also provide a way to conceptualize the interconnections of images of Muslims – which erase and harm – which echo what is occurring within Guantánamo Bay. Agamben's work follows Carl Schmitt's (1922) concept of the 'sovereign', defined by Schmitt as 'he who decides on the state of exception' (Schmitt quoted in Agamben, 2005: 1). For Agamben, sovereignty emerges precisely at the moment when legal structure is suspended and thus comes into being through the suspension of law itself. The protagonist placed outside of law is, for Agamben, *homo sacer* – a life that is 'bare life'. Distinguishing *bare life* from *qualified life*, Agamben demonstrates the constitutive power of law as subjects are turned from bare life (biological minimum life), through civil rights and citizenship, into qualified life (a thinking and meaningful life caught in political and national communities). De-realized through privation of rights and citizenship, bare life enters a suspended zone, exiled from political existence and human community, becoming a 'living dead man' (1995: 131).

For this to occur, however, and for it to be tolerated, *homo sacer* (specifically here, the Muslim-Other) placed outside of 'law' must appear to belong 'there'. In other words, they must, in the general public's imagination, warrant the unchecked violence which is made possible through the operation of sovereign power. What makes this possible, I'm suggesting, are the cultural imageries which collectively constitute the Other, imageries which assign to them a chain of signifiers which provide the very grounds for their legal excommunication. Specifically here, I am suggesting that the legal stripping of Muslims in Guantanamo is enabled through the dominant images of the Muslim, who is rendered *homo sacer* through strategic representational framings.

Such framings are discernible throughout *The Siege,* where, frame after frame, the figure of the Muslim, through the constitutive power of mass media, is deprived of the humanizing qualities necessitated for a qualified life. The film's construction of the Muslim-Arab terrorist as outside of reason, someone who cannot be negotiated with or compromised with, places the Muslim outside of political community. In contrast, the Western protagonist is always embroiled in political life as they navigate the complexities of politics and ethics. Rendered outside of political (human) community, the Muslim's biological-minimal life is contrasted to the politically qualified life of the Westerner, a thinking-meaningful subject (Agamben, 1995: 7). Once again outside of human frames, the Muslim's de-realization (a human who is not quite human) serves to endlessly justify the film's conclusion that extremism should be viewed as something inherent to Islam, a quality essential to a body of people, and this necessitates the punitive policies – from torture to internment camps – showcased through the film.

The significance of a narrative that reduces the Muslim to *homo sacer* should not be understated, particularly at a time when the internment of Muslims is currently being realized at Camp Delta. The (concentration) camp is, for Agamben, the site where the state of exception is fully realized and normalized, representing a stable spatial arrangement where martial law is the rule rather than a temporary exception at times of particular crisis (1995: 169). Referencing the Jewish concentration camps, Agamben describes how the 'denationalized' Jew was 'stripped of every political status and reduced wholly to bare life', thus allowing a brutal power to confront pure (bare) life without mediation (171). The propaganda and the imagined dangerousness of the Jew inscribed through the images and narratives at the time reduced, in the national consciousness, the Jew to bare life; the constitutive powers of law and cultural meanings working in and through one another, naturalizing the Jew's internment.

Given the Bush administration's lack of regard for international and domestic law, it is not difficult to see the parallels between the camps of Nazi Germany and Camp Delta and the Nazi propaganda representing the Jew and the contemporary imageries which constitute the Muslim. The 'enemy combatants' who defy legal classification and protection, have been placed at the mercy of a sovereign power which has the self-allocated authority to detain indefinitely. The stateless detainees have effectively entered Agamben's 'suspended zone', no longer recognizably human, reduced to nothing but bodies, to bare life. The resonance of the terrorism script and the images of the Muslim which are so vital to that script, no doubt make commonsense these authoritarian policies, yet, the suffering unleashed through their implementation is well documented. Testimonies of freed detainees illustrate the horror of the psychological and physical conditions of the camp. Rose (2004) notes the extent to which these testimonies are mutually corroborating and details the routine violence experienced by those detained. Tarek Dergoul, one of the British men released is quoted:

> … I heard a guard talking into his radio, 'ERF ERF ERF' [Extreme Reaction Force], and I knew what was coming… They pepper sprayed me in the face, and I started vomiting; in all I must have brought up five cupfuls. They pinned me down and attacked me, poking their fingers in my eyes, and forced my head into the toilet pan and flushed. They tied me up like a beast and then they dragged me out of the cell in chains, into the rec[reation] yard, and shaved my beard, my hair, my eyebrows'
>
> (quoted in Rose, 2004: 71)

These testimonies have had seeming little effect in the US. These stories are not front-page news, and, when they appear at all, they appear in out of the way places, easy to ignore, to pass over as unimportant. Mostly, though, they are absent. The marked passivity and indifference toward this suffering on the part of the American mainstream media, press and public is striking (Dixon, 2004), and speaks, I would suggest, to the efficacy of a script which puts the Muslim outside human eligibility. As *The Siege* solidifies a set of preferred orientalist meanings around Muslim identity, it powerfully reinvigorates established frameworks for apprehending reality. Intersecting with other cultural representations, political processes and institutional practices, this film contributes to a dominant culture which naturalizes and concretizes meaning around Islam and the West. The interconnections between symbolic power and the power exercised through legal strategies are here devastatingly illustrated. As prisoners indefinitely confined to Guantánamo Bay exist in an indefinite 'state of exception', no longer covered by any legal or civil rights, their suffering and vulnerability is nullified by a brutalizing cultural discourse. Mutually supportive, cultural and institutional enactments reduce the Muslim to a set of familiar orientalist qualities, outside of frames of the human, and these are processes which require deconstructing if we are to understand how legal protections can be so easily abandoned with such catastrophic results.

Methodological reflections

Seeing the image: media literacy

I show *The Siege* regularly as part of one of my classes. Toward the beginning of the term, and before students embark on reading the texts on semiology, orientalism and terrorism, I ask in a general way if they have previously seen the film and, if so, what they thought about it. Invariably, many of them have, and most enjoy the film. To most of my students the film is a pretty realistic, though exaggerated, representation of contemporary terrorism and the questions around counter-terrorism which emerge. Namely, how do we as a 'free' society fight terrorism while protecting our civil liberties and the (minimal) rights of those whom we are against?

For the most part, then, students are quite uncritical in their viewing, absorbing into their consciousness the underlying mythical assumptions of the film. They identify with the 'moderate' Denzel Washington character, having sympathy with the good Muslim, while their views about Muslims in general are confirmed. Mostly, they are critical of the internment camps and torture, though they understand the need for them in states of emergency, perhaps because these young adults came of age in a post 9/11 era, where terms like 'terrorism', 'torture', 'water-boarding' and more are part of their everyday lexicon.

We then read, amongst other things, seminal texts by Said, Saussure and Barthes, and as we do so we deconstruct, collectively, contemporary Western images of the Muslim found in news, film, fiction and more. At the same time, we view images and narratives which humanize the Muslim: images of war and internment and devastation, images, then, which do not obscure great suffering. As a class, we then watch the film, and for many of the students who have viewed it before, it is often a completely different experience. No doubt this is in part because they are in a classroom setting, surrounded by peers and a professor who underscores the importance of a critical reading, but in part, too, because the students are actively deconstructing, or, to put in Barthes (1972: 11) terms, they are looking with a view of seeing the 'ideological abuse' of the image.

What follows is always a rich debate, a confessional, of sorts, where some students reveal their easy enjoyment of films like *The Siege*, and how easily the film's preferred meanings are accepted and incorporated. When invited to look in a different way, with a view to gleaning the subliminal ideological underpinnings of cinematic imagery, the viewing experience is transformed. More often than not students later report that they cannot consume media in the way they did before the course, that they are more aware of how their reality is constructed, of how these narratives position them in relation to questions of their own identity, as well as justice and injustice. They have found, through a critical examination of an image, a way into the script.

Film analysis is one method of making the script visible. It is a means to denaturalize everyday meanings, which circulate unnoticed by most of us, including my students; it is a way to make apparent meaning's artificiality and partiality, and, as such, showing films can be a valuable teaching tool. Philosopher Slavoj Zizek makes clear the utility of cinema in the documentary *The Pervert's Guide to Cinema* (Fiennes, 2006), stating in interview:

> In order to understand today's world, we need cinema; literally. It's only in cinema that we get that crucial dimension which we are not yet ready to confront in our reality. If you are looking for what is, in reality, more real than reality itself, look into cinematic fiction.
>
> (quoted in *Time Out Online*, 2006)

For Zizek film requires exploration for it affects the psyche and society in complex ways, yet, it is also a window into exploring 'reality'. To my students, film analysis renders the familiar unfamiliar, it illustrates the capacity of symbolic power to shape their deeply held thoughts, and in understanding that interconnection – between images and their own views – they are able to appreciate the significance of a culturally produced script, which infringes upon not only *their* consciousness, but also, more widely, upon a *public* consciousness.

There are many ways to approach the cinematic image, and various theoretical orientations – as examples, structuralism, poststructuralism, psychoanalytic, feminist, and more – stress varying points of emphasis. Methodologically, approaches range from the more quantitative content analysis to the more qualitative focus on aesthetics, from a focus on who says what and to whom, to an analysis of the experience of the audience: the lighting, the music, the collective strategies which make a film compelling, interesting and immersing. Using film thus enables a range of readings, providing a way into many subject areas which span (and blur) disciplinary boundaries. Here, I have given emphasis to the semiotics of a film, of images in motion, with a view of revealing the tacit politics of meaning-making.

The work of theorist Roland Barthes (1972) encourages a way of looking which considers how meaning comes to *appear as natural*; in short, to explore the image's contextual devices which anchor the polysemy of the image, which coaxes the audiences into a preferred reading. An approach fostering a way of 'seeing' which unravels the cultural assumptions embedded in the image, makes it possible for a form of cultural reflexivity to emerge, an ongoing awareness of the political underpinnings of an image which circulate as natural meaning. Yet, this politicized reading positions *me* in the text, as this sort of analysis necessarily begins with recognition 'of an ideological objection or an awareness that the sign system carries assumptions that appear natural but are actually historical' (Gaines, 2002: 320).

Dominant strands of criminology would no doubt eschew such a politicized analysis. Within cultural criminology, however, there has been a call for a repoliticization of the discipline (Carter and Weaver, 2003; Ferrell *et al.,* 2004), to engage with questions of justice and injustice. The case study explored here hints at the urgency of this endeavour, to engage at the level where meaning is made, for, as I have suggested throughout this essay, the consequences of meaning-making can be devastating. A politicized deconstruction accentuates the importance of infiltrating the script; this is simultaneously a means to intervene in the script, a means to help unravel a cultural sensibility where images of terror have been connected to wider social anxieties, mobilized through the spectacle of terror which have deep emotional and psychical resonance (Valverde, 2006).

The interpellative function of these representations – the way in which they maneuver us into various subject-positions, how they help to discipline meaning and orchestrate our thoughts and feelings in relation to justice and injustice – can be gleaned through this deconstructive approach. Left intact, these meanings collaborate with a contemporary disciplinary-machinery which undoubtedly benefits from the terrorism script as it is thus configured. In a mass media-society understanding how these meanings are made and employed is crucial. This is important as a social researcher, but this way of seeing has wider resonance beyond the parameters of criminology and academia more generally. Fostering media literacy which draws on this form of deconstruction, has the potential to politicize not only criminology but, more vitally, a viewing public whose collective consciousness matters. Film analysis as part of teaching practice is one method to help in the cultivation of this form of reflexivity. Indeed engendering a critical gaze in student-citizens – with the hope that this way of seeing permeates the walls of the classroom – is certainly in line with a broader project which seeks to make visible the awesome capacity of symbolic power to affect the psyche and society.

Conclusion

Much cultural work is required for us to consent – either directly or through passivity and indifference – to what occurs at a political level. Cultural myths powerfully help to shape our perceptions of law and order, safety and security, of victims and perpetrators; their veracity is of not much consequence and has little to do with how compelling they are to us on an emotional level (Zizek, 1989). It is crucial to understand the cultural processes at work in the (re)creation of specific mythical frames and to understand and attend to these frames, since they decide, in a compelling way, what we can hear and what meanings are intelligible. Textual analysis of cultural representation and imagery provide a means to understand the wider cultural conditions in which they are deployed, while at the same time they reveal the signifying processes integral to creating a context which is inhospitable to alternative interpretations of meaning. The meanings of signs occur within a social and cultural context, and successful communication requires recognition of the vocabulary and its attendant decoding rules. Changing those rules with questions of justice in mind requires that we understand those rules.

This is not to ignore alternative and subversive interpretations and avenues for meaning-making, and indeed cultural criminology with its phenomenological orientation is well situated to engage at the level where meanings are consumed and negotiated (Ferrell and Sanders, 1995). Rather, it is to underscore that under certain institutional and discursive conditions collective meanings become devastatingly stabilized within specific contexts. Attempts to resignify Islam in the West are not without example, and acts of resistance *are* being performed: from poetry authored by some Guantánamo detainees (see Falkoff, 2007) to testimonies from released prisoners dramatized in documentaries and theatre productions (see, for instance, the play *Guantánamo: 'Honor Bound to Defend Freed'*); from hunger strikes, to suicide attempts, which might be read as subversive performances which seek to articulate something of the despair and suffering experienced by the detainees. Yet, the potentiality of meanings of these acts is currently constrained by a foreclosing hegemonic field which limits what can be said and what can be thought. In the current climate, a symbolic force that demarcates the speakable from the unspeakable silences these alternatives; a form of metaphorical sovereign power seemingly seeping its way out of Guantánamo's walls, diffusing through cultural and political representations, stabilizing meanings to the extent that alternative discourses and understandings are rendered implausible. The voice of the Muslim has been historically and contemporarily deauthorized; the Muslim does not speak from a recognizable human subject position: neither human in fiction nor in Guantánamo. Travelling through existing frames, their utterances wither as they are enunciated in a cultural field which silences and deletes.

Deconstructing this cultural milieu is hence vital, for, as Furedi (2007) suggests, this amorphous racism, driven by a narrative of fear, invites us to regard terrorism as incomprehensible, senseless and beyond reason. Speculation and fantasy have become legitimate forms of threat assessment, and the dramatization of the threat offers an invitation to terrorize our 'enemies'. Too often criminology collaborates with the apparatus of social control by reifying uncritically social categories and the assumptions of powerful institutions, thus failing, Ferrell *et al.* (2004: 2) write, 'to move us toward social arrangements less poisoned by fear, violence, and exploitation'.

While it is beyond the scope of this essay to detail the collaboration of criminology with intensified social control, specifically in relation to terrorism and counter-terrorism, it is worth concluding by suggesting that if we are to take issues of justice seriously, then we must animate an engaged criminology which does not shy away from examining the political processes which flow through cultural texts. Instead, we should seek to expose the interrelationship of mass mediated meanings and dominant institutions, spotlighting their regulatory and performative capacity, while making clear their very real ramifications. Indeed, as working criminologists, we must be always painfully reflexive of our own role in perpetuating 'knowledge' and a current sociocultural climate within which real people suffer.

References

Agamben, G. (1995) *Homo Sacer: Sovereign Power and Bare Life,* Stanford: Stanford University Press.

Agamben, G. (2005) *State Of Exception,* Chicago: University of Chicago Press.

Amnesty International (2003) *Holding Human Rights Hostage,* Amnesty International: United States (24 December 2003).

Barthes, R. (1972) *Mythologies,* New York: Noonday Press.

Bourdieu, P. (1991) *Language and Symbolic Power,* Cambridge: Polity Press.

Brown, M. (2008) 'Aftermath: Living with the Crisis: From PTC to Governing Through Crime', *Crime, Media, Culture,* 4(1): 131–6.

Butler, J. (2004) *Precarious Life: The Power of Mourning and Violence,* New York: Verso.

Carter, C. and Weaver, C.K. (2003) *Violence and the Media,* Milton Keynes: Open University Press.

Chomsky, N. (2001) *9–11,* New York: Seven Stories Press.

Cole, D. and Dempsey, J. (2002) *Terrorism and the Constitution: Sacrificing Civil Liberties in the Name of National Security,* London and New York: New Press.

Dixon, W. (2004) 'Introduction: Something Lost: Film after 9/11', in Dixon, W. (ed.) *Film and Television after 9/11,* Carbondale: Southern Illinois University Press, pp. 1–28.

Dyer, C. (2003) 'Law Lord Castigates US Justice: Guantánamo Bay Detainees Facing Trial by "Kangaroo Court"', *The Guardian Online* (26 November 2003).

Falkoff, M. (2007) *Poems From Guantánamo: The Detainees Speak,* Iowa City: The University of Iowa Press.

Ferrell, J., Hayward, K., Morrison, W. and Presdee, M. (2004) 'Fragments of a Manifesto: Introducing Cultural Criminology Unleashed', in Ferrell, J. *et al.* (eds) *Cultural Criminology Unleashed,* London: Routledge, pp. 1–12.

Ferrell, J. and Sanders, C. (eds) (1995) *Cultural Criminology*, Boston: Northeastern.

Fiennes, S. (2006) *The Pervert's Guide to the Cinema.*

Furedi, F. (2007) *Invitation to Terror: the Expanding Empire of the Unknown,* London: Continuum.

Gaines, E. (2002) 'Semiotic Analysis of Myth: A Proposal for an Applied Methodology', *The American Journal of Semiotics*, 17(2): 311–27.

Hayward, K. and Young, J. (2004) 'Cultural Criminology: Some Notes on the Script', *Theoretical Criminology,* 8(3): 259–73.

Herman, E. and Chomsky, N. (2002) *Manufacturing Consent,* New York: Pantheon.

Jackson, R. (2005) *Writing the War On Terrorism: Language, Politics and Counter-Terrorism,* Manchester: Manchester University Press.

Kramer, R. and Michalowski, R. (2005) 'War Aggression and State Crime', *The British Journal of Criminology,* 45: 446–69.

Kuhne, H. (2006) 'Terrorism Rediscovered: The Issue of Politically Inspired Community', in Freilich, D. and Guerette, R. (eds) *Migration, Culture Conflict. Crime and Terrorism,* Burlington: Ashgate Publishing.

Landy, M. (2004) 'America under Attack: Pearl Harbor, 9/11, and History in the Media', in Dixon, W. (ed.) *Film and Television after 9/11,* Carbondale: Southern Illinois University Press, pp. 79–100.

Lewis, J. (2005) *Language Wars: The Role of Media and Culture in Global Terror,* Ann Arbor. MI: Pluto Press.

Meeuf, R. (2006) 'Collateral Damage: Terrorism, Melodrama and the Action Film on the Eve of 9/11', *Jump Cut*, no. 48, Winter.

Rafter, N. (2007) 'Crime, Film, and Criminology', *Theoretical Criminology,* 11(3): 403–20.

Rose, D. (2004) *Guantánamo: The War on Human Rights,* London and New York: The New Press.

Ross, J.I. (2007) 'Deconstructing the Terrorism-News Media Relationship', *Crime, Media, Culture,* 3(2): 215–25.

Said, E. (1970) *Orientalism,* New York: Vintage.

Said, E. (1997) *Covering Islam: How the Media and the Experts Determine How We Should See the Rest of the World,* New York: Vintage.

Schofield, K. (2004) 'Collisions of Culture and Crime: Media Commodification of Child Sex Abuse', in Ferrell, J. *et al.* (eds) *Cultural Criminology Unleashed,* London: Routledge, pp. 121–32.

Shaheen, J. (2001) *Reel Bad Arabs: How Hollywood Vilifies a People,* New York: Olive Branch Press.

Smith, A. (1994) *New Right Discourse on Race and Sexuality,* Cambridge: Cambridge University Press.

Time Out Online (2006) *'The Pervert's Guide to Cinema' – Slavoj Zizek interview* London: Time Out. 6 October 2006. http://www.timeout.com/film/news/1439/#

Valverde, M. (2006) *Law and Order: Images, Meanings, Myths,* London: Routledge.

Young, J. (2004) 'Voodoo Criminology and the Numbers Game', in Ferrell, J. *et al.* (eds) *Cultural Criminology Unleashed,* London: Routledge, pp. 13–28.

Zizek, S. (1989) *The Sublime Object of Ideology,* London: Verso.

Zwick, E. (1998) *The Siege.* Distributed by 20th Century Fox.

Chapter 8

Framing the crimes of colonialism

Critical images of aboriginal art and law

Chris Cunneen

'Painting is our foundation. White man calls it art' Galarrwuy Yunupingu. (quoted in Isaacs, 1999: xi)

Introduction

This chapter considers images of crime and law, and what we, through the lens of cultural criminology, might learn of the nature and experiences of crime represented through the image. Cultural criminology opens a new space for understanding crime, especially where the image is produced by those who are victims of crime and simultaneously without access to other channels of communication within mainstream social and political institutions. The images considered in this chapter are particular: Australian Aboriginal art. These artworks function on two levels, as an expression of Aboriginal law and, more extensively, as a critique of the imposed colonial law. Both in traditional and contemporary society, Aboriginal art is a powerful medium for expressing Aboriginal law and culture.

Aboriginal art plays a special role in understanding law in a society that did not rely on the written text. In this context, the image has sacred standing quite distinct from the commodity status of art in contemporary capitalist societies. Art also provides an important material expression and critique of the colonizing process, both as an historical record of events such as massacres, segregation and the denial of civil and political rights, and as an ongoing contemporary postcolonial critique of the outcomes of colonization, dispossession and racial discrimination. Aboriginal artists are constantly engaging colonialism, law and the criminal justice system as subject matter for their art. The production of the image is a tool of resistance.

There is a sense in which Indigenous art *unhinges* colonial law as an abstract expression of power and grounds it firmly in the lived experiences of Aboriginal people. For the cultural/critical criminologist, art becomes a rich source of ideas, documentation and insight into the inner workings of an oppressive state formation and the modes of resistance engendered by oppression. The image becomes a critical tool in both deconstructing oppression and in understanding the political dynamics and contours of resistance. Methodologically, the image becomes both a window on the experiences of victimization (particularly in the cases of state crime considered in this chapter), and a source of documentation of disturbing criminal events (such as mass murder) where the criminal justice institutions of the colonial state have chosen to ignore or deny the existence of such events.

Focus

Interpreting aboriginal artwork through cultural criminology

I have approached Aboriginal art as part of an ongoing project in relation to broadening our understanding of the 'state crimes' of colonial regimes and the potential for reparations for historical injustices against Indigenous people in Australia (Cunneen, 2005, 2008). The origins of this research derive from two somewhat disparate strands of influences and thoughts about the production and function of the image. The first is an interest in the technologies and 'arts' of resistance. In particular, this was sparked by an interest in some of the academic work on political murals in Northern Ireland. Cultural criminology provides the opportunity to shift the epistemological priority given to certain forms of knowledge, and to treat seriously the importance of the image in understanding state crime and political resistance. The second strand has been the role of art in Indigenous society as an expression of law. I have been interested for sometime in debates around the recognition of Aboriginal customary law and the way in which the debate often trivializes the expression of law in a society that does not rely on written texts. It seems self-evident that various forms of art – such as painting, sculpture, dance and song – will have a special place in reproducing social, moral and religious meanings. In short, if law is not reproduced through the written text it will be reproduced in other forms. Cultural criminology offers the potential to revalorize alternative conceptions of the expression of law, that is an understanding of law constituted through the image, rather than law constituted and reproduced as written text. Let us look at these two strands of influence in more detail.

An understanding of the northern Irish murals has been influenced by the extensive work of Rolston (2001, 2003, 2004). A key concern has been the role of the murals as public art in imagining community and reaffirming particular identities. The public murals also reinforce and recreate specific historical narratives and meanings. As Rolston (2004: 118) states, 'through these cultural artefacts they articulate their political hopes and fears, their view of their own identity, their hopes of their past and future, and the political obstacles which they see facing them currently or in the future'. I draw three interconnected points from this literature. First, the art work is not seen as simply Art but is clearly bound-up with political activity. The work is both artistic (that, it has a clear aesthetic value) and self-consciously political. The aesthetics and the politics are arguably one. Secondly, the artists are organic to their communities. Their politics is part of the culture and politics of the community they represent, and it is integral to those politics. The art and the artists can be seen more specifically as organic in a Gramscian sense, as growing out of a political constituency and speaking to and for that community. Thirdly, the art has the power to articulate and celebrate historical and political causes and aspirations. In Sivanandan's (1990) terms, it is part of the way 'communities of resistance' develop, understand themselves and maintain solidarity and support.

The example of the murals of Northern Ireland leads more generally into the literature on the technologies and arts of resistance. Scott (1990: xi) discusses how shared critiques of domination occur among 'subordinates' outside the immediate control of the dominant. The subordinate are likely 'to create and defend a social space in which offstage dissent to the official transcript of power relations may be voiced'. There is a difference between what is said in the face of power to what is said 'offstage' – this is the 'hidden transcript' which is produced for a different audience than the public transcript. The extent to which these transcripts are hidden will vary on a range of factors. When the affronts of power are 'suffered systematically by a whole race, class, or strata, then the fantasy [of revenge and confrontation] can become a collective cultural product' (1990: 9). The work of historians like EP Thompson (1974) also has influenced our understandings of resistance. Thompson was interested in the popular discontent, riot and disorder among working class and rural poor. He was interested in the traditions of counter theatre and theatrical symbolism and 'the acts of darkness'. Similarly, Bakhtin's (1984) celebration of carnival and riot as part of medieval folk culture, of the process of turning the 'world inside out' presented new understandings of resistance – an understanding we attempted to apply in a study of leisure-based antipolice riots (Cunneen *et al.*, 1989). Overall these lead to a focus on the cultures of resistance among the subordinated – to what Scott calls the 'infrapolitics of subordinate groups' that constitute various forms of resistance (1990: 19). These broad approaches to the cultures of resistance provide a context for the analysis of Indigenous art.

The second strand to the argument involves a consideration of Aboriginal art as a powerful medium for expressing Aboriginal law and culture. Aboriginal art plays a special role in understanding law in a society that did not rely on the written text. Stated simply, this is the idea that we can see Aboriginal art as 'law'. By 'law', I mean the body of rules that govern a society, rules that generally reflect moral and ethical principles, which proscribe certain forms of behaviour, and are enforceable through sanctions or punishment.

As lawyers or criminologists, we see and understand the following as law.

Crimes Act 1900

Part 3 – Offences against the person

Division 1 – Homicide

17 (Repealed)

17A Date of death

(1) The rule of law that it is conclusively presumed that an injury was not the cause of death of a person if the person died after the expiration of the period of a year and a day after the date on which the person received the injury is abrogated.

(2) This section does not apply in respect of an injury received before the commencement of this section.

18 Murder and manslaughter defined

(1) (a) Murder shall be taken to have been committed where the act of the accused, or thing by him or her omitted to be done, causing the death charged, was done or omitted with reckless indifference to human life, or with intent to kill or inflict grievous bodily harm upon some person, or done in an attempt to commit, or during or immediately after the commission, by the accused, or some accomplice with him or her, of a crime punishable by imprisonment for life or for 25 years.

(b) Every other punishable homicide shall be taken to be manslaughter.

(2) (a) No act or omission which was not malicious, or for which the accused had lawful cause or excuse, shall be within this section.

(b) No punishment or forfeiture shall be incurred by any person who kills another by misfortune only.

19 (Repealed)

19A Punishment for murder

(1) A person who commits the crime of murder is liable to imprisonment for life.

(2) A person sentenced to imprisonment for life for the crime of murder is to serve that sentence for the term of the person's natural life.

(3) Nothing in this section affects the operation of section 21 (1) of the *Crimes (Sentencing Procedure) Act 1999* (which authorises the passing of a lesser sentence than imprisonment for life).

(4) This section applies to murder committed before or after the commencement of this section.

(5) However, this section does not apply where committal proceedings (or proceedings by way of ex officio indictment) for the murder were instituted against the convicted person before the commencement of this section. In such a case, section 19 as in force before that commencement continues to apply.

(6) Nothing in this section affects the prerogative of mercy.

20 Child murder – when child deemed born alive

On the trial of a person for the murder of a child, such child shall be held to have been born alive if it has breathed, and has been wholly born into the world whether it has had an independent circulation or not.

21 Child murder by mother – verdict of contributing to death etc

Whosoever, being a woman delivered of a child is indicted for its murder, shall, if the jury acquit her of the murder, and specially find that she has in any manner wilfully contributed to the death of such child, whether during delivery, or at or after its birth, or has wilfully caused any violence,the mark of which has been found on its body, be liable to imprisonment for ten years.

For our purposes the content is almost unimportant. It can be 'seen' immediately as law. If we look closer we can understand it as law: it defines and proscribes certain behaviours and establishes a set of penalties for offences. As criminologists, we may be critical of it, or we may see it as a positive expression of moral values in a liberal democracy, or we may be indifferent and prefer to count the number of times the law was breached and by whom in what circumstances.

However, can we understand the following painting from the Pintupi man Yala Yala Gibbs from central Australia as law? And what would we make of it as criminologists?

Figure 8.1 Yala Yala Gibbs Tjungurrayi *Kaarkurutinytja, Lake McDonald* (1997). © Estate of the artist. Licensed by Aboriginal Artists Agency 2008.

The painting by Yala Yala Gibbs and another by Anatjari Tjampitjinpa called the *Tingari Cycle at Tjuwal* (1989), which is not reproduced here, describe Pintupi law (see Isaacs, 1999: 41–43). The paintings relate to the Tingari ceremonial cycle, a journey undertaken by a group of Creation Ancestors. The Tingari took human and animal forms and travelled over vast areas of the desert performing rituals and singing into being animals, plants and natural features. The Tingari laid down social custom and law as it should be practiced. The two paintings by Pintupi men map Tingari journeys. Water sources are fundamentally important, and these Tingari journeys plot the whereabouts of soaks, rock holes and ancient wells (Isaacs, 1999: 40). They are both topographical and ethical maps. They represent spiritual and environmental connections.

The role of art as the expression of law has been recognized is various ways in relation to Aboriginal land claims under Western property law (through the concept of native title), and this is a complex subject in itself. Suffice to state here, that some Aboriginal communities have been using art to document their country and their traditional ownership of the land when making land claims. Perhaps the most well know of these is the Spinifex claim in Western Australia. Here the community produced two large canvasses: one representing men and the other women which covered people's relationships to the whole land area under claim. The paintings were included in the native title agreement which was negotiated with government (Winter 2002: 64; Crane, 2002: 14–15). The point I want to establish here is the particular relationship between art and law in Aboriginal society – and the different significance of art in Indigenous society compared to the concept of art as individual artistic and imaginative expression which is favoured in the West. For Aboriginal people, art can be a material expression of law.

The image as a political and historical voice

The remainder of this chapter focuses on analysis of Aboriginal art in the context of colonial law and the fundamental human rights abuses that arose as a result of the colonial process. It is here that Aboriginal art provides a unique window on state crime and the colonial process. Aboriginal artists are constantly engaging colonialism, Anglo-Australian law and the criminal justice system as subject matter for their art. As Kleinert and Neale (2000: vii) note, 'It is clear that Australia's Indigenous people have used 'art' to reaffirm their autonomous concerns, and they have deliberately sought to engage in dialogue with the colonizing society'.

As a critique of the colonizing process, Aboriginal art can be seen as a polysemic voice, providing for differing types of narratives around a central theme of the colonial experience, while at the same time reaffirming the separate validity of Indigenous culture, history and identity. At one level, Aboriginal art is a voice for Aboriginal people. As the artist Gordon Bennett stated, 'I found the language in which I was most articulate to be the visual language of painting, and it was through painting that I found a voice' (quoted in McLean and Bennett, 1996: 27). There is a link with the traditional role of art as a key form of cultural expression, and perhaps reinforced by the more limited access Indigenous people have had to the dominant written culture of the colonizer.

Indigenous art also provides an historical voice for Aboriginal people. Art provides documentary evidence that certain things occurred (such as massacres) or that certain relationships were and are in place (such as the relationship to land). This challenges the view that Indigenous people in Australia do not have historical recording of the past, because they do not have written records. As the artist Lin Onus has stated, 'Some people write the history. I can't write, so I paint instead' (quoted in Isaacs, 1989: 28). As discussed further in the following section, such accounts of the past through art are particularly important around contentious issues like colonial massacres.

Aboriginal art is also profoundly and often self-consciously political. At times it can provide a direct critique of various aspects of the non-Indigenous political and social order. As Leslie Griggs, an artist who learnt to paint in prison stated, 'I find [painting is] the best way to get back at the system without leaving myself open to prosecution' (quoted in Mclean, 1998: 109). Or as Galarrwuy Yunupingu stated, 'Our painting is a political act' (quoted in Isaacs, 1999: xi).

An example of the bridging of traditional art and modern Aboriginal political claims against the colonial state can be found in the Yirrkala Bark Petition (1963) and the Barunga Statement (1988). Both are powerful artistic and political statements.

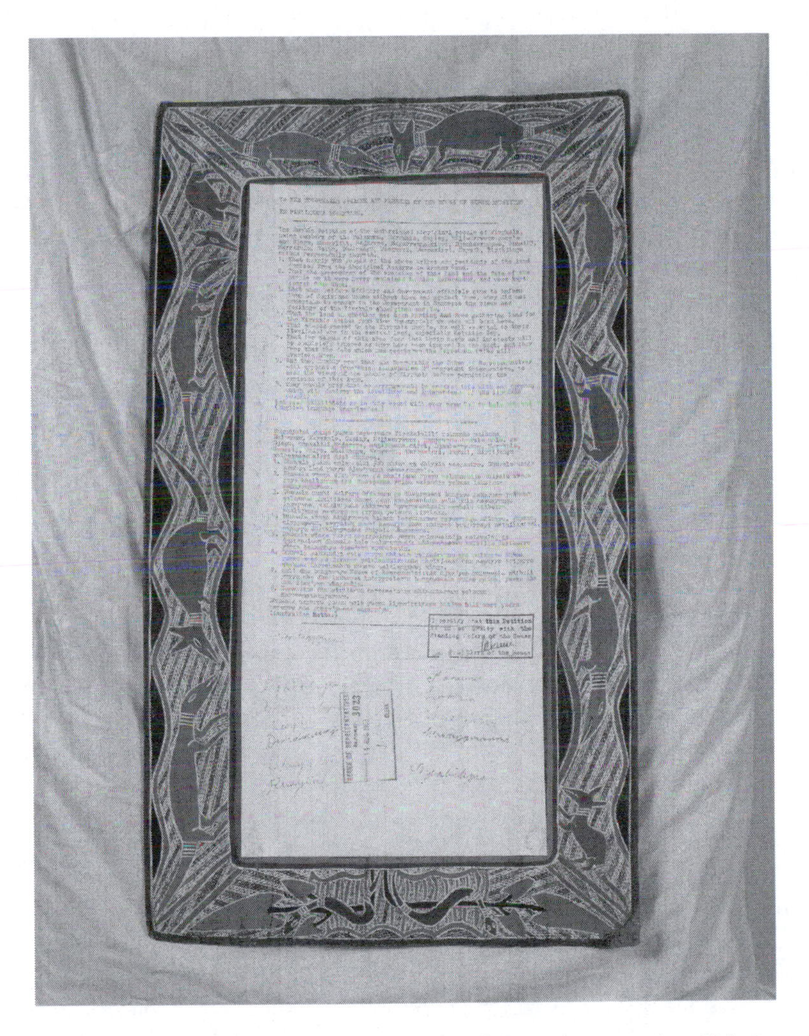

Figure 8.2 Section of the Yirrkala Bark Petition. © Buku Larrngay Art, Yirkalla and Parliament House Australia.

The Yirrkala Petition was an appeal, a petition to the imposed colonial law to recognize Aboriginal rights to land and an expression of Indigenous law of the land. 'It was not an ordinary petition: it was presented as a bark painting, and showed the clan designs of all the areas that were being threatened by the mining company … It showed that we were not people who could be painted out of the picture or left on the edge of history' (Yunupingu, 1993).

The Barunga Statement was made in 1988 (the year of the Australian Bicentenary) and presented to the then Prime Minister Bob Hawke by the Northern and Central Land Councils of the Northern Territory (Morphy, 1998: 258). The Statement called on the government to negotiate a treaty with Aboriginal people that recognized prior ownership of the land, continued occupation of the land by Aboriginal people and their sovereignty. It is a statement about the recognition of Indigenous law, culture and political sovereignty. It is a basic claim for Indigenous self-determination. The artistic work on the Barunga statement represents the various language groups or Aboriginal nations which constitute the two large Land Councils in the Northern Territory.

Both the Yirrkala Bark Petition and the Barunga Statement can be recognized as fundamental documents in the development of a postcolonial Australian politics. They represent Indigenous political demands which are couched in the terms that a modern liberal state comprehends, as well as providing a clear statement of Indigenous understandings of people, culture and place, and they do this partly through a medium of Indigenous art.

The crimes of the colonial state

As I have argued elsewhere (Cunneen, 2008), modern state building had an element of criminality against Indigenous peoples embodied in its foundational core. In other words, state crime is not an incidental or accidental element in the history of the modern state. The colonial context places state crime at the core of the modern state. Many contemporary states are built on crimes committed against colonized and enslaved peoples. Indigenous people have been victims of profound historical injustices and abuses of human rights which can be understood in the context of state crimes committed in pursuit of colonial domination. At the highest level is the claim that particular colonial practices against Indigenous peoples constituted genocide. Below genocide are claims of mass murder, racism, ethnocide (or cultural genocide), slavery, forced labour, forced removals of children and forced relocations of communities and nations, the denial of property rights, systematic fraud and the denial of civil and political rights.

Many of the harms against Aboriginal peoples in Australia relied on colonial law for their legitimacy. Many were essentially aimed at destroying Indigenous culture and identity. For this reason, it is important to see how Indigenous history and identity is being explored in Indigenous art, particularly in its understandings of the colonial and neocolonial experience. In this sense, Indigenous art provides those with an interest in critical and cultural criminology an insight into the experiences and understandings of the colonial state. Contemporary Indigenous art in particular captures the aggression of the colonial state in its impact on Indigenous peoples – as the aggressive violence of genocide and terror, and as the aggressive project of *civilizing* the native through various forms of 'protection' and assimilation. Common themes emerge from Aboriginal artist which provide a voice and a level of evidence and narrative about historical injustices, human rights violations and crimes of the colonial state.

The crime of genocide has been levelled against colonial regimes in their treatment of Indigenous peoples in Australia and the Americas (Churchill, 1997). There are well documented massacres of Aboriginal people in Australia in the late eighteenth and nineteenth centuries. There was never any doubt at the time that the Indigenous people and the colonizers were indeed at war in parts of southeastern Australia (Goodall, 1996), in Tasmania during the 1820s and early 1830s (Reynolds, 1995) and in Queensland during the mid to later half of the nineteenth century (Reynolds, 1993). In some cases, this 'war' amounted to genocide (Moses, 2000).

Aboriginal art has been an important tool for reproducing knowledge about massacres – particularly where the existence of mass murders was denied by colonial authorities. The work of artists contributes to the evidence and continuity in knowledge of local accounts by Indigenous people of massacres that are not necessarily recorded or acknowledged in any colonial official documentation. Art becomes a material dimension to the oral history and oral testimony of Indigenous people. There is thus a materiality to historical accounts separate from the written historical documents that tend to privilege the accounts of the authorities. For criminologists interested in state crime, the image functions as an evidentiary tool for the existence of officially sanctioned crime.

For example, there has been longstanding official denial of the massacres of Indigenous people in the Kimberleys of Western Australia during the early twentieth century. In late 2002 and early 2003, Gija artists from the Kimberleys staged an exhibition at the Ian Potter Gallery in Melbourne called *Blood on the Spinifex* to specifically highlight their oral history of massacres in the region. The *Blood on the Spinifex* exhibition depicted three massacres at Mistake Creek, Bedford Downs and Chinaman's Garden.[1] Artists Queenie McKenzie and Rover Thomas from the Kimberleys have also depicted various massacres in the region in their artwork (Isaacs, 1999: 131; Kleinert and Neale, 2000: 236–37; Arthur and Morphy, 2005: 217).

One of the paintings from the *Blood on the Spinifex* exhibition is Timmy Timms *Bedford Downs Massacre* (2000). The painting reveals a site where in

1 Blood on the Spinifex 14 December to 16 March 2003, Ian Potter Museum of Art, Melbourne. Artists: Paddy Bedford, Goody Barrett, Rameeka Nodea, Lena Nyadbi, Rusty Peters, Peggy Patrick, Desma Sampi, Freddy Timms, Timmy Timms, Phyllis Thomas. Guest curator Tony Oliver, Arts Adviser, Jirrawun Aboriginal Art Corporation.

1924 a group of Gija people were massacred. The men had been convicted by a local court of killing a bullock on Bedford Downs Station. They were sent back to the station with 'tickets' hung around their necks as a sign they were guilty. Some of the men discarded these tickets before they got back, but others chose to keep them. On their return those who still had their tickets were taken to a remote location and told to chop wood. After working, the men were given a meal poisoned with strychnine and died. Their bodies were burnt with the wood they had chopped that morning. Two men had refused to eat and made their escape. These two, along with two women who had followed the party and also witnessed the killings, returned and told their story to their people (Art Gallery of New South Wales, nd: 140).

Aboriginal artists who have depicted massacres in other parts of Australia include Robert Campbell Jnr whose *Map of the Massacre of Blacks on the Macleay Valley* (1990) details past rapes, murders and poisoning of waterholes in the area of New South Wales (see Art Gallery of New South Wales (nd: 38–39).

One of the most powerful and frequent themes in contemporary Indigenous art is the depiction of deaths in police and prison custody. In some cases, this is linked historically with the massacres of Indigenous people by colonial authorities. Harry Wedge's painting *British Justice* (Ryan, 2004: 101) captures the meaning and understanding of what 'justice' meant for Indigenous people. It was painted at the time the Royal Commission into Aboriginal Deaths in Custody was conducting hearings throughout the nation. The painting shows a British trooper with sword drawn standing next to a distorted Aboriginal figure hanging from the gallows.

Oscar of Cooktown's work from the late nineteenth century bridges the divide between historical massacres and contemporary concerns about deaths in custody. The work of Oscar is known from a single small sketchbook dating from the end of the 1800s. Oscar had been taken by police as a boy and placed on a cattle station near Camooweal in northwest Queensland. His drawings deal with a range of issues, of particular interest are the depictions of the Native Police. His work shows the 'dispersal' of Aboriginal people by Native Police (see *Dispersing usual way. Some good shooting (1890s)* (Roberts, 2005). As is evident is his sketches, and from other contemporary accounts, 'dispersal' meant shooting or killing Aboriginal people in locations where they were seen as being a 'problem' (Cunneen, 2001).

The sketch reproduced here shows Native Police lynching an Aboriginal person and is simply described as 'police boys doing duty'.

Images of deaths in custody were particularly pronounced in Aboriginal art during the 1980s and early 1990s. This was the period when there was widespread Indigenous political agitation for a national inquiry into the issue and saw the eventual establishment of the Royal Commission into Aboriginal Deaths in Custody (1987–1991) (see Johnston, 1991).

Trevor Nickolls' painting *Deaths In Custody (1990)* is based on a photograph which appeared in a Brisbane daily newspaper of an Aboriginal person held in

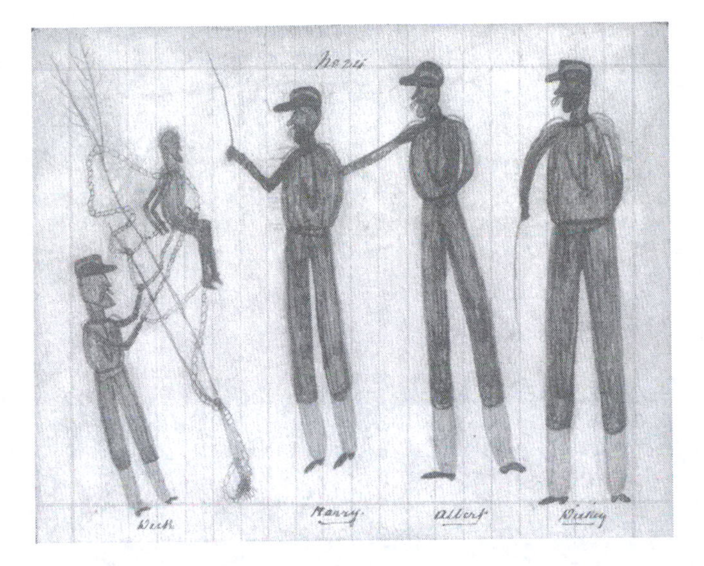

Figure 8.3 Police Boys Doing Duty (Lynch Law) Drawn by Oscar, Cooktown. c1899. Photograph George Serras, National Museum of Australia. Reproduced with Permission.

custody in a cage. It is confronting painting of an Aboriginal man caged in a cell. On the back wall is an image of a hanged Aboriginal man set against an Aboriginal flag. Les Griggs' painting *Deaths In Custody* (undated) shows a traditional Indigenous background overlaid with police batons, handcuffs and two nooses. Robert Campbell Jnr's *Deaths In Custody* (1987) (reproduced here) dates from the year the Royal Commission was established. In four frames, it shows an Aboriginal man being placed in a van by police, then placed in cell, then hanging in the cell and finally in a coffin ready to be buried.

Gordon Bennett's 1993 painting, *Ask a Policeman*, deals with the issue of deaths in custody. The painting is captured 'place rope around neck and pull – if you need help ask a policeman' (McLean and Bennett, 1996: 59). Pam Johnston's *Untitled* shows five black figures hanging and asks 'What do you call five black-fellas in a police cell? A black mobile.' In smaller lettering at the bottom of the painting is written 'Whose laughing?' (Art Gallery of NSW, 1989: 107).

Sally Morgan's *Greetings from Rottnest* shows an assortment of happy tourists with sunglasses and cameras (Milroy, 1996: 71). The painting provides 'another view of Rottnest Island. Now a popular tourist resort, it was once a prison where many Aboriginal people died and were buried' (Milroy, 1996: 70). Like much of her work, an underlying theme is that Australian prosperity is largely built on Aboriginal suffering.

Figure 8.4 Robert Campbell Jnr *Deaths In Custody* (1987). Courtesy of the artist and Roslyn Oxley9 Gallery, Sydney.

Following on from both massacres and deaths in custody, is the broader question of genocide. Fiona Foley's *The Annihilation of the Blacks* (1986) uses a traditional sculptural form found in Cape York (Morphy, 1998: 293), but changes the traditional content to comment on the issues of Aboriginal deaths. The title's use of 'annihilation' strongly suggests the theme of genocide. Given the timing of the work and the hanging bodies, the sculpture also connects clearly to the issue of deaths in custody.

Foley's reference to a traditional sculptural forms which suggest abundance, wealth and prosperity, suggests that the abundance for the non-Aboriginal Australia (shown by the white figure observing the hanging black figures) relies on the destruction of Aboriginal society.

Sally Morgan's screen print simply called *Another Story* (1988) also suggests that the abundance, wealth and prosperity of colonial Australia was built on the genocide of Indigenous peoples. Morgan notes, 'An alternative view of the Australian Bicentenary. On 26 January every year, two stories are told: the European Australian story of colonizing and conquering Australia and our story of invasion and survival. This print depicts how the pastoral industry was built on Aboriginal slave labour' (quoted in Milroy, 1996: 24). The print shows a pretty cottage with a white picket fence built on a mound of Aboriginal bodies.

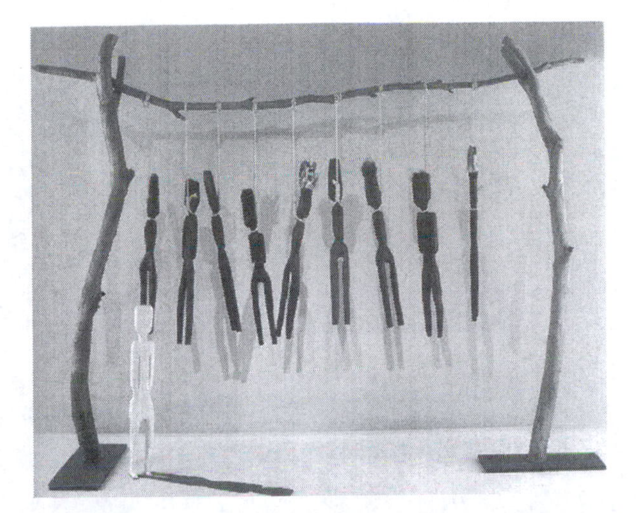

Figure 8.5 Fiona Foley *The Annihilation of the Blacks* (1986). © Niagara Gallery. Reproduced with permission.

Morgan's *Terra Nullius* also deals with the issue of genocide. She notes, 'Terra Nullius is Latin for "land belonging to no one", which was how Europeans classified Australia when they arrived. This picture plays on the meaning of terra nullius to show the reality of our suffering. If terra nullius wasn't true in 1788, later genocide tried to make it so. The rainbow serpent represents our survival, our spirituality, our hope' (quoted in Milroy, 1996: 48).

Perhaps one of the most striking artistic interpretations of genocide in Australia can be found in a work by artists from Ramingining in central Arnhem Land. The installation is called *Aboriginal Memorial 1988*. The work consists of 200 painted hollow-log coffins which are used in this community for interring the bodies of those who have died. The work has one log coffin for each year of the 200 years of colonization. The hollow log coffins from Arnhem land were first displayed at the Sydney Biennale of 1988. The installation was intended as a Bicentennial memorial for Aboriginal people who died in the colonial encounter. The installation is now part of the permanent collection at the National Gallery of Australia, Canberra.

The rule of law and the denial of civil, political and equality rights

Despite the view that Aboriginal people were British subjects, the processes of colonization required a suspension of the rule of law in relation to Indigenous people. Different treatment on the basis of race became justified. For example,

Figure 8.6 Sally Morgan *Terra Nullius* (1989). © The artist. Reproduced with permission.

Aboriginal people were still publicly executed in Western Australia decades after the practice of public executions had ceased for non-Indigenous people. Violence became accepted as a normal and justifiable way of dealing with Indigenous people. Racial differences were used to justify the use of brutal punishments. For Aboriginal people, floggings and the use of neck and leg chains remained in use until the 1930s (Cunneen, 2001).

During the period of 'protection' and the later policies of assimilation, racial discrimination remained firmly entrenched. The critique of notions of the rule of law and equality before the law is captured succinctly in Gordon Syron's

Figure 8.7 Ramingining Artists Aboriginal Memorial 1988. © Ramingining Artists. Licensed by VISCOPY, Australia 2008.

Judgement by His Peers which shows a courtroom judge, jury and lawyers who are all Aboriginal and a lone offender who is white.

Racial discrimination provided an overarching basis to governmental law and policy towards Indigenous people. Racialized constructions of Aboriginality changed during the eighteenth, nineteenth and twentieth centuries: in Australia this move was away from notions of barbarism to views about a race 'doomed' to extinction. Indeed, competing views about race were often prevalent at the same time. However, what is important is that racialized constructions of Indigenous people inevitably facilitated discriminatory intervention. In Australia, institutionalized and legalized discrimination reached a peak during the 'protection' period of the twentieth century. Racism provided a foundational logic to many of the harms that subsequently developed, including the denial of basic civil and political rights.

Settler colonial states put in place many restrictions on the civil and political rights exercised by Indigenous peoples and thus the foundations of liberal democracies in countries like Australia were built on various exclusionary measures which denied the enjoyment of citizenship. In Australia, the exclusionary practices included numerous legislative controls and restrictions on movement, residence,

Figure 8.8 Gordon Syron's *Judgement by His Peers*. © The artist. Reproduced with permission.

education, health care, employment, voting, worker's compensation and welfare/ social security entitlements. These restrictions continued well into the later part of the twentieth century.

Many of the developments which we associate with the rise of modern social welfare-oriented liberal democracies during the course of the twentieth century need to be considered against the backdrop of a range of exclusionary practices which were essentially derived from the colonial experience. For example, Aboriginal people were largely excluded from the right to social security: a number of federal statutes explicitly disqualified Aboriginal people from receiving government entitlements claimable by non-Indigenous Australians, including invalid, aged and widows pensions, maternity allowances and child endowment. These discriminatory laws remained in effect until the 1960s, and discriminatory restrictions on eligibility for social security benefits for Aboriginal people were not completely lifted until 1966.

However, it was the case that Aboriginal people could become eligible for citizenship benefits if they could demonstrate they were 'civilised' – which entailed giving up their Aboriginality. Sally Morgan's screen print *Citizenship* was completed in 1987, the year before the Bicentenary. It is a commentary on the 'dog tags' (citizenship papers) of Western Australia.

During the first half of the twentieth century, many Aboriginal people had been segregated on government reserves or church-run missions as part of a 'protection' policy. After 1945, the protection regimes began to break down with a new emphasis on assimilation. Ideas about cultural assimilation came to the fore and largely replaced ideas of a biological basis to racial inferiority. However, cultural assimilation was still based on a view of the inferiority of the native – now defined more in terms of culture rather than biology. The ultimate goal had not changed: the disappearance of Aboriginal people as a distinct group of people.

There were many facets to the colonial expectations of the disappearance of Aboriginal people. One was to collect the cultural artefacts and human remains of Aboriginal people in the interests of science and as museum pieces to display the material life of 'primitive' peoples. Countering the colonial scientific interest in Indigenous peoples as a doomed race and primitive relic has been the political activism around the return of human and cultural remains to Aboriginal people, in particular from the collections in Britain, Germany and the USA. Indigenous artists have also taken up this theme. Judy Watson's three 1997 paintings titled *Our Bones in Your Collections*, *Our Hair in Your Collections* and *Our Skin in Your Collections* are example of this work (Art Gallery of New South Wales, nd: 168).

Figure 8.9 Sally Morgan *Citizenship* 1987. © The artist. Reproduced with permission.

Life on the missions and reserves was meant to reconstitute the culture of Aboriginal people as assimilated into white society. Julie Dowling's *This Side of the Fence* shows an image of colonial expectations. The painting was made from an original photograph and shows Dowling's grandmother and other family members. The photo was used to demonstrate to the Native Welfare Department that the family were 'assimilated' into white society. Dowling writes, 'The other side of the fence is about the fence as a symbolic divide between a 'civilised' and 'uncivilised' view of my family. Our family was positioned as those of the acceptable few as seen by the authorities of the time' (http://www.artplace.com.au/exhibsprevious/Warridah-Dowling.html).

More generally, one of themes which runs through the artwork concerned with the protection period and later assimilation is the depiction of what Morrison (2006) has referred to as 'civilised space'. According to Morrison and following Hobbes' *Leviathan*, civilized space is seen as a modern realm of civil society where humanity can flourish in a civilized way under the watchful eye of the sovereign (2006: 18). The protected realm of the modern sovereign allows for inhabitable space and ordered territory to develop. At least in some instances, the colonial project is to bring an ordered and ordering civilized space to the colonial subject who lacks civilization and modernity. As Bauman notes the

> suppression and physical or cultural extermination of defeated minorities never given the chance to write their own histories came to be recorded and retold as an edifying and uplifting story of progress or of a civilizing process: of a gradual yet relentless pacification of daily life and purification of human interaction from violence (cited in Morrison, 2006: 54).

Assimilation is also about assimilating space in the interests of a legal bureaucratic regime that denies the vibrancy and validity of Indigenous culture. Elaine Russell's work captures this ordering of space and cultural life in *Inspection Day* (Art Gallery of New South Wales nd: 129). The vibrant and colourful style belies a concern to depict the assimilation intentions of ordered space under the gaze of the white welfare inspector. Other examples of Indigenous artists working on the theme of mission life include Robert Campbell Jnr, Roy Kennedy and Ian Abdulla (see Isaacs, 1989: 19; National Gallery of Victoria, 2002: 22; Arthur and Morphy, 2005: 124).

Perhaps the most distressing and destructive part of the civilizing mission to reform 'natives' was the forcible removal of children from their families and communities. The policy has been referred to as genocide and has been subject to litigation and demands for reparation (for a summary see Cunneen, 2008). Because of the widespread effect on Aboriginal communities, it is perhaps not surprising that it has been widely examined by Indigenous artists.

Indigenous women artists in particular have dealt with themes arising from the Stolen Generations. Many of these works are incredibly personal and poignant. Brenda Croft's work is titled *She Called Him Son* (1998). Her father was a member of the Stolen Generation and first met his mother just before she died. The image is based on the only photograph of their reunion. The image states in the centre,

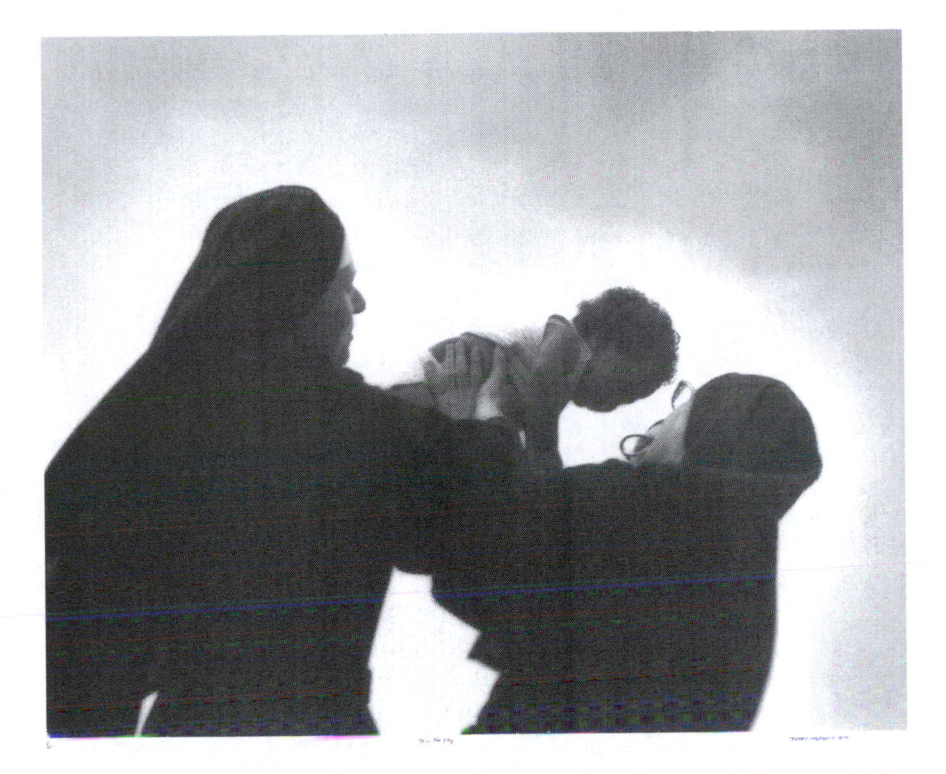

Figure 8.10 Tracy Moffatt *Up in the Sky*, 9, from a series of 25 images. Courtesy of the artist and Roslyn Oxley9 Gallery, Sydney.

'She called him son', at top right, 'They said she had given him away' and at the bottom left, 'He never really knew her'.

Many Aboriginal artists have dealt with the trauma and pain caused by the forced removal of Aboriginal children from their families and these include Julie Dowling (Arthur and Morphy, 2005: 124), David Fernando (Art Gallery of New South Wales 1989: 106), Sally Morgan (Kleinert and Neale, 2000: 703), John Packham (National Gallery of Victoria, 2002: 23), Jacob Stengle (Cochrane, 2001: 113) and Tracy Moffatt (Moffatt, 1998: 41). Above is the powerful image by Moffatt depicting the role of the churches in Aboriginal child removal.

Methodological reflections

What can we make of the use of these images in our understanding of crime and law? Analysis of these images through a cultural criminology perspective provides the opportunity to break out of the positivist epistemological straight jacket that has tended to dominate both criminological and legal theory and practice.

In the particular instance that has been the focus of this chapter, a cultural perspective focusing on the image has enabled a repatriation of Indigenous knowledge and critique. Indigenous cultures utilize rich and complex oral and artistic traditions as an essential part of the communicative process. Yet, through traditional criminological approaches these forms of communication would remain unrecognized. As Young has noted, the domain of preferred objects of analysis in criminology have traditionally been limited and static (Young, 2008: 18).

The central methodological reflection of this chapter is the importance of the image as a source of knowledge in understanding state crime. There are few examples where the two have been brought together: one is Morrison's (2004) discussion on photography and genocide; and to a lesser extent David Garland's (2005) use of an exhibition of lynching postcards as part of his discussion on the relationship of lynching to punishment in the US. In contrast to the image, writing, record keeping and official documentation have been an essential part of imperial culture. Indeed, record keeping was integral to the project of colonization: it is the tool for describing, itemizing and controlling the colonized Other. It is also the stuff of mainstream criminology – for example, the crime figures which endlessly repeat the offending rates of minority peoples. Further, the legal process itself tends to construct, reinforce, prioritize and legitimize particular forms of knowledge, particularly written documentation, as evidence, while dismissing other communicative processes as uncertain, unreliable, partial and impermanent.

Perhaps most importantly the discounting of the image as Aboriginal 'evidence' silences and avoids fundamental questions over the meaning of the rule of law in colonial settler democracies: questions about the extent of theft, murder, dishonesty and racial discrimination by government and their agents are left unasked. The Indigenous image may be 'unsettling' of the basic claims to the political, legal and moral legitimacy by colonial power. Further, an analysis of Indigenous art can indicate new ways of thinking (Foucault, 1970), a break between two systems of thought. The artistic forms of the political demands in works like the *Burunga Statement* and the *Yirrkala Petition* are indicative of a postcolonial hybridity. They are representative of an epistemological break between both Western and Indigenous modes of political discourse.

Cultural criminology's approach to the image can provide an inherently radical critique of law and criminology's privileging of particular epistemological claims to validity (e.g. written documentary evidence). It can open a new space for understanding and critique. Combined with a theoretically informed postcolonial understanding of the long-term impact of colonialism, cultural criminology might provide a methodological avenue for understanding and analysing people's experiences which is not reliant on the official inscriptions and records of government – records which, not surprisingly, do not reveal the levels of abuse, deprivation and racism for which government was responsible.

The approach I have taken here is somewhat different to many discussions on the role of the image in criminology. I have taken an approach that stresses the literality of the image, rather than its affective or emotive meanings (Valier and Lippens, 2005; Young, 2008). While I do not discount the polysemous nature of the image, I am also interested in what the image stands for in a literal sense. Undoubtedly, the images will provoke various experiences and emotions in the viewer. However, I am interested in the artist's statement through the image of their colonial and postcolonial experiences. The works reproduced in this chapter are not simply images *of* victims of crime (Valier and Lippens, 2005) but rather images *by* collective victims of state crime.

Conclusion

These images bring an Aboriginal voice to our understanding of crime and punishment: the crimes of the colonial state and the search for redress and reparations for the abuses arising from the processes of colonialism. For minorities that have been systematically excluded from mainstream institutions, it is not surprising that alternative communicative modes have increased importance. For Aboriginal people, the use of image provides an expression of the human rights and state crime abuses which arose from the colonial process and legally entrenched racial discrimination.

The image then provides a powerful voice for those who may not be able to utilize the language of law or academia. To fail to consider this voice is to deny a source of evidence and knowledge. It is to privilege one form of knowledge (written) over another (image). Cultural criminology provides the opportunity to consider the cultural production of knowledge in its broader manifestations, and by doing this, it provides the opportunity to hear the voices of those outside the traditional corridors of power.

Finally, the study of the image in cultural criminology stimulates some thought about the *value* we attach to different types of knowledge in criminological discourses. Is the painting of a mass murder by state police (which is based on the oral testimony of a survivor) of little value in the absence of official state documentation of the behaviour of its own functionaries? Is a painting of the emotional distress caused by the forced removal of a child of less value in understanding victimization, than the report of a child psychologist? As Borrows has noted in the context of Canada,

> [Indigenous] people have ... used pictoglyphs, wampum belts, masks, totem poles, button blankets, culturally modified environments, birch bark scrolls, burial disturbances, songs, ceremonies and stories, to name but a few, to remember and interpret what happened in the past
>
> (Borrows, 2001: 18).

Cultural criminology provides an opportunity to reappraise the epistemological foundations of criminology and to open up new understandings of the nature of power and resistance.

Acknowledgements

The author would like thank the Aboriginal Artists Agency for use of the image of Yala Yala Gibbs painting Tjungurrayi; Buku Larrngay Art, Yirkalla and Parliament House Australia for use of the image of the Yirkala Bark Petition.

References

Art Gallery of New South Wales (nd) Tradition Today, Indigenous Art in Australia, Art Gallery of New South Wales, Sydney.

Arthur B. and Morphy, F. (2005) *Macquarie Atlas of Indigenous Australia,* Macquarie Dictionary, Macquarie University.

Australian Perspecta (1989) Catalogue from exhibition 31 May – 23 July, Art Gallery of NSW, Sydney, 1989.

Bakhtin, M. (1984) *Rabelais and His World*, Bloomington: Indian University Press.

Borrows, J. (2001) 'Listening for a Change: The Courts and Oral Tradition', *Osgoode Hall Law Journal,* 39 (1): 1–38.

Churchill, W. (1997) *A Little Matter of Genocide: Holocaust and Denial in the Americas, 1492 to the Present*, San Francisco: City Lights Books.

Cochrane, S. (2001) *Aboriginal Art Collections. Highlights from Australia's Public Museums and Galleries*, St Leonards: Fine Art Publishing.

Crane, S. (2002) *Pila Nguru. The Spinifex People*, Freemantle: Freemantle Arts Centre Press.

Cunneen, C., Findlay, M., Lynch, R. and Tupper, V. (1989) *The Dynamics of Collective Conflict*, North Ryde: Law Book Company.

Cunneen, C. (2001) *Conflict, Politics and Crime. Aboriginal Communities and the Police*, Sydney: Allen and Unwin.

Cunneen, C. (2008) 'State Crime, the Colonial Question and Indigenous Peoples' in Smuelers, A. and Haveman, R. (eds) *Supranational Criminology: Towards a Criminology of International Crimes,* Antwerp: Intersentia Press.

Cunneen, C. (2005) 'Colonialism and Historical Injustice: Reparations for Indigenous Peoples', *Social Semiotics*, 15(1): 59–80.

Cunneen, C. (2008) *State Crime, the Colonial Question and Indigenous Peoples*

Foucault, M.(1970) *The Order of Things*, London: Pantheon.

Garland, D. (2005) 'Penal Excess and Surplus Meaning: Public Torture Lynchings in Twentieth Century America', *Law and Society Review*, Vol 39(4): 793–833.

Goodall, H. (1996). *Invasion to Embassy. Land in Aboriginal Politics, 1770–1972*, St Leonards: Allen and Unwin.

Isaacs, J. (1989) *Aboriginality: Contemporary Aboriginal Paintings and Prints*, St Lucia : University of Queensland Press.

Isaacs, J. (1999) *Spirit Country. Contemporary Australian Aboriginal Art*, South Yarra: Hardie Grant Books.

Johnston, E. (1991) *National Report, 5 Vols*, Royal Commission into Aboriginal Deaths in Custody, Canberra: Australian Government Printing Service.

Kleinert, S. and Neale, M. (2000) *The Oxford Companion to Aboriginal Art and Culture*, Melbourne: Oxford University Press.

Kerr, Joan (1996) 'Colonial Quotations: Reinventing the Original', *Art and Australia*, 33(3), Autumn: 376–87.

McLean, I. (1998) *White Aborigines: Identity and Politics an Australia Art*, Cambridge: Cambridge University Press.

McLean, I. and Bennett, G. (1996) *The Art of Gordon Bennett,* Sydney: Craftsman House.

Milroy, J. (1996) *The Art of Sally Morgan*, Ringwood: Viking.

Moffatt, T. (1998) *Free-Falling*, New York: Dia Centre for the Arts.

Morphy, H. (1998) *Aboriginal Art*, London: Phaidon Press.

Morrison, W. (2004) '"Reflections with Memories": Everyday Photography Capturing Genocide', *Theoretical Criminology*, 8(3): 341–58.

Morrison, W. (2006) *Criminology, Civilisation and the New World Order*, Milton Park: Routledge-Cavendish.

Moses, D. (2000) 'An Antipodean Genocide? The Origins of the Genocidal Moment in the Colonisation of Australia', *Journal of Genocide Research,* 1: 89–106.

National Gallery of Victoria (2002) *Indigenous Australian Art in the National Gallery of Victoria*, Melbourne: National Gallery of Victoria.

Reynolds, H. (1993) The Unrecorded Battlefields of Queensland, in H. Reynolds (ed.), *Race Relations in North Queensland*, Townsville: Department of History and Politics, James Cook University.

Reynolds, H. (1995) *Fate of a Free People*, Ringwood: Penguin.

Roberts, T. (2005) *Frontier Justice. A History of the Gulf Country to 1900*, St Lucia: University of Queensland Press.

Rolston, B. (2001) '"This Is Not a Rebel Song": The Irish Conflict and Popular Music', *Race and Class*, 42(3): 49–67.

Rolston, B. (2003) 'Changing the Political Landscape: Murals and Transition in Northern Ireland', *Irish Studies Review*, 11(1): 3–16.

Rolston, B. (2004) 'Visions or nightmares? Murals and Imagining the Future in Northern Ireland', in B. Cliff and E. Walshe (eds) *Representing the Troubles. Texts and Images, 1970–2000*, Four Courts Press.

Scott, J.C. (1990) *Domination and the Arts of Resistance*, New Haven: Yale University Press.

Sivanandan, A. (1990) *Communities of Resistance*, London: Verso.

Thompson E.P. (1974) 'Patrician Society, Plebian Culture', *Journal of Social History*, VII: 382–405.

Valier, C. and R. Lippens (2005) 'Moving Images, Ethics and Justice', *Punishment and Society*, 6(3): 319–33.

Winter, J. (2002) *Native Title Business. Contemporary Indigenous Art*, Brisbane: Keeaira Press.

Young, A. (2008) 'Culture, Critical Criminology and the Imagination of Crime', in T. Anthony and C. Cunneen (eds) *The Critical Criminology Companion*, Leichhardt: Federation Press, pp. 18–329.

Yunupingu, G. (1993) 'The Black White Conflict', in *Aratjara: The Art of the First Australians*, Cologne: DuMont.

1988 Australian Biennale: From the Southern Cross: A View of World Art c. 1940–88, catalogue from exhibition, Biennale of Sydney and The Australian Broadcasting Commission, Sydney, 1988.

Chapter 9

'Drive it like you stole it'

A cultural criminology of car commercials

Stephen L. Muzzatti

> A commodity appears, at first sight, a very trivial thing, and easily understood. Its analysis shows that it is, in reality, a very queer thing, abounding in metaphysical subtleties and theological niceties.
>
> (Marx, 1965/[1867]: 71)

Introduction

Over the last decade or so cultural criminologists have been fascinated by the processes and products associated with what they have variously described as the 'commodification of violence' (e.g. Presdee, 2000; Ferrell, Hayward and Young, 2008) and the 'marketing of transgression' (Hayward, 2004). This visual representation of crime and transgression is, they argue, not only central to the production of news, but is also now a vital component of the entertainment media – gripping the collective imagination of television viewers, moviegoers, internet browsers, video-gamers and other audiences. To a certain extent, of course, there is nothing intrinsically new about the use of this type of imagery in the service of consumerism – certainly, crime and violence have been used to sell cinema passes, TV sets, video games and music for decades. However, what is new, as Ferrell, Hayward and Young illustrate, is the force and range of these 'illicit' messages (2008:140) and the effect this has had on the tectonic landscape of the late modern entertainment media. In particular, there appears to be a far greater willingness among *mainstream corporations* to utilize allusions to crime and transgression to give their products edgy appeal whilst still serving the conservative interests of consumer capitalism and its control functions.

This interplay of advertising, consumption and control in late modernity is multifaceted, and ephemeral. One of cultural criminology's many strength lies in its adroit treatment of this fleeting yet ever-present tangential. Negotiating the landscape of transgressive imagery and its role in contemporary consumption practices must include an examination of advertising, because contemporary consumerism and its concomitant control functions would simply not exist were it not for advertising in its myriad forms.

Advertising is ubiquitous and its influence omnipresent. Indeed, it is likely the single most influential agent of socialization in late-modern societies. Its scope and impact is tied to enormous fiscal expenditures. According to the advertising industry's own calculations, spending on advertising in 2006 topped over $150 billion in the US and $385 billion worldwide, the latter predicted to exceed $500 billion by the end of the decade (Price Waterhouse Coopers, 2008). This type of spending buys a great deal of exposure. For example, in countries like Canada, the US and the UK, young people, averaging (a conservative) two hours of television daily will see between 20 and 40 thousand commercials in a given year (CBC, 2008), to say nothing of the other ads they are exposed to in public spaces, on the internet and increasingly in schools. When considered in combination with the amount of product placement they encounter in their favourite video games, films, TV programmes, social networking websites and music videos, it is not surprising that 78 per cent of British 10-year-olds list shopping as one of their favourite activities and display an intimate familiarity with between 300 and 400 brands (Hall, Winlow and Ancrum, 2008: 94). For corporations, the stakes are extremely high as they compete for children's markets worth £30 billion in Britain, $1.9 billion in Canada and $30 billion in the US, to say nothing of the estimated $1 trillion in family spending that they are estimated to influence (ibid; Robertson, 2005; CBC, 2008).

As the following slice of text from the fictional and highly stylized video/PC game *Grand Theft Auto IV* poignantly illustrates, at least when it comes to youth oriented narratives about the vicissitudes of late modernity, it is frequently the case that consumption itself is now *the* strategy employed to demarcate, compartmentalize, and control the general public (see relatedly Bauman, 1987: 49–69; 2007: 30–39):

> What does the American Dream mean today? For Niko Bellic, fresh off the boat from Europe, it is the hope he can escape his past. For his cousin, Roman, it is the vision that together they can find fortune in Liberty City, gateway to the land of opportunity. As they slip into debt and are dragged into a criminal underworld by a series of shysters, thieves and sociopaths, they discover that the reality is very different from the dream in a city that worships money and status, and is heaven for those who have them and a living nightmare for those who don't.[1]

In other words, unlike pre-deindustrialized generations in which social worth was determined through the relationship to the means of production and other stratified forms of social meaning, today our selves and our subjectivities are increasingly determined through our consumption practices (see Hayward and Yar, 2006). For the sociologist Zygmunt Bauman (2007: 30–39) this transformation

1 www.gta4.net

has only served to intensify inequality. According to Bauman, late modern consumer society is now polarized between, on the one hand, indemnified, privileged and dutiful consumers, and, on the other, the increasingly swollen ranks of the marginalized and criminalized classes, who, either as a result of inability of unwillingness, have failed to acquiesce to the hegemonic dictates of consumerism. The first of these groups, the 'Seduced', naturally exhibit the requisite desire and fixation required by unmediated consumer societies. More important, though, they are in a position to satisfy their desire through continual cycles of unreflexive hyper-consumption. Standing in stark contrast to the 'Seduced' are the 'Repressed', a group that embody what one might describe as the *collateral damage* of consumerism; this throng of uncommoditised or failed consumers represent an ever-growing, marginalized mass who, through negligence or wilfulness, fail to adequately acquit themselves of their consumer 'duties'. Put bluntly, the 'repressed's' insufficient and/or disreputable consumption patterns do not satisfactorily integrate them into the acceptable echelons of consumer society. What is of importance in terms of this chapter (and something often overlooked by Bauman) is the way in which advertising's ideological work serves not only to incessantly remind us of this distinction, but also acts to control and manipulate us by illustrating the consequences of lax or ineffectual consumption work (Muzzatti, 2008).

In his influential work on crime and consumer culture, Keith Hayward (2004) illustrates that the products and services we acquire and access through our consumer exercises are the primary indices of identity. Following this line of thought, this chapter will map out a cultural criminology inspired approach to reading the images used in advertisements for cars and car-related services (specifically car insurance). My decision to focus on car adverts was influenced not only because of the vast numbers of cars in late-modern societies, but also because cars frequently feature in an array of crime-media texts.

Focus

Consuming images of automobiles in adverts

Cars, cars... everywhere cars, ...

North America and Western Europe are indisputably car-centric cultures. Recent statistics illustrate that almost 90 per cent of all cars manufactured worldwide are purchased by their populations (Best, 2006). The manufacture of automobiles and related parts and services are thus major components driving what is left of our multibillion-dollar industrial economies. The long-standing and ever-increasing ubiquity of the automobile in our culture is undeniable. In short, cars, and perhaps even more relevant to this chapter, *images* of cars, are simply unavoidable: advertisements for them fill newspapers, television, magazines and websites; giant automobile billboard ads are a common sight in both town and country and even public services are now reappropriated as advertising space, with car ads festooned on the sides of subways, streetcars, buses, light-rail transit and other public transportation conveyances and property. While real cars streak and (ever more frequently) crawl along the highways that crisscross the nation, images of cars stand as silent sentinels alongside these asphalt ribbons; a relentless reminder to the already fixated (and distracted) driver of the requisite commodity fetish. This, of course, is in addition to the highly fetishised images of cars that, while not openly recognized as advertisements, fill the storylines of our television programmes, feature films and video games and have a host of books, magazines, internet sites and television channels devoted to them.

In such an environment, it is unsurprising that car ownership is not only an indicator of an individual's social and economic worth, it is also part of a game of distinction and 'identity value' – a game that ultimately serves to imbue individuals with a narcissistic sense of who they are (Ewen, 1977, 1988; Lasch,1979; Best, 2006).

A final prescient element we must consider before delving into specific examples of imagery in car adverts is the way in which cars feature in a host of diverse crime-media texts. Indeed, the examples from both the 'entertainment' and 'news' media (if such a distinction can still truly be made in our late-modern times) are legion. From stories about the stolen car and car parts market (which is second only to illicit drugs in the amount of money it generates within the underground economy)[2] to live news helicopter footage of high-speed police chases, from reports of drunk drivers and 'road-rage' to illegal street racing and bank-robbery 'get-away' cars, automobiles are central to numerous crime-news narratives. They are perhaps an even more prevalent image in the entertainment media. Car chases, crashes and explosions are a staple feature of many Hollywood blockbusters, with films featuring illegal street racing and risk-laden driving practices now constituting a distinct action movie sub genre (see *The Fast and the Furious* series). Cars also play central roles in a host of TV programmes (both 'reality' and dramatic), music videos and video games (see for example the MTV 'car makeover' show *Pimp My Ride*, or the *Carmaggedon* video game series).

Certainly, the economic, cultural and criminal significance of the automobile under prevailing late-modern conditions makes adverts for cars and related products/services an obvious site for the articulation of highly stylized visual presentations – and an area ripe for analysis by cultural criminologists. What follows are some select examples of the way car advertisements reflect some of the features of an unmediated consumer society, and in particular, the Baumanian categories of the 'seduced' and the 'repressed' as alluded to earlier.

The advertisements cited in the subsequent sections are all quite mainstream, airing on primetime network television. Moreover, while the cars themselves

2 See Statistics Canada (2008) and United States Department of Justice, Federal Bureau of Investigation (2006).

Figure 9.1 Billboard for Mercedes M-Class SUV: Consumerism's Orwellian double-speak.

vary in cost and prestige from mid-range through lower-end luxury models, the ads are for cars targeted toward the 'average' car buyer (i.e. not specialists, tuners or sports car enthusiasts). It is also worth noting that ads with extreme, over-the-top (and all too obvious) imagery, such as Audi's 2009 A6 commercial featuring actor Jason Statham reprising his roles in car centric movies such as *The Transformer* and *Death Race*, were deliberately avoided. Instead, the selected commercials were chosen for their somewhat mundane style and imagery. Indeed, as was noted earlier and documented elsewhere, while it is certainly the case that car chases, gunfire, explosions, riots and other extreme images are now more commonplace than they have ever been in commercials, they still only constitute a relatively small percentage of all advertising images. Because cultural criminology is sophisticated and nuanced, it is best suited for finely detailed work. In short, rather than bludgeoning the most egregious targets, cultural criminology is employed here as a means of delicately excavating the discreet and judicious ideological work of advertising – images that regularly pass unnoticed.

THE SEDUCED AS EDGEWORKER – NORMALIZING THE EXTREME: SPEEDING AND THE LEXUS IS 350

A good deal of the carnivalesque is driven by the need to feel alive in a highly controlled yet highly unstable environment (Presdee, 2000; Hayward, 2004: 163). The desire of late-modernity's subjects to seize control coalesces visually with consumerism's inherent 'pursuit of the now' in Lexus' 'Moments' advertising campaign. The commercial for the luxury IS 350 model powerfully blends a series of clips from 'life's moments' (a child's birthday party, convocation ceremonies, a wedding, etc.) in the grainy, overexposed style of home-movies with images of the car quickly negotiating a series of bends before accelerating rapidly along a straight-stretch of open roadway. A superimposed time of '0–60 in 5.3 seconds' dominates the screen while miniscule text ('Driving simulator') scrolls across the bottom. An ambient synthesiser provides musical accompaniment to the voiceover encouraging the narcissistic pleasure of the now through speed-induced euphoria:

> 'There's fast, ...scary fast, ...and then there's 'remember this moment for the rest of your life' fast. Pursue the moment.'

The advertiser's obvious intention is to enlist the appetites of the 'Seduced'; 'established' audiences sprawled on expensive leather chesterfields across the country with a message that strikes an inviting balance between the somewhat sedate, if not elitist aphorism 'You've worked hard. Now treat yourself' and the too crass 'Work hard. Play hard' theme better suited to a more hedonistic (and younger) demographic audience. However, a fugitive reading of this text inspired by cultural criminology's sensibilities proves not only illuminating but also highly entertaining. Clearly, the target audience is so incarcerated within a stifling upper-middle class life characterized by banality, boredom and soul-crushing conformity that a stolen moment of driving an expensive car too fast is the only thing that reminds them of the humanity lost to mindless (though perhaps in this instance, relatively well paid) wage-slavery and endless consumption work.

THE SEDUCED AS TUTOR – ILLUSTRATING THE FUTILITY OF RESISTANCE: OFF-ROADING AND KIA SPORTAGE

Not unlike the Lexus commercial cited earlier, the advertisement for Kia's SUV (sports utility vehicle) relies upon images of speed to draw the audience's attention, though in this instance the setting is comprised of rural lanes and swampland, not winding bends and open roads. Another notable difference is the way the visceral pleasure of speed is used in conjunction with other emotions (see relatedly Lauer, 2005). While the Lexus ad pairs it with a warm and fuzzy nostalgia, the Kia SUV commercial employs targeted farcical humour, specifically an 'othering' of Goth youth. The humour plays to generational and

Figure 9.2 Lexus IS 350: Preferred vehicle of the 'Seduced'.

urban-rural differences. However, it also, more cunningly, distinguishes between those who willingly embrace consumption and those who (at least on some levels) attempt to resist its insidious grasp.

Set in the Louisiana bayou, the commercial begins with three sullen male Goths (apparently members of a stranded band called 'The Reptiles') looking disconsolately at a flattened tire on their tour bus. Conjuring up an idealized version of the 'South', drums, banjo and fiddle music herald the arrival of a fifty-something moustachioed local, adorned in a work shirt and straw hat. Skidding his silver Kia Sportage SUV to a halt on the gravel road and leaning halfway out of the window, he enthusiastically asks 'Hey, wanna' lift?' in a thick Cajun accent. As the music accelerates so does the SUV. The vehicle speeds through the bayou, deftly manoeuvred by the 'raging-cajun' whose hoots and howls of 'Aiyeeee,…!' serve as auditory exclamation marks for his pronouncements: 'Man you look a little pale – I think you use too much sunscreen', and 'I'll turn that frown upside down. – You have to cheer-up a little bit'. As the Sportage careens around dirt-road corners, bounces over rises and ploughs through muddy swamp water, the three Goths begin to experience the pleasures of SUV ownership and off-roading. As the commercial nears conclusion, the three Goths, barely able to contain their joy and grinning widely, join the local in the 'hootin'

Figure 9.3 Kia SUV: A long way from the Louisiana bayou.

'n' hollerin''. Clearly, 'The Reptiles' have been schooled in an important lesson in consumption, as has the audience: 'The 2008 Kia Sportage – Freedom starts at $21,695'.

NOBLE SAVAGES BRIEFLY MISTAKEN FOR THE 'REPRESSED': DODGY NEIGHBOURHOODS AND THE VOLKSWAGEN JETTA SPECIAL EDITION

Sharing elements in common with Kia's Sportage advertisement, this commercial centres on the interaction between the 'Seduced' and others who teeter on the brink of disreputable and insufficient consumption. However, unlike either the Kia or the Lexus ads, this commercial does not employ any images or allusions of speed and extreme driving. Instead, the VW remains parked for all but the very last short scene of the commercial, and once the car is moving, it appears to be doing extremely slowly. Also noteworthy is the fact that, unlike the previous examples (and indeed most car commercials), the moving vehicle is not shot externally. Instead, the audience only sees the serene driver – shot from an interior mounted camera. Interestingly, in this commercial the fetish which lies at the core of consumerism is not veiled beneath the artifice of 'love', 'fulfilment',

Figure 9.4 VW Jetta in a "dodgy" neighbourhood: Will 'The Club' deter the Repressed?

'family togetherness', 'friendship' or other images of a highly desirable social life which the market promises but cannot supply. Rather, it is the fetish, the fixation itself which is placed at the forefront of the Jetta advertisement.

Set in an anonymous quasi-deserted American urban nightscape, this commercial begins with a shot of a very ordinary looking 30-something man in khaki pants and button-down shirt stepping out the door of a corner shop carrying a paper bag of groceries. Shifting quickly from a look of surprise and mild fear on his face, the camera then focuses in on a black Volkswagen Jetta parked by the kerb that we are to assume is his. In shadowed light, we see two dark figures peering into the car from the driver's side window and front windshield. As the owner halts mid-step, the two figures straighten up and acknowledge his presence. As they step forward into the light cast by the lone street lamp, they reveal themselves as two 'toughs' – presumably the Mutt and Jeff of opportunistic car theft. The first of them is tall and slightly overweight with greasy hair and is adorned in ill-fitting jeans (plumber, not gansta' style), nylon windbreaker and has a slightly Eastern-European look about him. The second 'foiled thief' is smaller in stature and squirrely-looking. He is dressed in the chav's uniform; tracksuit bottoms with matching jacket and backwards baseball cap. No doubt paralysed by the fear that the unsavoury duo will likely forgo the simple car theft for assault and robbery the Jetta owner stands immobile as the larger man leans in toward him. In a deep voice tinged with a slight (and hence unidentifiable) accent, he haltingly says, 'That's a pretty hot car'. With his eyes averted and hands folded before him like an errant schoolboy he continues, 'On Friday nights some of us get together behind the Dairy Freeze to look at cars. You should come.' The commercial ends with a dashboard mounted shot of the VW owner driving away with a smile on his face while the two toughs, still standing in the street, shrink from view in the back windshield. Robbery and beating averted, it is clear to the audience that the Jetta owner is not only relieved, but is also quite pleased. He is safe, and has reaped the reward (albeit minor in this instance) of his consumption work. He will drive back into his world, satisfied that he had accomplished important work in providing a lesson in consumerism to the working class car enthusiasts. Equally clear is that it is highly unlikely that he will drop by the Dairy Freeze this, or any other Friday night.

THE REPRESSED AND THE SEDUCED AS ROAD HAZARDS: GREY POWER INSURANCE AND SAVVY CONSUMERS

Combining elements from both the Kia and Volkswagen advertisements, this set of two commercials for Grey Power Insurance[3] direct our attention to the differences between the ad world's Seduced and 'others'. However, unlike all the previous examples (and indeed most commercials) these ads feature senior citizens as protagonists – no doubt, because it is this group that comprises the target demographic. These two commercials also diverge from the aforementioned examples insofar as they do not construct failed or insufficient consumers as simply in need of tutoring, or indeed as rehabilitateable – they are simply 'others'. Nor for that matter is there any allusion to the need for traditional social control for the others. Instead, the audience is left to deduce that the market (in this case, the insurance industry's actuarial tables, risk assessments and the concomitant differential pricing) will inevitably serve to discipline the 'others'. The commercials focus almost exclusively on the virtues of sustained responsible consumerism and promises further rewards to this particular subset (50 yrs of age and older) of the Seduced.

Situated at an indistinctive suburban intersection, these two commercials both begin by focusing the audience's attention on a senior man and woman in a nondescript mid-sized sedan easing the car to a halt at a stop sign. As the male driver

3 Grey Power Insurance is a specialty insurance coverage offered solely to drivers over 50 years of age by the Trafalgar Insurance Company of Canada. It is part of the multinational ING Group.

checks to his left and right for cross-traffic, the two commercials deviate slightly; in the first, he hears a honking horn, while in the second, he hears loud heavy metal music. The scenes in the respective commercials then shift. In the first, the audience sees a demonstrably annoyed 40-something woman attired in a business suit pounding on the horn of her pristine champagne coloured car while leaning out of the window shouting, 'C'mon already! Let's gooooo!'. The second commercial shows a poorly caricatured male heavy-metal fan in a black leather jacket and spiked leather wrist bracelet driving a rusting, smoking hulk. In stark juxtaposition to the business woman in the first ad, he is not focused on the elderly couple in the car ahead, and in fact seems oblivious to all around him, undoubtedly distracted by his loud music and leaking exhaust fumes (and drugs that no doubt he has been smoking). Following the presentation of the respective road hazards, the two commercials synchronize with a shot of the bemused and long-suffering driver, and a voice-over announcing 'You don't drive like him[/her] – so why should you pay the same insurance rates?!' and the company's phone number and website. The protagonists and the target audience are reminded of the benefits of their Seduced lifestyle, while they are simultaneously warned of the threats posed by consumerism's inner demons; the overly integrated Seduced and the inadequately integrated Repressed.

Methodological reflections

One of the most appealing elements and I would suggest greatest strengths of cultural criminology is its methodological diversity. In contrast to the quantitative regimen of numerical alchemy (see Young, 2004; Ferrell, Hayward and Young, 2008, particularly Plates 6.1 and 6.2) that dominates most American (and perhaps to a slightly lesser extent, British and Canadian) criminology, cultural criminology is propelled, in part, by a methodological openness and creativity that is frequently marginalized and often maligned in orthodox ('administrative') criminology, sociology and indeed most of the 'social sciences'.

Cultural criminology offers revamped terms of engagement with the spheres of crime and transgression through edgy counter-current methodologies that directly confront the convenient fictions which privilege quantitative analysis and circumvents its disciplinary madness.

Driven in part by an anarchic resistance to the staid, carcereal shackles of the Home Office's (Solicitor General's or National Institute of Justice's) institutional review board protocols which operate in service of the State and 'building a better mousetrap', and in part by a genuine desire to celebrate the long and illuminating legacy of undermining the false subject-object bifurcation, cultural criminology embraces a plurality of methodological ontologies and epistemologies. The use of content and discourse analysis as well as field ethnography as primary research strategies thus gives cultural criminology an edgy, counter flow which prioritizes the aesthetic and emotive over the detached sterility of numerical alchemy.

While cultural criminology's methodological toolkit is rife with creative instruments, including a long-rich history of critical ethnography and edgework (Irwin, 1977; see also Ferrell and Hamm, 1998), many cultural criminologists have rediscovered other qualitative orientations which are attuned to the nuances of visual imagery and style – the present collection being perhaps the most recent manifestation of this development. As a result, the fieldwork tradition that dominated much early cultural criminology is now augmented by a cultural and media studies-inspired deconstruction of images. In keeping with the overall theme of this collection, this chapter has sought to utilize media methods to unpack images of the car in late modernity, specifically though not exclusively in advertisements for the models themselves.

Advertising is an extremely well-funded 'desire machine' (Corner, 1999: 105) which capitalizes on the cultural meanings associated with the mythologies of late-modernity. It does so, in part, by dynamically and emotively linking '*images*' of a desirable social life (such as fun, happiness, friendship, excitement, success, freedom, etc.) with a specific product in such a way as to inexorably bind them – at least until we encounter the next ad (Muzzatti, 2008). Advertising thrives on mythological discourses, but relies almost exclusively on *visual* representations to ensure connectivity and solidify the audience's emotional investment. Because most advertising is image-based, the images employed are not merely decorative, but are themselves integral structural ideas. The move from being passive consumers of images to active interrogators involves both an intellectual and political commitment, as well as a methodological apparatus that is as illuminating as it is invigorating. Marguerite Helmers' (2006: 26–35) work on visual culture provides students of cultural criminology with a concise methodology for analysing images. It is presented in the following section, in a slightly modified and condensed form, as a strategy commensurate to the weighty task of decoding the visual presentation of advertisements.

i) *Record your initial impression:* This first step requires that we transform the emotionally imbued image into a written text. For example, as addressed earlier in this chapter and elsewhere (see Hayward, 2004 and Ferrell, Hayward and Young, 2008), in an attempt to generate the appropriate amount of 'noise', advertisers increasingly rely upon a broader range and more forceful tone in the transgressive images they now employ. Therefore, unlike more traditional ads which rely upon the 'warm and fuzzy', (or the 'nostalgic', the 'patriotic', the 'romantic', the 'homey', etc.) our initial impressions will likely be more sublime (e.g. illicit excitement, humiliation, loathing, shock or decadent pleasure).
ii) *Contextualize the image:* Here we draw upon our knowledge of the world around us and our cultural capital to socially situate the image. This involves framing the text we created in the first step with the particular insights provided by critical theory, generally and cultural criminology, specifically. In this instance, we can begin by considering the contributions of Frankfurt

School theorists Max Horkheimer and Theodor Adorno (1972) to our understanding of the role played by the culture industries in transmitting corporate consumerism's destructive values. From there we can easily transition to incorporate the work of contemporary cultural criminologists, such as Presdee's (2000) investigation into the 'carnival of crime' and Hayward's (2004) exacting analysis of the ways that transgression is marketed and violence is commodified.

iii) *Identify the symbolic:* Building upon that which we accomplished in our contextualization, this step asks us to accelerate our excavation of the ad's symbolic representation of ideas; an iconographic decoding. This means that we must recognize the interplay between both the literal elements of the ad (i.e. its manifest content, such as a stretch of deserted roadway in the city) as well as the symbolic elements (i.e. its latent content, such as the absence of police traffic enforcement apparatus) in the construction of meaning (the freedom to drive fast). Part of this involves the relatively simple task of identifying 'what's there' and 'what's missing'. For example, consider Figures 9.5, 9.6 and 9.7, three images from the same TV broadcast that were captured only seconds apart. The first two, images from a commercial for the 'reality'-TV show *Canada's Worst Driver,* play upon the decadent and narcissistic voyeurism that is the hallmark of 'reality' television. In this instance, we are encouraged to take pleasure in the pratfalls and buffoonery of bad (i.e. 'other') drivers – not unlike the case of the aforementioned Grey Power commercials. In this case, dangerous driving habits such as failing to check wing-mirrors (let alone blindspots), following too closely, speeding, aggressive lane changing, braking too hard or too late are all part of a packaged spectacle sold to us as 'reality' entertainment. Sadly, it is the third image, which appeared immediately after the commercial as part of the regular news broadcast which truly illustrates the reality of bad driving.

It is also integrally important to be able to approximate a dominant-hegemonic or approved reading of the ad so that we can then contrast it with an oppositional or fugitive reading inspired by cultural criminology (see Hall, 1993; Muzzatti, 2006). For example, a dominant-hegemonic reading of the ad might excite us (as it is indeed intended to do) by promising the thrill of acceleration in the sleek, high-performance of a sports coupe. Examined this way, the ad invites us as an audience to imagine ourselves in the driver's seat, revelling in the seductive pleasure of excessive speed (and all that that entails), free of the encumbrances posed by speed-limits, traffic signals, police officers or other hindrances to our velocity-oriented fun, such as pedestrians, bicyclists and other road users. The ad's 'success' is premised largely in part, if not exclusively, on the audience employing just such an approved reading. In contrast, the success of cultural criminology's project rests with our ability to employ a fugitive reading as a means of illustrating the dissonance of consumer culture and putting forth an alternative epistemology. In this particular instance, there are a profusion of entry

Figures 9.5, 9.6 Farce and fatalities: two sides of dangerous driving.

Figure 9.7 Farce and fatalities: two sides of dangerous driving.

points and options ranging from the personal and social costs of unsecured debt (most people cannot pay cash for a sixty thousand dollar luxury sports coupe), to environmental concerns (pollution from cars and the oil industry) to the ravages of deindustrialization (why is an urban street devoid of people at midday?!) through state-corporate crime (tax-payer funded multibillion dollar 'bail-out' packages for the North American auto industry) and bleak, vicious, dystopian futures (the inevitable effluvia of a consumer society's ongoing war against people).

The analysis of crime, media and popular culture is undeniably one of the most significant and potentially illuminating areas of criminological inquiry. As residents of late modernity, we are subject to an increasing array of mediated texts in forming our ideas about crime, transgression and control – advertisements are simply a recent addition. Moreover, because the meanings associated with crime, transgression and control are so fluid and ephemeral, it behoves us as students of cultural criminology to equip ourselves with a variety of navigational instruments and analytical tools. Certainly, as this chapter has laboured to illustrate, critical theory's penetrating analysis and media-studies' effervescent methodologies can provide us with as much (if not more!) interesting criminological insight than a stale government report, moribund textbook or indecipherable mainstream journal article.

Conclusion

The intersections of the legitimate and the illicit interweave along a multiplicity of intersecting axis; pain and pleasure, accommodation and resistance, privacy and public display, approved and fugitive meanings, intertextuality and reification. As subjects of late-modernity, we are surrounded, even infused with advertising's imagery and the concomitant messages of not only the requisite consumption work, but more so, the formation, fortification and periodically the transmogrification of our identities through our consumer exercises. Part of what cultural criminology refers to as 'the crime-culture nexus' is inextricably bound to this consumerization of the means to identity (Hayward, 2004: 4–5; Hall, Winlow and Ancrum, 2008: 107) and hence rightfully constitutes not only an appropriate, but also much needed area of inquiry. This is particularly true when the primary mirror of identification is based upon bifurcated images of the 'Seduced' and the 'Repressed', romanticized images of transgression and crime and allied conspicuous disobedience.

Modern advertising's production of desires and insecurities relies heavily upon its ability to successfully transmit to the target audience palatable and appealing images (images, which it has itself created and/or appropriated). While this process has been occurring for many decades, and has accelerated rapidly in the twenty-first century, what is new is the ways in which the creation and expression of identities via the celebration of consumer goods have all but supplanted other more traditional forms of identity expression. Additionally, the conduits through which advertisers strive to swell the ranks of Bauman's (2007) 'Seduced' masses have become increasingly serpentine, moving from commercials, infomercials and traditional product placement through advertainment, 'anti-advertisement' advertisements, 'real-life' product placement, branding, culture-spying, cool-hunting, brandalism, viral marketing and corporate-*bricoleur* YouTube postings. So too, the sophisticated visual imagery and iconography of ads have changed considerably in the last few years. While it is still the beautiful, urbane, nauseatingly normal upper middle classes whom disproportionately populate the scripted worlds of advertisements, their behaviours, in keeping with the cultural 'mainstreaming of the extreme' that began in the mid-1990s, have become edgier, even defiantly and joyously transgressive in the advertisements of recent years. These characters have been joined in the ad-world by a growing number of consumerism's collateral damage – the 'Repressed'. These latest entrants sometime serve the predictable functions of buffoons, straw men and foils, but are also cast as consumption's newest eager beavers, willingly seeking the tutelage of and serving as apprentices to the Seduced denizens of the advertisement's mediated world.

As Hall and his colleagues poignantly theorize, these 'latter-day saints of consumption' are the advertising industry's iconic representation of whom and what we should be; ultra-cool and super-hip nonconformists for whom resistance is but one more credit card charge away (2008: 96). Under these conditions, cultural criminology's efforts to prioritize the image become an ever more salient component of its broader political and intellectual project.

As Mike Presdee (2000: 15) reminds us, the 'debris of everyday life' is the data of cultural criminology. We need not seek out the most exotic, esoteric or heinous examples of popular culture for scrutiny. Indeed, as I have attempted to illustrate with my chosen commercials, there is a great deal to be learned about the subtle and routinized disciplinary ordinances of late modernity by examining the ordinary and conventional images that confront us almost at our every turn.

References

Bauman, Z. (1987) *Legislators and Interpreters: On Modernity, Post-Modernity, and Intellectuals,* Cambridge: Polity.

Bauman, Z. (2007) 'Collateral Casualties of Consumerism', *Journal of Consumer Culture,* 7(1): 25–56.

Best, A. (2006) *Fast Cars, Cool Rides: The Accelerating World of Youth and Their Cars*, New York: New York University Press.

Canadian Broadcasting Corporation (2008) 'Pester Power: Your Child's Inner Consumer', http://www.cbc.ca/health/story/2008/12/22/f-barwick.html. Last accessed on 02 February, 2009.

Corner, J. (1999) *Critical Ideas in Television Studies*, Oxford: Oxford University Press.

Ewen, S. (1977) *Captains of Consciousness: Advertising and the Social Roots of Consumer Culture*, Toronto: McGraw-Hill.

Ewen, S. (1988) *All Consuming Images: The Politics of Style in Contemporary Culture,* New York: Basic Books.

Ferrell, J. (2003) 'Speed Kills' *Critical Criminology,* 11(3): 185–198.

Ferrell, J. and Hamm, M. (eds) (1998) *Ethnography at the Edge: Crime, Deviance, and Field Research,* Boston: Northeastern University Press.

Ferrell, J., Hayward, K. and Young, J. (2008) *Cultural Criminology: An Invitation*, London: Sage.

Hall, S. (1993) 'Encoding, Decoding', in S. During (ed.) *The Cultural Studies Reader,* London: Routledge, pp. 90–104.

Hall, S., Winlow, S. and Ancrum, C. (2008) *Criminal Identities and Consumer Culture: Crime, Exclusion and the New Culture of Narcissism*, Devon: Willan.

Hayward, K. (2004) *City Limits: Crime, Consumer Culture and the Urban Experience*, London: Glasshouse Press.

Hayward, K. and Yar, M. (2006) 'The "Chav" Phenomenon: Consumption, Media and the Construction of a New Underclass', *Crime, Media, Culture*, 2(1): 9–28.

Helmers, M. (2006) *The Elements of Visual Analysis*, Toronto: Pearson/Longman.

Horkheimer, M. and Adorno, T.W. (1972) *Dialectic of Enlightenment,* New York: Herder and Herder.

Irwin, J. (1977) *Scenes.* Beverly Hills: Sage Publications.

Lasch, C. (1979) *The Culture of Narcissism: American Life in an Age of Diminishing Expectations,* New York: Norton.

Lauer, J. (2005) 'Driven to Extremes: Fear of Crime and the Sport Utility Vehicle in the United States', *Crime, Media, Culture*, 1(2): 149–68.

Marx, K. (1965/[1867]) *Capital: A Critical Analysis of Capitalist Production (Vol. I)*, Moscow: Progress Publishers.

Muzzatti, S. (2006) 'Cultural Criminology: A Decade and Counting of Criminological Chaos', in W. DeKeseredy and B. Perry (eds) *Advancing Critical Criminology: Theory and Application*, Lanham: Lexington Books, pp. 63–81.

Muzzatti, S. (2008) 'They Sing the Body Ecstatic: Television Commercials and Captured Music', in M. Pomerance and J. Sakeris (eds) *Popping Culture*, 5th edn, Toronto: Pearson, pp. 191–201.

Presdee, M. (1994) 'Young People, Culture and the Construction of Crime: Doing Wrong *vs*. Doing Crime', in G. Barak (ed.) *Varieties of Criminology: Readings from a Dynamic Discipline*, London: Praeger, pp. 179–88.

Presdee, M. (2000) *Cultural Criminology and the Carnival of Crime*, London: Routledge.

Presdee, M. and Vaaranen, H. (2004) 'Stories from the Streets: Some Fieldwork Notes on the Seduction of Speed', in J. Ferrell *et al. Cultural Criminology Unleashed*, London: Glasshouse, pp. 245–48.

Price Waterhouse Coopers (2008) 'Global Entertainment and Media Outlook: 2008-2012' http://www.pwc.com/extweb/pwcpublications.nsf/docid/5AC172F2C9DED8F5852570210044EEA7. Last accessed on 27 January, 2009.

Robertson, H. (2005) 'Marketing to Kids', *Canadian Forum,* 74(845): 10–15.

Statistics Canada (2008) 'Motor vehicle theft in Canada, 2007', *Juristat* 85-002-x.

United States Department of Justice, Federal Bureau of Investigation (2006) *Crime in the U.S.: Motor Vehicle Theft*, Washington, DC: Government Printing Office.

Young, J. (2004) 'Voodoo Criminology and the Numbers Game', in J. Ferrell, K. Hayward, W. Morrison and M. Presdee (eds) *Cultural Criminology Unleashed*, London: Glasshouse Press, pp. 13–27.

Chapter 10

Staging an execution

The media at McVeigh

Bruce Hoffman and Michelle Brown

Introduction

> ... it is essential that they [new theoretical models] emerge from the lives of criminologists and criminals alike. While a theory's analytical elegance is one measure of its value, by equal measure it should take shape as an elegant story that captures the gritty particularities of everyday experience.
>
> (Ferrell *et al.*, 2004: 2)

Just as cultural criminologists seek to come to terms with the 'lived experience' of participants in crime and social control (Katz, 1988; Hayward and Young, 2007), so too does cultural criminology point us inward, directing us to become more critically aware of our own lives as criminologists. This directive, which we already knew in theory, became unavoidable for us after June 2001, over the weeks and months that followed our participation as criminologists at the execution of the Oklahoma City bomber Timothy McVeigh.

As researchers interested in media practices, social movements and the cultural dimensions of law and punishment, we had travelled to Terre Haute, Indiana and filmed the activity of the media, protesters and other participants during the twenty-four hours prior to the execution. Like the other media present, we had limited access to the event. Most were restricted from witnessing the execution first-hand, and many reported from the periphery, lacking admission to the official press area on the prison grounds. Moreover, like the media assembled, we also had to respond to the relative lack of content at the event. Standing alongside conventional news reporters and working in parallel, we developed a new appreciation for the contexts and decisions in which reporters produce and reproduce conventional understandings of punishment. As we became aware of how our own frames of understanding were shifting in the immediacy of the context – contingent upon who was present, what aspects of the event were accessible, and the interpretations and opinions given – we became more sensitive to how reporters were seeking to both improvise and rely on conventional routines and frames in response to contingency.

Our attempts to understand the processes through which other media were representing events heightened our own awareness of our identity as criminologists caught up in culture. As the day drew on, we found ourselves increasingly challenged: to understand and ultimately justify our own presence and responsibilities as criminologists at the execution. On the one hand, as events unfolded around us, we found ourselves struggling to comprehend what was significant. Just as the news media fell back on familiar patterns of meaning, we became aware of how our camera was seeking out images structured by the theoretical frameworks we carried (quite literally, in fact, with copies of Austin Sarat's *When the State Kills* and Craig Haney's powerful, personal account 'Psychological Secrecy and the Death Penalty' packed inside our camera bag). How did theory shape the process by which we responded to the event, and how was it shaping the story we would later want to tell? [1] As criminologists, why were we there and what did we seek to produce? What, if anything, distinguished us from the citizen spectator? What might it mean to bring back sociological theory to criminology at an execution? In what follows, we reflect on how we sought to understand what was happening around us; the significance of our own peripheral position, seemingly at the sidelines of the execution (a nonetheless central vantage point for most of media coverage of the event), and the subsequent life of the films that emerged.

On the other hand, we also had to confront the possibilities, limitations, and dangers of visually representing the execution – even and especially through the liberating new technologies of digital filmmaking. The 'digital revolution' in media technology increasingly makes it economically affordable and technologically possible for even a single person to produce a feature length film, thus opening up new possibilities for those wishing to engage in what has been called 'news-making criminology,' or criminology that actively seeks to challenge and destabilize dominant frames of meaning (Ferrell, 1996; Barak, 1988, 1994, 2007). In this respect and others, cultural criminology has served as the central site for a criminology of the image. What that image means as well as what it means to produce those images in contexts marked by the limits of representation, contexts marked by death, is central to our concerns – and anxieties as filmmakers. The thoughtless, unreflexive use of criminological images is, as Ferrell puts it, 'ugly criminology,' sadly misinformed and misunderstood (2006). What cultural criminology has increasingly moved toward instead is an alternative framework: one dependent upon 'a philosophical reorientation toward image and representation – a reorientation that engages symbolic meaning with some degree of honesty and sophistication, that promotes human immersion in the symbolic

1 Hayward and Young define social theory as the linchpin of cultural criminology when they argue that 'Most fundamentally, cultural criminology seeks to *bring back sociological theory to criminology*; that is to continue to (re)integrate the role of culture, social construction, human meaning, creativity, class, and power relations into the criminological project' (2007: 103).

environment under study, that acknowledges the essentially symbolic construction of all windows and all worlds…' (Ferrell, 2006: 263). Our efforts at the McVeigh execution were directed at just such a reorientation within the context of capital punishment and the production of images surrounding it.

In the end, we find that all of these aspects of our experience at Timothy McVeigh's execution – our attention to media practices, a reflexive understanding of criminology, and new media technologies – are tightly bound to one another. While the new digital technologies open up the possibility of news-making in new and exciting ways, this can be only the case if we come to understand – and challenge – how conventional cultural practices and narratives shape and reproduce interpretations of events. Indeed, the hegemonic power of these practices extends to criminologists who are reflexively bound by the conventions and frames of the mass media (Giddens, 1979, 1990). At the McVeigh execution, we found that few activities are as intense and as eye-opening as having to film the event on our feet, requiring us, as criminologists, to attempt to understand and participate in the construction of images as they unfolded. Possessing the same equipment as the organized media and occupying the same peripheral position at the events, how would our constructions differ? As activists gave us the same strategic sound-bites that they were giving the media, as residents told their well-rehearsed jokes and commentaries on the proceedings and as media representatives fell into the same rote presentations in our interviews that they gave during their broadcasts, how would we distinguish our images from theirs? And did we have the foresight to capture images that would enable us to do so?

Focus

Documentary filmmaking as cultural criminology

Social documentary has played an important and longstanding role in extending and challenging traditional social scientific approaches. The question about what an image may convey that a written text cannot continues to haunt the social sciences. Like all products of science, such as graphs or statistics, documentary film images are focused translations of reality, requiring special care in their interpretation. Yet, because images are such powerfully persuasive accounts, conveying such a strong illusion of mirroring reality, there are, perhaps, special obligations for researchers who choose to rely on images in their construction of events. Early on in our study of the media at the execution of Timothy McVeigh, we found ourselves – and our original scientific aims – challenged in this regard.

Anticipating spectacle

When we initially decided to film the execution, our intention was not to study the media but the crowds and protest activity that promised to emerge. Not only was the execution of Timothy McVeigh, the Oklahoma City bomber who had rejected appeals to hasten his own execution date, but it was also to be the first federal execution in nearly forty years. As Sarat has argued, McVeigh's execution is central to debates about the proper place of capital punishment in American culture: 'It is used as the ultimate trump card, the living, breathing embodiment of the necessity and justice of the death penalty. Even people normally opposed to, or indifferent about, capital punishment find themselves drawn to it in McVeigh's case' (2001: 11). Several months before McVeigh's execution, abolitionist groups scheduled a seventy mile march from Indianapolis to Terre Haute for the federal executions of David Paul Hammer and Juan Raul Garza, which were subsequently stayed by then President Clinton to review racial disparities in the administration of the death penalty. The confluence of McVeigh with the return of the federal death penalty was widely expected to bring out throngs of activists and onlookers.[2] The expected carnival that was anticipated by media and experts alike is captured in this news story, widely circulated prior to the execution by the Reuters news service:

> Death penalty opponents and proponents, hate groups, religious believers, opportunists and the merely curious are expected to be among demonstrators outside the Indiana prison where Oklahoma City bomber Timothy McVeigh is to be executed. Federal prison authorities in Terre Haute have prepared a battle plan employing hundreds of anti-riot officers and separate demonstration areas to contend with potentially rowdy protesters voicing their opinions on the grassy prison grounds. "It's going to be reminiscent of early executions before there got to be so many," said Stephen Bright, a death penalty expert and director of the Southern Centre for Human Rights. "It's a high-profile case, which tends to bring out the dark side of the human spirit. There are those in favour of executions, who one would hope would view it as sad and tragic, as opposed to the celebrations and beer parties that go on," Bright said. Ku Klux Klansmen could show up in full regalia, and a group of Catholic nuns plan to hold a 168-minute prayer service to honour the 1995 bombing victims… (Reuters 03 May 2001).

Just like ourselves, the news media were also anticipating the arrival of the protesters. Over 1400 media had applied for licenses to cover the execution in Terre Haute, and their satellite trucks stretched across the prison grounds and their press passes, illustrated with representations of fire and judgment that resembled rock concerts, visibly distinguished them from ordinary spectators (Plate 10.1).

Many other satellite trucks also lined the periphery of the prison, their engines humming in residential lawns turned into parking lots and staging areas by enterprising citizens. One resident would later tell us – in a catchy sound bite that was

2 However, such activities were downplayed by Amnesty International, which encouraged local, as opposed to national or on-site demonstrations.

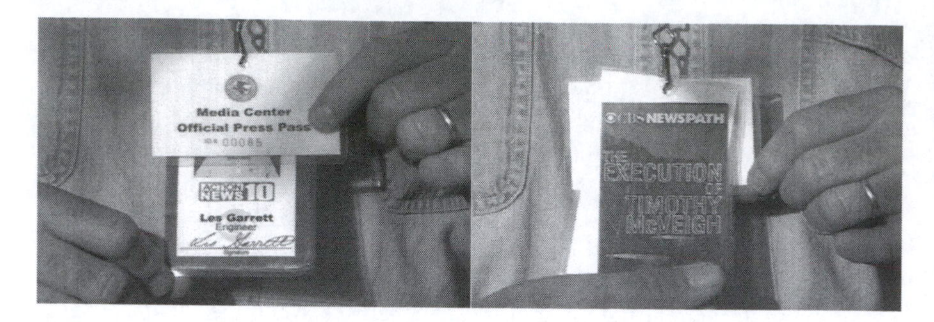

Figure 10.1 Action News 10 Press Pass.

told to and broadcast by countless other news crews – that 'For years they've made me pay for parking ... now it's *my* turn to make *them* pay *me*!' In fact, many of the news crews had arrived weeks and even months before 11 June, and had interviewed the same residents multiple times. A single provocative demonstrator could be assured attention by numerous news crews (Figure 10.2). By the day of the execution, many crews had taken to interviewing one another for content, crafting stories about the experience of waiting, and were eager for the change of pace that the protesters and the execution itself would bring.

The federal prison had prepared for the protests as well, having detailed protocols drawn up on how to handle protest activities. More than responding to events, the state would also direct events, as was evident as we pulled off US Interstate 70 and were met by a blinking road signs telling protesters where to assemble: 'Pro-Demonstrators * Use Voorhees Park * Anti-Demonstrators * Use Fairbank Park' (Figure 10.3). The state had begun to structure the terms and process of protest and its consequent representation.

Arriving in Terre Haute

Upon our arrival in Terre Haute, it was clear that the anticipated masses had failed to materialize for the event. Save for police and the Indiana National

Figure 10.2 Lone Activist Portrayed as Jesus for the Evening News.

Figure 10.3 Electronic Sign Directs and Divides Protesters.

Guard, the park for 'anti-demonstrators' was all but empty; a father and son fishing in a nearby river directed us across town to a church where protesters were preparing for a scheduled march along the prison grounds. There, it was clear that media heavily outnumbered the protesters, as was wryly observed by an organizer who announced over his bullhorn: 'For those of you actually here to demonstrate, please gather, like, over here…' Protesters, for their part, were organized and media savvy while engaging in 'prime time activism,' moving from press conference to press conference with well-rehearsed statements; and several reporters commented on their collectively assembling during news cycles (Ryan, 1990). Among them were cultural criminologists protesting the execution in keeping with the politics, more broadly, of criminology.[3] Despite their efforts,

3 In November 1989, The American Society of Criminology formally adopted the following policy position with regard to capital punishment:

> Be it resolved that because social science research has demonstrated the death penalty to be racist in application and social science research has found no consistent evidence of crime deterrence through execution, The American Society of Criminology publicly condemns this form of punishment, and urges its members to use their professional skills in legislatures and courts to seek a speedy abolition of this form of punishment.

See http://www.asc41.com/policyPositions.html.

however, it was clear to us that one key aspect of their message was recontextualized by the media: the protesters, who carried towering puppets pairing Uncle Sam (reading 'Stop Me Before I Kill Again') with Jesus ('What Would Jesus Do?') were clearly demonstrating against the power of the state. The media, however, through their narratives and editing, would neutralize this critique, by representing their protests as not against the state but as a point of view needing to 'balanced' against 'pro-demonstrators' – other citizens – in an abstract debate over the death penalty. This binary logic, framed as 'balance,' is central to the containment of death penalty discourse in the United States.

Meanwhile, in the 'pro-demonstrator' park, no one had gathered. Well, almost no one: three local teenagers, encouraged by the blinking road signs, had brought cardboard signs to the park and seemed at once shocked and elated by the media presence. 'There's CNN!' one of them shouted, grabbing the arm of another while pointing to the Satellite Truck that had just pulled up. The three of them stood aside a local reporter and her camera operator as they waited for their 'live' interview on the evening news (Figure 10.4). In front of them stood an impressively long line of the world's media, each patiently waiting for their chance to interview the sole demonstrators in the park whose voices would be transformed into the 'pro-' position in a debate (Figure 10.5). As the teenagers repeatedly commented on their nervousness and surprise at having become, in their words, 'three celebrities,' the reporter sought to calm them and coach them on what to say.

Figure 10.4 Three Demonstrators Represent the "Pro-" Position.

Figure 10.5 World Media Line Up Before the Evening News Cycle.

It remains to this day difficult to assess, in fact, how many protesters were ever present as media accounts diverge so dramatically, in many instances citing hundreds or even thousands of people. The best estimates indicate there were never more than twenty protesters at the pro-death penalty staging area and not more than two hundred at the anti-death penalty sites. While there was an obvious lack of activists at the events, we found our attention shifting throughout the day to the ways in which their activities were being responded to and represented by the vast numbers of media present. How were they handling the relative lack of demonstrators? How were they interpreting the event?

Interviewing the media

The news media that we interviewed included local, regional, national, and international reporters, as well as many of their camera operators and engineers. We were also able to interview local residents about their experience with the media. We sought to interview the media about the questions that they were asking and their own perceptions of themes addressed and unaddressed by the news industry, as well as film the media across the broad spectrum of their activities: as engineers set up equipment and reporters interviewed residents, demonstrators, and spectators; filed their live updates; edited their sequenced news packages; and, above all, waited for something to happen.

With the camera reversed, only a few reporters – notably those working for large media conglomerates, such as Gannett and CNN – were unable to step out of their professional on-air personalities, answering our questions with the studied gravitas of their newscasts. In general, however, reporters expressed both candidness and not a little discomfort at being the subject of an interview. Many reporters expressed during the interview that 'they were usually the ones asking the questions', or that they had never been asked their views on their profession before. One reporter concluded that 'I've never given an interview where I said what I believed.' These responses are especially interesting in that when beginning our interviews, reporters overwhelmingly assumed that we would be asking them the same question that they were asking their respondents, 'are you for or against the death penalty?' Some would even begin stating their opinions before the first question was asked! Instead, we sought to engage them in a dialogue about their profession: what questions they were asking; how they would select the stories and interviews that made it onto the air; how they would frame the events; what themes they could address well; and themes that were hard to get it. In most instances, these questions were responded to in a way that led into candid discussions of their industry. Reporters explained to us how little time they had to gather and present the news; their frustration at the constraints of their news packages; and in general, presented their reporting as an effort to attain quality against the pressures and constraints of the news industry.

Reporters were also surprisingly open with us about their personal observations and misgivings about the coverage of the execution. For example, when interviewing the three young residents supporting the execution – surrounded by a queue of the world's media who would do the same – a local reporter told our camera that she thinks that 'it's important to know that there are just three people here … these kids will be on everyone's news, but it's just three people.' Despite these concerns, however, such observations were not incorporated into her own newscast in which their voices were decontextualized and made to speak for a 'side' in an abstract debate about the death penalty. Another reporter, previously critical of the media's ability to get at the truth, stood gazing at activists gathering for a vigil on the prison grounds, negotiating with his camera operator what might be a credible exaggeration of the number of protesters to include in his morning report.

Above all, we were struck by the reflexive self-monitoring of the reporters. Just as reporters sought sound bites for their news reporting, so too did some reporters monitor their speech for us, seeking to give us good sound bites and scolding themselves for 'violating the ten-second rule,' referring to the succinct passages they themselves were seeking and anticipated that we would need for our own editing. Sometimes, they even searched for more interesting or provocative ways of restating their points. Similarly, when asked what questions they were asking, most responded quickly that they themselves chose the questions based on what they thought their audience wanted to know, or – identifying with the audience – asking questions that they themselves wanted to know. For most reporters, these led to the uniform questions: 'why are you here' and 'what is your opinion on the death penalty.'

Following our interviews, several engineers and reporters invited us into their satellite trucks to watch their recorded or edited broadcasts. The interviews and final edited reports of protesters were virtually interchangeable, constructed around montages that juxtaposed protesters into 'pro' and 'anti' positions. Deeper sociological questions, including questions about the power of the state or about the society which created McVeigh, were left out.

Virginia

We learned that the execution had taken place in the same way that the reporters with whom we were standing with did: from Katie Couric's newsfeed on *Today* transmitted across their radios in the morning rain. It was an unusual moment during the morning's proceedings, in which the activity of the reporters stopped, ceasing their interviews and broadcasts, and, instead, listening to Couric's uncharacteristically somber narration.

Immediately after the execution was announced, reporters began submitting their final reports and the engineers and reporters began packing up. As we – and the media engineers – were putting away our cameras and preparing to leave Terre Haute, we were approached by a reporter that we had been trying to interview that morning. Tired and emotionally drained, we initially questioned whether we should conduct the interview. However, she persuaded us, and it turned out to be the most complex and substantive discussion that we had in Terre Haute. Virginia's interview wove back and forth between the execution and her activities as a reporter, the recent death of her brother and her experience with suffering, the imagined pain of McVeigh's victims and family, and the duties and restrictions of the state in ways that are complex and contradictory. As an interview, Virginia's fatigue from the experience led to an unusual forthrightness and a sudden emotive ability to contextualize the execution through her own experiences with loss and pain in a way that challenged the conventions of the media. Through her own proximity to pain, she was able to articulate the logic of violence and disregard that undergirds the mechanics of death in capital punishment. We attempted to represent this complexity by including nearly eight minutes of the interview with minimal editing in our film, conveying both our own exhausted questions and Virginia's complex answers. Juxtaposed against the quick, conventional editing of the first half of the film, Virginia remains the focus for our students and audiences; and for our students in particular, she often challenges the expectations of what a reporter should be. In retrospect, this opening up of a debate and discourse that had been consistently closed off in the hours prior to the execution was only possible because of two factors. One, the interview occurred in the aftermath of the culmination of state violence and the completion of McVeigh's execution. Everyone was now aware that someone had just been killed. Two, the interviewee had an unknown proximity to death and this experience opened up a space in which to recognize the pain of others. Virginia's interview remains the only instance within our footage where the violence of the state could be foregrounded in any substantive way.

Methodological reflections

Methodological reflection on recording and editing the film

> The future of the cinema no longer lies in its past.
>
> (Wim Wenders, 2001)

> To me the great hope is that now these little 8 mm video recorders and stuff have come out, some ... just people who normally wouldn't make movies are going to be making them, and – you know – suddenly, one day, some little

> fat girl in Ohio is going to be the new Mozart – you know – and make a beautiful film with her little father's camera-corder – and for once the so-called professionalism about movies will be destroyed. Forever – you know – and it will really become an art form.
>
> Francis Ford Coppola, in Bahr and Hickenlooper 1991, *Hearts of Darkness* (1991)

Several years ago, German filmmaker Wim Wenders and American Francis Ford Coppola both provocatively argued the 'digital revolution' in cinema opened up dramatic new possibilities for both filming and storytelling. We have often thought about these statements following our experience in Terre Haute. At the McVeigh execution, we had the same equipment as the media, often leading to confusion among those we were interviewing. 'Which station did we represent?' Such similarities lead to reflection: what does differentiate us from them? For Wenders, nothing about the 'digital revolution' inevitably leads to a break with the past narratives, for digital films can simply emulate and replicate conventions. Ideologies may be reproduced and 'ugly' criminologies may persist. However, Wenders argues that new technologies enable dramatic new possibilities, quite possibly by being located outside of the studio system that dictated funding, equipment, editing, and were tied to audience reception. In an age when anyone can be a rebel with a Canon, what will differentiate the stories and narratives composed from those that have been told in the past?[4]

Our lived experience with the media (and as the media) at the execution of McVeigh significantly shaped our understanding of culture, criminology and the image, and what it means to practice an image-making criminology sensitive to culture. As we discuss in the following section, these understandings are of two sorts. On the one hand, over experience helped illuminate for us how everyday media practices work: including the ways in which diverse reporters critical of their profession nevertheless reproduce institutional logics and frames. On the other hand, our engagement sensitized and challenged our own work as criminologists. The experience of needing to understand the events we were involved in, as they emerged, and to find a way to represent and film these understandings on the go, made us aware in a new and urgent way of how frames of meanings were structuring both the reporters and camera operators as well as us and our own understandings. The further challenge of editing these recordings in a way that challenges representations while constructing new forms further served to

4 Such questions have also been taken up by filmmakers such as the Danish collective DOGME 95. Their manifesto asks filmmakers to democratize cinema by taking 'The Vow of Chastity' and using only handheld cameras, unaltered locations and sounds and minimal production to challenge existing conventions and create new cinematic forms. (DOGME 95 principles also inspired a musical staring Björk centering around an execution, Lars von Trier's *Dancer in the Dark*.) See http://www.dogme95.dk/the_vow/vow.html.

make us aware of what we were unable to capture due to the limitations of our understanding at the time, the invisibility of the practice at the event and the simple, stark fact that executions occur at the limits of representation. What follows are a series of meditations and theoretical insights on these predicaments.

1. *Individualizing Opinion.* First, participation at the event made it clear to us how much media reporters were seeking and emphasizing observer opinions in their representations, juxtaposing them into the frame of a 'debate' on the death penalty. Such questions and their editing created a debate structured around individual responsibility. Did McVeigh deserve to die for killing or is killing absolutely wrong? Emphasis on individual opinions constructed the death penalty as a matter of individual debate, but did not allow for alternative frames, such as the society that created Timothy McVeigh or the role of capital punishment in shaping American society, let alone the media's role in mediating interpretations. (Indeed, when we ourselves were interviewed by a regional station, the tape of our own interview was cut off mid-sentence, just before the words 'and the culture that shaped Timothy McVeigh.') In this way, dominant ideologies surrounding the death penalty are reproduced, relying heavily upon individualistic understandings of crime and punishment (Haney, 1997; Sarat, 2001).
2. *Framing 'Balance.'* Second, the questions of reporters to activists, uniformly consisting of the question 'are you for or against the death penalty,' were not going to reveal alternative ways of understanding the event. While abolitionists often framed their opposition in terms of their opposition to state practices – not in opposition to death penalty supporters – invariably the media packaged protesters and supporters as a contest between two opposing sides. Often, this was understood as the imperative of 'balance' – to be fair to both sides of the 'debate' – but assuming the terms of the debate in advance. Such a framework inevitably positions 'sides' as irreconcilable – a zero-sum game, where as Judith Butler writes, 'the framework for hearing presumes that the one view nullifies the other' (Butler, 2004: 13). In such a context, sociological explanation itself is suspect, 'as if to explain these events would involve us in a sympathetic identification with the oppressor, as if to understand these events would involve building a justificatory framework for them' (13). This, in fact, is exactly how discourse is closed off.
3. *The Structuring Absence of the State.* At the event, however, few protesters opposed to executions were actually arguing at 'pro' death penalty advocates; rather, their opponent was more frequently the state that kills. But the killing state was largely invisible due to the normality of social control in everyday life. The detailed protocols of the state structured most aspects of the execution in a naturalized form of bureaucratic regulation: including directing traffic; dividing the protesters by assigning them to distant parks where they were to demonstrate; giving them rules to abide by when marching

past the prison; running shuttle buses to escort protesters to a candlelight vigil on a far corner of the prison grounds; and restricting these protesters from carrying umbrellas and other implements in the name of security. At the execution, the state's power was, consequently, both subtle and omnipresent, particularly governing behaviour and access. For instance, at the main road adjacent to the prison grounds, citizens knew to walk or cycle only on the far side of the street. Nevertheless, a powerful tension permeated the prison grounds. Would there be a bomb? A shooting? A raid by McVeigh's supporters? Imagined by protocols and government, such scenarios had led to the cancellation of school and the closing of public buildings prior to the execution. Around 3:00 a.m., their wish was granted: as narrated to us by a young college student on bicycle, the sudden flashing lights of a dozen police vehicles we were witnessing were mobilized by a driver, suspected to be drunk, who had pulled to the side of the road at night to gaze across prison grounds. On the grounds themselves, a series of tents set up were rumoured among the media to conceal rapid response teams, thought to be seated in their vehicles, ready to roar out on a moment's notice. Consequently, while the experience of state power was pervasive and often the talk of indirect conversation, it proved difficult to capture in any transparent way on film. Rather, the careful regulation and choreography of the potential spectacle surrounding the execution embodied at the microlevel, in its anticipation of a dangerous potentiality that never materialized, what it means to govern through crime (Hall *et al.*, 1978; Simon, 2007).

4. *Subverting Convention: Sound Bites.* While most interviewees expressed regret at the time pressures of their work – both in the pace of filming events and interviews, as well as in their restricted broadcast time – only a few criticized their reliance on the sound bite as a key element of their narratives. When asked how they selected their material for their reporting, many reporters and engineers somewhat defensively explained that our own editing would proceed the same way – 'you'll take what you need, and leave the rest on the cutting-room floor'. We did, in fact, find this to be a disturbing challenge for our own editing [as well as this article]: would our constructions reproduce the illustrative reliance on the attractive sound bite? This proved especially difficult for our final interview with Virginia, a discussion framed immediately after the execution about pain, suffering, and death. How would we avoid reproducing the very conventions which appeared to be closing off any deliberative or substantive debate about capital punishment in the United States?

Overall, our experience led us to consider how we might construct an alternative story, avoiding the dependence on constructions of personal responsibility, exposing the media's reliance on 'balance', illuminating the role of the state, and avoiding the reliance on dominant conventions like the sound bite. We found, when we returned home, that we had much material to work with for some of these questions, due to the theoretical focus and critical questions we brought with us and were able to realize at the event. However, other topics – in particular, the role of the state – we were unable to represent, due to their invisibility at the event and our inability creatively to find a strategy of representation in real time. This kind of experience made us acutely aware of the importance of theoretical preparation and praxis: self-consciously using theory to anticipate, structure, and help make sense of experience, while remaining open to happenings that challenge and surprise theoretical understandings (cf. Taylor, 1985). Most critically, we ultimately chose to tackle the issue of representation through an alternative narrative style that explored issues of time, juxtaposing the standard editing of the news profession with an alternative and contextualized long take: that of our most complex and challenging interview, our final one with Virginia.

Showing the film

Not unlike Al Gore's travelling slide show on the environment,[5] our footage from the McVeigh execution has lived many lives, in many forms – especially in conjunction with our university teaching and public showings. Before it became a film, parts of the footage were selected and woven together to discuss a wide range of class themes. Eventually, a variety of different films were made out of the material, depending on the context and audience. These versions were shown in classrooms, public lectures, media cooperatives, and film festivals, enabling an open and diverse discussion. When Howard Zinn came to visit Seattle, we gained permission to film his public discussion and publicly asked him questions about the McVeigh execution, resulting in additional footage to add to the collection.

As a polished film, the documentary is still a bit rough – probably not ready for commercial distribution – but for our purposes of challenging and generating reflection and discussion with local audiences, the film has continued to surprise us. In the age of the Internet and YouTube, wide distribution is possible, although we are left with lingering fears about disembedding our footage from local contexts of discussion, potentially allowing it to be used in other unpredictable ways. However, just as the contradictions of capital punishment lead the government to take such measures to control its message – including controlling the satellite stream of the execution, a point well understood by satellite operators at the execution – for our film, we believe – and hope – that the roughness and contradictions left within the footage in some way fortifies it, guaranteeing that no single interpretation – or simplistic interpretation – can win out (cf. Jasanoff, 1996).

5 See *An Inconvenient Truth* (2006).

Conclusion

> As I have argued, death, whatever its cause, marks the limits of representation. Films can neither capture death nor help us know what cannot be known. We can and do watch others die without being able to capture death's meaning or significance.
>
> (Sarat, 2001: 247)

In the study of capital punishment, the image holds special significance. And the media, as the producers of these images, hold special powers. Capital punishment depends, as Craig Haney argues, upon the concept of psychological secrecy: the condition that the public learns only selected details about the life and death of the person executed (Haney, 1997). These details are largely framed by immediate time pressures and heavy reliance upon industry conventions and audience expectations by news media, as we witnessed. The resulting images are consistently ugly criminology, representations ripped out of complex cultural contexts. An alternative frame begins with a stark acknowledgment. As Sarat marks it, any and all efforts to represent death are fundamentally failures. In this way, the only 'successful' representation is one which, as Butler writes, 'not only fail[s] to capture its referent, but *show[s]* this failing' (2004: 146). American media are practically and institutionally organized in a manner which prevents this failure from achieving any visibility. Rather than opening up identification in a way that might expose the problematic, inherently open-ended relationship between representation and death, closure is the conventional and hallmark ending of any news story covering an execution. The image (re)solves all. To this end, we hope that our film fails – and fails in a manner that is productive and useful for those who still reside in the killing state.

The film, Staging an Execution: The Media at McVeigh, *can be found online at Ohio University's Center for Law, Justice and Culture: http://www.ohio.edu/lawcenter/films/mcveigh.html. Special thanks to the Comparative Law and Society Studies Center at the University of Washington for a grant that facilitated its development.*

References

Bahr, F., with G. Hickenlooper (Screenwriter and Director) (1991) Hearts of Darkness, A Filmmaker's Apocalypse [Film.] Zaloom Mayfield Productions in Association with Zoetrope Studios.

Barak, G. (1988) 'Newsmaking Criminology: Reflections on the Media, Intellectuals, and Crime', *Justice Quarterly,* 5: 565–87.

Barak, G. (ed.) (1994) *Media, Process, and the Social Construction of Crime: Studies in Newsmaking Criminology*, New York: Garland.

Barak, G. (2007) 'Doing Newsmaking Criminology From Within the Academy', *Theoretical Criminology,* 11: 191–207.

Butler, J. (2004) *Precarious Life: The Powers of Mourning and Violence*, New York: Verso.

Dogme 95 (1995) 'The Vow of Chastity': http://www.dogme95.dk/the_vow/vow.html. Last accessed on 18 November, 2007.

Ferrell, J. (1996) *Crimes of Style: Urban Graffiti and the Politics of Criminality,* Boston: Northeastern University Press.

Ferrell, J. (2006) 'The Aesthetics of Cultural Criminology', in Arrigo, B.A. and Williams, C.R. (eds) *Philosophy, Crime, and Criminology*, Urbana, IL: University of Illinois Press.

Ferrell, J., Hayward, K., Morrison, W. and Presdee, M. (2004) 'Fragments of a Manifesto: Introducing *Cultural Criminology Unleashed*,' in Ferrell, J., Hayward, K., Morrison, W. and Presdee, M. (eds) *Cultural Criminology Unleashed*, London: Glasshouse Press.

Giddens, A. (1979) *Central Problems in Social Theory: Action, Structure, and Contradiction in Social Analysis,* Berkeley, CA: University of California Press.

Giddens, A. (1990) *The Consequences of Modernity*, Stanford, CA: Stanford University Press.

Hall, S., Critcher, C., Jefferson, T. and Roberts, B. (1978) *Policing the Crisis: Mugging, the State, and Law and Order*, London: Macmillan.

Haney, C. (1997) 'Psychological Secrecy and the Death Penalty: Observations on "the Mere Extinguishment of Life"', *Studies in Law, Politics, and Society,* 16: 3–69.

Hayward, K. and Young, J. (2007) 'Cultural Criminology', in Maguire M., Morgan, R. and Reiner, R. (eds) *The Oxford Handbook of Criminology,* 4th edn, Oxford: Oxford University Press.

Jasanoff, S. (1996) 'Beyond Epistemology: Relativism and Engagement in the Politics of Science', *Social Studies of Science,* 26: 393–418.

Katz, J. (1988) *Seductions of Crime*, New York: Basic Books.

Ryan, C. (1990) *Prime Time Activism, Media Strategies for Grassroots Organizing,* Boston: South End Press.

Sarat, A. (2001) *When the State Kills: Capital Punishment and the American Condition.* Princeton, New Jersey: Princeton University Press.

Simon, J. (2007) *Governing Through Crime*, New York: Oxford University Press.

Taylor, C. (1985) 'Understanding and Ethnocentricity', in Taylor, C., (ed) *Philosophy and the Human Sciences: Philosophical Papers 2*, Cambridge: Cambridge University Press.

Wenders, W. (2001) 'A Universe to Discover: What the New Technologies Offer to Us', http://www.wim-wenders.com/news_reel/2001/0101article.htm. Last accessed on 23 January, 2008.

Chapter 11

Fighting with images

The production and consumption of violence among online football supporters

Damián Zaitch and Tom de Leeuw

> ...people seek to have their photographs taken – feel that they are images, and are made real by photographs.
>
> (Susan Sontag, *On Photography,* 1979)

Introduction

With a few notable exceptions, mainstream criminology has shown no real sustained interest in the cultural meanings of images. According to Mariana Valverde (2006), in a recent book on images, law, and order, this reluctance to engage with the visual has much to do with the primacy of nineteenth-century enlightenment thinking within fields such as criminology and jurisprudence. Traditional social science, she claims, has only trusted 'hard facts', while image analyses have been largely dismissed as lacking objective value. Even social constructionist or critical approaches within criminology have privileged face-to-face interaction or discourse analysis as their primary methods for gathering data. However, a change is clearly under way, as various cultural criminologists have begun undertaking what Prosser (2003) calls *image-based research* (e.g. Carney, 2004; Young, 2005, 2007; Valverde, 2006; Ferrell *et al.*, 2008). In a recent issue of the journal *Crime, Media, Culture*, the editors argue that 'the visual constitutes perhaps the central medium through which the meanings and emotions of crime are captured and conveyed to audiences. Indeed, we would suggest that it is the visual that increasingly shapes our engagement with, and understanding of, key issues of crime, control and order' (Greer *et al.*, 2007: 5). This is clearly the case. We can no longer afford to neglect the force of the image, whether in relation to our specific understanding of crime and punishment, or more generally in terms of the way the visual media shape our perceptions and influence the way we construct and present our identities.

Despite the reluctance to fully integrate the image into criminology, it is possible to note several areas of research where an interest in the image has featured: most notably as a research 'tool' to gather data (visual ethnography), as the specific focus of research (media and cultural studies), or as a control and surveillance technology (police photography and closed circuit television-CCTV).

However, as a result of cultural criminology, other new image-based fields of study are fast emerging, including (especially in Europe) the study of football supporter violence; due, no doubt to the huge popularity and strongly mediatised character of football itself across at least three continents. Several studies have highlighted how football supporters are presented in traditional media such as newspapers, sport magazines or TV news (Hall, 1978; Salerno, 2005; Poulton, 2005). Others meanwhile have begun to point out how 'fantasy football hooliganism' – the expanding range of hooligan-related entertainment products, including television documentaries, 'real' videos, 'hoolie' novels and biographies, films and video games – all offer packaged experiences of 'transgression' to various groups with diverse tastes, preferences and tolerances for violence (Poulton, 2007).

In this chapter, we follow a different but related path: instead of focusing on media constructions or the commodification of hooligan material per se, we explore how images are produced, used and shared by online football supporters. More specifically, we analyse images placed on Argentinean and Dutch football supporter websites in a bid to understand not only what these images 'mean' or represent, but also what they actually 'produce' (Carney, 2004) in terms of football supporter identity construction. In what follows, we focus on how uploaded images are being used by football supporters to *invent* and *present* themselves in a whole host of self-styled, so-called 'bad ass' roles: including hooligan 'warriors', marginalized drug-addict thieves, anarchist lawbreakers – even as members of hierarchical street gangs and criminal organizations.

After introducing our research, the cultural value of 'violent' images will be discussed by highlighting some of the issues and aspects associated with pictures, including the highly stylized way in which supporters portray themselves; the celebration and aggrandizement of alcohol and drugs within young male cultures and the constant reference to particular sorts of outlaws, gangsters and criminals. This will be followed by some reflections on the value of this type of research method for cultural criminology more generally. The chapter will end with some conclusive remarks and will highlight some issues for further exploration.

Focus

Researching images of football supporters on the Internet

Football supporters increasingly belong to virtual communities that actively interact with each other online in blogs and supporter sites. They use cyberspace to gather information, make appointments, meet other supporters, build alliances, 'other' enemies, sell or consume commodities, show the results of real combats, insult the police, discuss political matters or show-off/perform as violent individuals. Images (photos, photomontages, banners or videos) play a central role in this process. These online images offer researchers an open window to study processes such as identity construction and the shifting patterns of masculinity within male subcultural groups defined by official myths, moral panics and different levels of criminalization.[1]

We collected our material from two parallel research projects on football supporters in The Netherlands and Argentina (Zaitch and De Leeuw, 2006; De Leeuw, 2007). Our goal was straightforward: to understand how supporters used the internet in both countries. To this end, we gathered texts and images from 20 different supporter sites during the first half of 2006.[2] In compiling our sample, we ensured that we covered both Dutch and Argentinean sites, including both large and small (sometimes second division) clubs, and (self) censored and uncensored sites. All sites accessed were either open or had some basic registration procedure, so images belonging to closed and protected sites remained, sadly, out of sight. A key selection criterion was indeed the quality and quantity of texts and images posted on these sites. We analysed the sites with a standard topic list, looking for material on the construction of collective identities and the ways in which users 'fight' and have fun in cyberspace. Hundreds of photos, photomontages and films were gathered and classified by topic.

A second study was based on ethnographic research conducted in the Netherlands in 2006 by one of the authors (De Leeuw, 2007). This research drew upon observations, face-to-face interviews with several 'hard-core' Dutch football supporters, and rigorous content analysis of the (mainly British) literary genre known as 'hooliporn' – popular hooligan writings for mass consumption including memoirs, autobiographies, fiction and journalistic accounts. Although the focus here is on the meanings and performances of images, we used the other material as necessary and useful context.[3] What follows is a brief descriptive summary of some of the more prominent themes identified by our research.

---

1 Although some studies have been undertaken on the social background and cultural practices of Argentinean and Dutch football supporters (Alabarces, 2003; Alabarces et al., 2005; Spaaij, 2006), none of them focus on the specific groups of supporters who use the Internet. Some research has been conducted on 'online' football supporters (Giulianotti, 2001; Poulton, 2007, Fafinski, 2007), but it mainly focuses on consumption patterns of supporters or the role of the Internet in 'facilitating' football-related violence.

2 We identified eight types of websites actively visited and used by football supporters. These were: a) Official football club sites; b) Official supporter sites; c) National or international supporter sites above club level; d) Unofficial supporter sites focusing on club or football issues; e) Unofficial supporter sites focusing on supporters themselves; f) Individual blogs; g) Unofficial sites on other activities indirectly connected with football; and h) Private commercial sites. Types a), g) and h) were finally discarded for the analysis.

3 Such background information is useful, because many of the images studied refer to real events and people captured 'out there' in bars, streets and in and around football grounds. That said, when drawing on this secondary material, we also recognized the many concerns that have been expressed about the veracity of much of this so-called hooliporn literature.

Photoshopped reputations: the online iconography of Dutch and Argentinean football supporters

Bricolage and reputation

Through techniques described by Goffman (1959) as 'impression management', individuals and social groups construct a particular collective image to present to others. Traditionally, football supporters have undertaken this process face-to-face in so-called reputational disputes (Spaaij, 2006). However, the Internet offers football supporters an alternative arena to build up or contest these reputations. Indeed, many of the images we identified are posted specifically for the purpose of representing memories and desires and building, manipulating and managing reputations (Emler and Reicher, 1995).

The 'raw' materials to construct the images used in these reputational disputes come from two main sources: either self-made private photos and videos produced with mobile telephones or video cameras, or publicly available photos and videos drawn from the media and the entertainment industry. Actual images found online often combine various sources and are heavily 'touched' and transformed with software such as *Photoshop*. Through this process of *bricolage* (Hebdige, 1979), meanings and effects of images are radically altered and reinvented, not only by a clear de/recontextualization of the images, but also by their physical transformation and manipulation.

Online football supporters function as *bricoleurs* as they appropriate and assemble, more often as an *ad hoc* and improvized response to their environment, various repertoires of signs, discourses and traditions, resignifying them and creating new discourses and different subversive messages.

For example, many groups utilize and identify themselves with images of roaring lions, barking pit bulls, raging bulls, killer bees, dirty rats, Chinese dragons, poisonous spiders, eagles, wild horses and crawling tigers. Other symbols include pirates and even prehistoric cavemen. This identification with wild, dangerous animals or 'barbaric' people – also evident in the case of Dutch supporters who would use symbols and characters from German and Scandinavian traditions and (Viking) mythologies – is based on the cultural conception of violence as an act of honour directly related to the body and an entrenched masculine identity. While they reinvent the meanings of animals or randomly grasp certain aspects from the Scandinavian Viking tradition, football supporters build, reinforce and question reputations.

These acts of *bricolage* are subversive, as they constitute the main way in which subcultures reveal and communicate their 'secret' or forbidden identities (Hebdige, 1979). They signify 'Others' as friends, enemies or part of the establishment. In the same way that Surrealist or Dada artists composed their collages, photomontages and 'ready mades' to disrupt and reorganize meaning, football supporters set online these digitally manipulated images and symbols (whether using Viking iconography, Al Pacino movies, real *graffiti* or home-made pictures) to construct reputations and convey messages full of irony, fun, anger and desire.

In this sense, then, the online images we studied do not seem to constitute so-called postmodern *pastiche* – at least not in the way Frederic Jameson dismisses much postmodern culture as 'blank parody'. *Pastiche*, Jameson argues, 'is, like parody, the imitation of a peculiar mask, speech in a dead language; but it is a neutral practice of such mimicry, without any of parody's ulterior motives, amputated of the satiric impulse' (Jameson, 1984: 65). The images we collected are definitely not neutral, they are imbued with a language that is very much alive, and they leave plenty of room for parody and social critique.

Dangerous portraits

The primary goal of these sites is to portray supporters as tough and dangerous individuals, committed to their club and skilled in fighting. Here, emphasis is placed on 'positive' values such as courage, freedom, strength, racial purity, loyalty and masculinity. For example, in many Dutch websites, in order to gain respect, it is necessary to participate in virtual showdowns in which self-proclaimed violent football supporters use pictures to manufacture and promote 'tough' identities and gain reputations. By triggering reactions and discussions around these 'dangerous' images and receiving recognition for their 'bad' reputations, they *become* hooligans. Ironically, although these images give 'face' to the underground subculture, the real faces of the protagonists are almost always anonymized. This could be interpreted as a strategy to avoid the Dutch cyber police, but in fact, this process is primarily an aesthetic choice: the black bars in front of their eyes add credibility to their constructed appearances as football villains.[4]

Most pictures show groups of approximately ten to thirty men. The supporters in the images are typically adolescents, in their late teens or young adults. In the Dutch context, they pose mostly in so-called casual clothing, the established garb for European hooligans since the early 1980s. Other common artefacts depicted in these images are bottles, cans or glasses of beer, club flags (including those incorporating ethnic or geographic signifiers) and umbrellas and other 'weapons' used during real world confrontations.

One image, for example, depicts a group of supporters of Dutch football team *Go Ahead Eagles*. Supporters are pictured in casual attire, posing behind flags of the Moluccas, a former Dutch colony that actively resisted colonial repression; an association that adds a frisson of political resistance to the hooligan mix. This image also illustrates the process of digital manipulation that frequently takes place on these sites: here the accentuation of the flag colours and the addition of the club and city name in the background. Often such images are captured outside or near football stadia (pubs, parks or prominent landmarks). Especially valued are images of the group taken in the hostile city centres of rival clubs.

---

4 Despite the fact that far less policing of Argentinean hooligan websites takes place, hardcore supporters also frequently cover their faces.

Portraits of the last category function as pictorial evidence of the courage of a group to show up in the 'belly of the beast'. Another common compositional trait in these images is the way the group is prioritized over the individual. Men are closely grouped together, symbolizing the solidarity and cohesiveness of the hooligan unit. Group strength is frequently further embellished by taking photographs in small spaces such as stairwells, corridors or in small pubs. The violent potential of these groups is likewise embodied in masculine postures such as brandishing fists or raising arms, while others prefer to adopt a cooler, more menacing demeanour in an attempt to project control, dominance and intimidation.[5]

These symbolic portraits are carefully read and scrutinized by opposing supporters on Dutch websites. Consider, for example, this posting by an NAC Breda supporter commenting on an image posted by Roda JC hardcore supporters:

> Nice site Boys. I only wonder why you didn't accept our invitation [to fight], considering the image of your group' season 05/06 NAC-RJC'! I'm still disappointed, while seeing this tough photo of your group!
>
> (BredaCasuals076, www.045crew.com, accessed 28 November 2006)

Argentinean supporters also frequently upload photos of themselves, but whilst there are a number of compositional and iconographic similarities with the imagery employed by Dutch online hooligans (see the following section), typically images on these sites take a different form. In contrast with the well-composed group portraits found on Dutch sites, it is rare for Argentinean supporters to self-consciously 'pose' for the camera as an organized violent/dangerous group. Instead, groups of supporters typically play a secondary role to either a focal object (e.g. a flag, banner or graffiti piece) or a particular individual (often a professional footballer or celebrity). Indeed, uploaded Argentinean photos tend to be much simpler, even mundane affairs; depicting groups of relatives or friends (often, young men and women together) happily posing in buses, stadia or private dwellings. These usually low-quality photos are seldom retouched or photoshopped. Another common strand of images on Argentinean sites are those of fans in more 'natural' settings as part of the *hinchada* (crowd of supporters). Popular here are long lens shots of well-known leaders or members of the *barras bravas* (hardcore supporter groups). The differing compositional nature of the images posted on these sites clearly has much to do with the cultural and social differences between Argentina and the Netherlands, for example differing degrees of individualization or notions of privacy, or particular relations with material artefacts or with celebrity.

5 Jack Katz (1988: 91), of course, identified very similar mechanisms for transmitting a sense of superiority in the pictures he analyzed of self-styled 'bad ass' gang members.

Celebrating alcohol and drugs

The majority of studies on football supporter violence indicate the existence of a 'culture of intoxication' among supporters and stress how the practices and meanings around alcohol and drug use are a constitutive part of their masculine universe (e.g. Armstrong, 1998; Garriga Zucal, 2005; Spaaij, 2006; De Leeuw, 2007). A great deal of the analyzed photos and images reflect this, depicting beer and wine drinking, marihuana smoking and cocaine sniffing in an extremely positive and celebratory light.

A category of photos prevalent on Dutch sites, portray groups of fans drinking large quantities of beer, either in pubs, bars or private parties. These images usually show smiling or singing supporters who pose for the camera with full glasses and bottles, sometimes with piled crates of beer in the background. Argentinean sites, however, show more intimate photos where small groups of supporters share a (litre) bottle of beer or red wine in public spaces. In these images, drinking alcohol is shown as a collective practice of inclusion or even a traditional *rite de passage* for many young men.

The celebration of alcohol and drunkenness is also revealed in images of flags, banners, tattoos and graffiti posted on the websites. The supporters of Godoy Cruz from Mendoza (Argentina) proudly call themselves *bodegueros* (wine makers), while the supporters of Quilmes are known as *cerveceros* (beer brewers). The positive status of these names becomes evident by accusing rival supporters of drinking water and celebrating their own status as *borrachos* (drunken). The paradigmatic case is the name of the *barra brava* of River Plate: *Los Borrachos del Tablón* (The Drunken of the Tribune). Figure 11.1 shows a large banner with the name and the symbol of a five-litre bottle of red wine. The photoshopped title

Figure 11.1 The Aguante (Resistance) *of River Plate.*
Source: www.barra-bravas.com.ar

above, *The Aguante* (Resistance) *of River,* tells the viewer that the colourful, crowded atmosphere and the banner dimensions should be interpreted as an evidence of loyalty, resistance and fighting skills – the three central elements behind the Argentinean notion of *aguante* (Alabarces, 2003; Alabarces *et al.*, 2005).

Many of the images discussed in the preceding section also feature explicit references to the use of illegal drugs, particularly marihuana. In Dutch websites, some images present supporters holding joints or sometimes larger quantities of raw marihuana. Instead of stressing 'drug use', these images frame supporters as either drug dealers or as proud Dutch citizens showing a high quality 'national' product. Cocaine is not directly referred to in these Dutch websites, although it is mentioned as the official 'riot powder' of Dutch hardcore supporters and is depicted (see Figure 11.2) through references to American gangster movies.

Drug images in Argentinean websites include portrayals of supporters smoking joints and sniffing cocaine during the match, depictions of the marihuana leaf, caricatures of famous individuals or celebrities (such as Che Guevara or Maradona) portrayed as comic marihuana-smoking supporters (see Figure 11.4). Many images of flags in stadia contain texts referring to the positive effects of drug use, but usually the connection is made between the drug and the club: i.e. the club is just another drug, and drugs are obviously positive since they allow supporters to be 'crazy', 'mad', 'blind', 'out of mind' or 'ruined'. Promoting illegal drug use in such images and, in the case of Argentina, in hundreds of lyrics posted online, we see the creation of strong symbolic markers used to establish boundaries with 'outsiders', particularly 'normal' people and the police. The identification between drugs and violence is romanticized within the world of supporters and makes explicit the often implicit statement *'No one likes us, we don't care'* (Robson, 2000). This contrast in the way in which drugs are presented reveals the different status of drugs in Argentinean and Dutch societies. While Holland seems to have largely normalized drug use, particularly marihuana smoking, drugs in Argentina are more strongly associated with notions of resistance and transgression.

Outlaw heroes, horror icons and criminal gangs

A further common theme revealed by our research into online sites was the profusion of gangster and horror movie icons. We identified a mass of filmic villains employed as symbolic markers and mascots by numerous real or imagined football firms. Characters were drawn from films such as *A Clockwork Orange*, *Fight Club, The Godfather*, *Scarface* and *The Deer Hunter*, through to more straightforward horror movies like *Friday the Thirteenth*, *Child's Play*, *The Texas Chainsaw Massacre* and *Nightmare on Elmstreet*.[6] Such *bricolaged* images typically fall into one of three categories.

6 Although the parallel appearance of these two cinematic genres might look odd, there are well-established commonalities between these two movie variants (see e.g. Don Diego, 2007).

Figure 11.2 Tony Montana, Feyenoord style.
Source: http://members.home.nl/danus/index1.htm

First, and most straightforward are photoshopped pictures of well-known gangster or horror movie icons, such as Fig 11.2's depiction of Tony Montana, the self-made gangster crime lord from Brian De Palma's *Scarface*. Here the movie poster is combined with the logo of the Dutch football club Feyenoord and finished with the inscription *'Hoolicore 3: 12 Hardcore/Jump Tracks for You Cocaine Motherfuckers'*. This image is actually the cover of an underground hardcore music CD compilation distributed via the group's website. Other Dutch sites utilize digital art featuring images of Mafiosi, American street and prison gangs like the *Vatos Locos* from the movie *Blood In Blood Out*, femmes fatales like *The Bride*, from the Tarantino movie *Kill Bill* (see the chapter by Alexandra Campbell, this volume), hero-monsters like *The Hulk* or antiheroes like the ultraviolent Alex DeLarge from Kubrick's *A Clockwork Orange*.

A second group of online images feature more constitutive figures, including amalgamations of everything from aliens to ghosts, corpses to transformed animal bodies. The Devil is appropriated by the 'Reds' of the Argentinean club *Independiente*, while several Dutch and Argentinean supporters present themselves as gravediggers, undertakers (Chacarita Juniors), the angel of death or even terrorists like Osama Bin Laden. The enduring theme of these images is their fusion of humour and violence, as exemplified in Figure 11.4.

The third and perhaps most interesting category of online images associated with filmic and televisual criminal heroes is the increased use of supposedly 'real life' cultural artefacts created both by supporters themselves and by media outlets keen to tap into the subcultural world of football violence. Currently, there exists a growing market for hooligan-related material, including widely available pseudo-documentaries (such as *The Real Football Factories*, a popular UK TV series presented by Danny Dyer, the star of the cult hooligan movie *Football Factory*), (auto)biographical books by 'legendary' hooligans and unofficial homepages about violent English football firms with names such as *Villains*, *Owls Crime Squad*, *Hit Squad*, *Bison Riot Squad* or *Seaside Mafia*. All this material is heaven sent for Dutch football firms who have a long tradition of re-appropriating English hooligan iconography.[7] It is perhaps no surprise, then, that this type of material now frequently features on Dutch supporter websites. This last category of image illustrates how closely interwoven is the reality of crime and its increasingly mediated representation. Cultural criminology, of course, is well positioned to understand this process of cultural 'loops' and 'spirals', as Ferrell, Hayward and Young have pointed out:

> ... contemporary culture can be conceptualized as a series of *loops*, an ongoing process by which everyday life recreates itself in its own image. The saturation of social situations with representation and information suggests that the linear sequencing of meaning is now mostly lost, replaced by a doppelganger world where the ghosts of signification circle back to haunt, and revive, that which they signify (2008: 130).

Our analyses suggest that this is certainly the case with online hooligan websites. In the following examples of Feyenoord supporters as *Vatos Locos* and Argentinean supporters as *Pibes Chorros*, we see considerable evidence of this looping process further blurring the dissolving boundaries between criminal fiction and criminal reality.

Vatos Locos

Alongside the aforementioned group who sought to identify with Viking traditions, a second organized faction of Sport Club Feyenoord (SCF) supporters emerged during the early 1990s (the high point of football violence in the Netherlands) calling themselves *Vatos Locos*. Inspired by the film *Blood In Blood Out* (1993), *Vatos Locos* chose to copy values, symbols and rituals from the Mexican prison gang depicted in the film, including a violent initiation ritual and an official membership tattoo. However, in terms of the current chapter, what is of particular interest is the visual reproduction of the group's 'criminal gang insignia' on the Internet.

7 It is common practice for Dutch firms to copy the English 'casual' style of clothing. Similarly, there is an established tradition of Dutch hooligans arranging meetings and photo opportunities with well-known British hardcore supporters in a bid to enhance their own hooligan credibility.

Figure 11.3 Blurring subcultures – Feyenoord's '*Vatos Locos*' Casuals.
Permission to republish granted to Tom de Leeuw

Our analysis identified several Feyenoord supporter websites containing images of prison style tattoos (typically located on the right forearm) consisting of the name *Vatos Locos* or simply *VT*. Other images employed the same Gothic calligraphy (see Figure 11.3) found in graffiti pieces in US Latino *barrios* (see Katz, 1988: 92);[8] while others depicted supporters communicating their affiliation by making (or 'flashing') 'V' and 'L' signs with their fingers. In all these examples, we see how US gang iconography – with its longstanding association with resistance and aggression – has been incorporated into Dutch hooligan subculture. What is of interest here, of course, is how images and cultural symbols can travel across continents, gain new meanings and histories and ultimately become new subcultural artefacts. Although the reputation of the Feyenoord *Vatos Locos* originates from real experiences and achievements, it is the circulation, reproduction and consumption of these gang images of *Vatos Locos* that really appeals to younger violent football supporters.

'Pibes Chorros' and the war against the police

Many Argentinean football supporters present themselves as '*pibes chorros*' (young thieves), a particular type of young offender who has been socially

8 Interestingly, this same typescript is frequently found on extreme right-wing and white-power movement websites.

constructed as 'extremely dangerous' - the toxic product of the systematic social exclusion of large parts of the Argentinian population during the 1990s. Neither local 'gangs' nor professional criminals, the '*pibes chorros*' are youngsters (very often minors) who have suffered extreme levels of marginalization (either living in slums or on the streets); are involved in violent muggings or armed robberies; use illegal drugs and alcohol; and who conduct their criminal activities in a spontaneous, unplanned fashion (Miguez, 2004). Some of these '*pibes chorros*' become local heroes because of the way they have resisted, survived or shown *aguante* to cope with everyday violence.

Numerous images celebrate and imitate the culture of intoxication of these marginalized youngsters. Likewise, their transgressive relationship to state authorities and the social order in general is also aggrandized in banners and murals. Figure 11.4, for example, shows part of a graffiti piece painted by supporters of Nueva Chicago, a small club with a well-known group of hardcore supporters. In this image, a Nueva Chicago supporter is portrayed smoking a joint with a skull full of marihuana; in one hand he has a thief bag and in the other a smoking gun. Such deviant rebels have become role models for hardcore supporters in Argentina, where the levels of violence in and outside football are high.

What is interesting here is the way in which large contingents of Argentinean hardcore supporters, regardless of their social background, now identify with this imagery and portray themselves as dangerous *pibes chorros*; as outlaw groups fighting against and resisting police repression. This identification of even middle-class supporters with underclass young violent thieves in photos, videos

Figure 11.4 Nueva Chicago graffiti piece.
Source: www.barra-bravas.com.ar

and all sorts of drawings clearly reflects the deep dissatisfaction with and distrust in state institutions in Argentina. Although we came across comparable Dutch hostility towards the police in online images that included taglines such as 'All Cops Are Bastards' (ACAB) and 'Fuck the Police' (FTP), this Argentinean visual violence has to be taken more seriously. For example, rather than just othering the police, numerous sites include videos of actual battles against the police, pictures of policemen running for their lives or photographs showing supporters proudly holding police clothes, caps or weapons stolen as 'trophies' during police-supporter clashes. What started out as just another hooligan symbol has now become a quasi-political cause, with many Argentinean football supporters finding in these 'real' *pibes chorros* a social model for autonomy, resistance and courage in the struggle against the incumbent political classes.

Methodological reflections

Next to more traditional qualitative research methods such as interviews or participant observation, the analysis of the meanings and effects of Internet images through the deployment of visual and virtual ethnographic strategies (Hine, 2000, 2005; Pink, 2007) can certainly add value to the study of the way in which football supporters construct, recreate and experience violent and masculine identities. Where traditional literature on football violence focuses on the aetiology of 'misbehaviour' and risk, image-based research provides more opportunities for understanding the complexity of football fandom in a late modern society in which consumption and media play a central role. Through the analysis of images, we found more insights into the subconscious meanings of violence as well as unearthing a specific aesthetics of violence. The Internet provided a rich environment for analysing different dimensions of this aesthetics, detail that would not be detected by only using more traditional (textual and face-to-face) qualitative methods of research.

Images often provide the necessary 'contextual' information to understand violent play and violent talk which is often lacking during interviews with football supporters. The wide range of images, texts, sounds or movie fragments, all social constructions in an endless but rather organized virtual space, provide conflicting angles and points of views on the social phenomena studied. They offer alternative 'layers' of meanings, and cause effects on those who produce and consume the images. In this sense, far from being mere 'data' to be gathered and interpreted, these virtual images have the power to create or trigger a wide range of social actions, from individual self-presentation and aesthetical expression to collective *othering* or even political action.

It should be stressed, however, that we approached football images and their unique grammar not merely as isolated social constructs to be analyzed 'on their own' (for example, by content analysis or semiotic interpretation), but we tried to make sense of them by looking at them as part of wider social interactions and power relations (place in the website, author(s), social reactions to the image, reception, circulation), and as *additional material* to be added to data from lived experience of football supporters, gathered by open interviews, face-to-face and virtual ethnography and the analysis of 'hooliporn'. In that sense, image analysis provides a fruitful way of building multidimensional research layers.

However, how exactly did we set about analyzing the images? We first spent some time scrutinizing websites and selecting images. Although collected and stored later in computer files, we always approached and analyzed the images in their context. In fact, we focused on three different aspects: content, form and context (this last one formed again by three dimensions: website, social interactions around the image and real-world events and performances). By doing this, we attempted to bring some structure into the analysis of images to overcome arbitrariness and superficial readings (Banks, 2007; Valverde, 2006; Pink, 2007). However, we did not treat those three levels separately – far from it. Instead, it should be recognized that they are closely intertwined and thus best approached together. Our goal was to avoid first impressions solely based on looking at the contents of the images.

In this way, we regard our approach as a combination of narrative and reflexive strategies in visual research. On the one hand, we approached images as data that can be used to construct visual stories that become 'the building blocks of an argument' (Stanczak, 2007). These images produced by football supporters are part of their narratives and can basically be researched by ethnographic methods. The challenge here is to combine face-to-face, virtual and visual ethnography to produce innovative and complex descriptions. On the other hand, it is imperative to follow a reflexive epistemology of visual research, which maintains that the meaning of images basically resides in the way actors (in our case producers and consumers of these football images) interpret those images, rather than in some inherent property of the images themselves (Stanczak, 2007: 11). We tried to do that by analysing context, reactions and consumption patterns of these images. Future research of this type, however, can go deeper still, using, for example, online photo elicitation techniques in which online supporters can be interviewed about particular images. In sum, our knowledge and understanding about crime can certainly expand if we are able to develop new and tailor-made methodologies to study images, and creatively combine them with existing traditional methods of data gathering.

Conclusion

For different reasons, late modern society has evolved towards a visual culture in which images communicate meanings and construct realities. Although the image has different meanings and purposes for different people involved in this process, together they directly or indirectly negotiate the meaning and boundaries of crime and crime control (Brown, 2006: 239; Young, 1996). Our interest in images of football violence on the Internet is therefore not meant as a safe alternative to an 'ethnography at the edge' (Ferrell, 1998). It is rather a step into one of the most important arenas for framing football violence, where reality and fiction intermingle via the exchange of specific imagery in and around the football hooligan subculture.

Before the era of the Internet, this subculture was less accessible in Western, industrialized societies. Despite media coverage and sporadic personal experiences with football violence in urban centres or stadia, outsiders had no insight into the making and remaking of transgressive practices and meanings. Personal images of fights, gatherings, nightlife experiences or 'away days' trips, only ever ended up in private photo-books and home videos of hardcore supporters. However, by the mid 1990s, these images had begun to circulate on the Internet.

This chapter has tried to analyse some of the meanings attached to these online images. We have understood them both as powerful devices for identity construction and reputation management, as well as bewildering examples of *bricolage* in which football supporters appropriate and resignify icons, photos, traditions or (deviant) social practices, subverting original or hegemonic meanings.

We claim that these images communicate desired and cultivated characteristics such as rivalry, fun, bravery, resistance, autonomy, solidarity, anger or passion by resorting to particular symbols like Vikings, monsters, gangsters, gangs, drug addicts, drunks and *pibes chorros*.

As a first, explorative attempt to analyse these images, we have remained descriptive and cautious about the comparison between Dutch and Argentinean supporters and websites. Despite several interesting commonalities around the use of deviant icons, real underdogs or fictional heroes by all supporters, we believe that more divergent patterns will also emerge – especially in two specific fields that clearly deserve further theoretical elaboration in any future studies of online football supporters.

The first area of interest is masculinity – a theme explored in more detail in our broader earlier research on virtual and real-life violence among football supporters (see Zaitch and De Leeuw, 2006; De Leeuw, 2007). With online images frequently making implicit and explicit references to 'hegemonic masculinities', homosexuality and the use of sexual imagery, such images can reveal much of interest about contested late modern masculinities and male identities in crisis in Argentina, the Netherlands and elsewhere (Faludi, 1999; Jefferson, 2002).

A second area ripe for further exploration is the particular relationship that exists between the 'virtual' and 'real' performances of football supporters – that is, between the fun, violence and consumption patterns that take place in and around the stadium and on the streets, and the various ways in which these activities are 'performed' online. In other words, to what extent do online images function to mimic or displace (or neither) offline social practices and identities. Moreover, does the relationship between offline and online experiences differ depending on the cultural context – especially in countries (like The Netherlands and Argentina) where there are clear differences in both the extent and effects of real football violence and the political and economic climate? These and other related questions concerning online imagery and its relationship to offline social behaviour represent interesting future lines of research for cultural criminology.

References

Alabarces, P. (ed.) (2003) *Futbologías. Fútbol, identidad y violencia en América Latina,* Buenos Aires: CLACSO.

Alabarces, P., Conde, M., Dodaro, C., Fernández, F., Ferreiro, J.P., Galvani, M., Zucal, J.G., Moreira, M.V., Palma, J. and Salerno, D. (2005) *Hinchadas.* Buenos Aires: Prometeo Libros.

Armstrong, G. (1998) *Football Hooligans. Knowing the Score,* New York: Berg.

Banks, M. (2007) *Using Visual Data in Qualitative Research*, London: Sage.

Brown, M. (2006) 'The Aesthetics of Crime', in Arrigo, B. and Williams, C. (eds) *Philosophy, Crime and Criminology*, Chicago: University of Illinois Press.

Carney, P. (2004) *The Punitive Gaze.* Unpublished doctoral thesis, London: Middlesex University.

Don Diego, C. (2007) 'Hits, Whacks, and Smokes. The Celluloid Gangster as Horror Icon'. in Silver, A. and Ursini, J. (eds) *Gangster Film Reader*, New Jersey: Limelight Editions.

Emler, N. and Reicher, S. (1995) *Adolescence and Delinquency: The Collective Management of Reputation,* Cambridge, MA: Blackwell Publishers.

Fafinski, S. (2007) 'In the Back of the Net: Football Hooliganism and the Internet', in Jewkes, Y. (ed.) (2007) *Crime Online*, Devon: Willan Publishing.

Faludi, S. (1999) *Stiffed: The Betrayal of the Modern Man,* London: Chatto & Windus.

Ferrell, J. (1998) 'Criminological Verstehen: Inside the Immediacy of Crime', in Ferrell, J. and Hamm, M. (eds) *Ethnography at the Edge. Crime, Deviance and Field Research*, Boston: Northeastern University Press.

Ferrell, J., Hayward, K. and Young, J. (2008) *Cultural Criminology: An Invitation,* London: Sage.

Garriga Zucal, J. (2005) 'Pibitos Chorros, fumancheros y con aguante. El delito, las drogas y la violencia como mecanismos constructores de identidad en una hinchada de fútbol', in Alabarces, P. *et al.* (eds) *Hinchadas,* Buenos Aires: Prometeo Libros.

Giulianotti, R. (2001) 'A Different Kind of Carnival', in Perryman, M. (ed.) *Hooligan Wars: Causes and Effects of Football Violence*, Edinburgh: Mainstream.

Goffman, E. (1959) *The Presentation of Self in Everyday Life,* New York: Anchor Books.

Greer, C., Ferrell, J. and Jewkes, Y. (2007) 'It's the Image that Matters: Style, Substance and Critical Scholarship', *Crime, Media, Culture,* 3(1): 5–10.

Hall, S. (1978) 'The Treatment of Football Hooliganism in the Press', in Ingham, R. (ed.) *Football Hooliganism: The Wider Context*, London: Inter-Action Imprint.

Hebdige, D. (1979) *Subcultures: The Meaning of Style*, London: Methuen & Co. Ltd.

Hine, C. (2000) *Virtual Ethnography*, London: Sage.

Hine, C. (ed.) (2005) *Virtual Methods. Issues in Social Research on the Internet,* Oxford: Berg.

Jameson, F. (1984) 'Postmodernism or the Cultural Logic of Late Capitalism', *New Left Review,* 146: 53–92.

Jefferson, T. (2002) 'Subordinating Hegemonic Masculinity', *Theoretical Criminology,* 6(1): 63–88.

Katz, J. (1988) *Seductions of Crime. Moral and Sensual Attractions of Doing Evil,* New York: BasicBooks.

Leeuw, T. de (2007) *Tussen Hobby en Haat. Identiteit en geweld tussen fanatieke voetbal-supporters in de consumptiemaatschappij*. Unpublished master thesis, Rotterdam: Erasmus University Rotterdam.

Miguez, D. (2004) *Los Pibes Chorros. Estigma y Marginación,* Buenos Aires: Capital Intelectual.

Pink, S. (2007) *Doing Visual Ethnography*, London: Sage.

Poulton, E. (2005) 'English Media Representation of Football-Related Disorder: Brutal, Short-hand and Simplifying', *Sport in Society,* 8(1): 27–47

Poulton, E. (2007) 'Fantasy Football Hooliganism', in Popular Media, *Media, Culture & Society,* 29: 151–64.

Prosser, J. (2003) *Image-based Research. A Sourcebook for Qualitative Researchers*, London: Routledge Falmer.

Robson, G. (2000) *'No One Likes Us, We Don't Care'. The Myth and Reality of Millwall Fandom*, Oxford: Berg.

Salerno, D. (2005) 'Apología, Estigma y Represión. Los Hinchas Televisados de Fútbol', in Alabarces, P. *et al.* (eds) *Hinchadas,* Buenos Aires: Prometeo Libros.

Sontag, S. (1979) *On Photography*, London: Penguin Books.

Spaaij, R. (2006) *Understanding Football Hooliganism. A Comparison of Six Western European Football Clubs*, Amsterdam: Amsterdam University Press.

Stanczak, G. (2007) 'Introduction: Images, Methodologies, and Generating Social Knowledge', in Stanczak, G. (ed.) *Visual Research Methods. Image, Society and Representation,* London: Sage.

Valverde, M. (2006) *Law and Order. Images, Meanings, Myths*, Oxon: Routledge Cavendish.

Young, A. (1996) *Imagining Crime*, London: Sage.

Young, A. (2005) *Judging the Image. Art, Value, Law,* London: Routledge.

Young, A. (2007) 'Images in the Aftermath of Trauma: Responding to September 11', *Crime, Media, Culture,* 3(1): 30–48.

Zaitch, D. and De Leeuw, T. (2006) '*Virtual Combats. Othering, fun and violence of Argentinean and Dutch supporters on the Internet'*. Paper unpublished presented at the second International Conference on Cultural Criminology, 12–13 May 2006, London.

Chapter 12

A reflected gaze of humanity

Cultural criminology and images of genocide

Wayne Morrison

> The holy Synod enjoins … that the images of Christ … are to be had and retained particularly in temples, and that due honour and veneration are to be given them; not that any divinity, or virtue, is believed to be in them, on account of which they are to be worshipped; or that anything is to be asked of them; or, that trust is to be reposed in images … but because the honour which is shown them is referred to the prototypes which those images represent… And the bishops shall carefully teach this, that, by means of the histories of the mysteries of our Redemption, portrayed by paintings or other representations, the people is instructed, and confirmed in (the habit of) remembering, and continually revolving in mind the articles of faith; as also that great profit is derived from all sacred images, not only because the people are thereby admonished of the benefits and gifts bestowed upon them by Christ, but also because the miracles which God has performed by means of the saints, and their salutary examples, are set before the eyes of the faithful; that so they may give God thanks for those things; may order their own lives and manners in imitation of the saints … But if any one shall teach, or entertain sentiments, contrary to these decrees; let him be anathema.
>
> (extracts 25th Session, Council of Trent, 1547)

> Cultural criminology uses the 'evidence' of everyday existence, wherever it is found and in whatever form it can be found; the debris of everyday life is its 'data'.
>
> (Presdee, 2000: 15)

Introduction

Cultural criminology and a hope for truth in images of atrocities

For the authors of *Cultural Criminology: An Invitation,* orthodox criminology (perhaps better labelled 'state-sponsored criminology') is devoid of passion and unable to grasp the reality of the human condition. Obsessed with quantitative methodology, it offers an illusionary and inconsequential 'aesthetics of authority',

Figure 12.1 Mother leading child through one of the rooms of the National War of Liberation Museum, Dhaka, Bangladesh, 2004. Photo: Wayne Morrison.

a 'triumph of the bureaucrat and the survey statistician' (Ferrell, Hayward and Young, 2008: 165). In a late modern world of radical imbalances in power, opportunity and wealth, 'objective' or 'scientific' criminology lacks the ability to visualize and put into frame the complexity of human reality, offering instead 'symbolic performances of scientific objectivity'; social harm becomes a packaged commodity. To anyone conscious of the hopes and aspirations of the then intellectual outlaws of the seventeenth and eighteenth century who criticized institutional structures of authority and are now celebrated as the 'father figures' of the enlightenment and modernity, this is a tragic tale.

The enlightenment is most usually represented as the drawing away of veil from human sight, of the ushering in of the ability to see accurately, to encounter reality free from the arbitrary interpretations of authority. Reason, not strictures of institutional power, was to be humanity's authority and emancipation was to follow. Modernity was the social, political, economic and cultural complex that was thereby enabled: a time of great change, of increased complexity and fluidity in modes of social life, of technological advancement, of concern for 'health', of enormous increases in population and medical treatments, of the freeing of human desire and the engagement of individuals and groups in circles of consumption. It saw also an increase in human ability, and (perhaps) willingness, to knowingly and deliberately rape, maim and kill other humans as directed by the state or associated bodies or with the acquiescence of 'civilized' states. A perplexing, often obscured, issue is what is the connection between modern, organized social life and mass atrocity? Is mass atrocity a minor fault, a fact that occurs when particular and historically specific groups have gone 'evil' as a result of some historically specific and contextually limited set of determining factors? On the other hand, is there some fundamental relationship between organized, civilized, modernity and atrocity? Is atrocity – and genocide – somehow modernity's dark twin? Perhaps not strangely, but quite understandably, this has not been an issue within the criminological imagination. A child of modernity, criminology was born in the contingent union of a faith in science and the Westphalia political-military compromise of the division of the recognized globe into a nation state system.

Born out of the horrors of intra-European religious wars, Westphalia doctrine (established subsequent to the Treaty of Westphalia, a name given to two treaties signed in1648) recognized sovereignty as the central organizing force of political life and took the nation state as a territorial state. It made securing conditions of social life for its subjects/citizens the reason for the state's existence. War was to be managed by matters of international agreement (i.e. between sovereign states), with noninterference in the affairs of another sovereign state a key principle. Affairs internal to the nation state were the matter of that nation's government, of policing. In time, it became accepted that legitimate government should be rational: i.e. its personnel should be officers performing their roles as defined by the appropriate legal norms and in accordance with the principles of good management.

Conventional criminology likewise offered an illusion of scientific led policing. Criminology was thus an applied science, an aid to the state in reducing (even solving?) the problem of crime. It was also meant to be independent, to be a multidisciplinary set of methods and theories that could be tested and reproduced or discarded on the basis of scientific criteria. Yet, criminology's ability to offer a truthful account of crime and criminality was and remains compromised by its ontological foundation: the ability of the nation state to define what 'crime' is. If states had the ultimate right to 'state' (i.e. to pass legislation that defined the nature of legal social relations) and thus the legitimate force to process, incapacitate and often kill those deemed 'criminal', then criminology's scientific endeavour was contaminated (for a full length account see Morrison, 2006).

Cultural criminology, rightly, locates mainstream criminology in terms of a cultural production, a matter of construction in which 'the method is the message'. As a result, we are confronted with state-sponsored representations of the crime problem, reinforced by 'symbolic performances of scientific objectivity' (Ferrell, Hayward and Young, 2008: 168). Scientific method – ideally – is the aspiration to authentically see, to enlighten, to attain and present data in such a way that others can understand the process of representation, trust the communicator and, perhaps, be inspired to join the enterprise. One of the founding 'fathers' of modern criminology, the Italian doctor Cesare Lombroso (1835–1909) described his moment of enlightenment, when having begun to study 'criminals in the Italian prisons', he was carrying out a postmortem on the famous brigand Vilella.

He found a strange 'depression' located 'as in inferior animals, especially rodents'. The effect was dramatic: 'At the sight of that skull, I seemed to see all of a sudden, lighted up as a vast plain under a flaming sky, the problem of the nature of the criminal – an atavistic being who reproduces in his person the ferocious instincts of primitive humanity and the inferior animals' (Lombroso-Ferrero, 1911: xi–xx). Lombroso preserved that skull in a glass presentation case on his study desk where it still stands in a small museum dedicated to ambiguous legacies of his scientific fundamentalism (see Morrison, 2004a). Mainstream criminology now regards that occasion as a false start and relegates the study of skulls to anthropology or forensic investigations. Yet, today there exist a number of other museums that still display skulls. In Figure 12.1, a mother leads her small child through a room with many skulls, human bones and photographs of human beings, flesh torn, cut and tied up.

Where is this place? This mother and child are walking through one room of a museum of conscience, a counter factual to conventional criminology dedicated to presenting atrocities committed in the name of the state, namely the events of 1971 in East Pakistan, now Bangladesh. At that time, under the guise of dealing with matters of internal affairs (and so, following Westphalia doctrine, not a matter of concern for other states), the West Pakistan military authorities attempted through violent military action to suppress political change and wipe out a sociopolitical elite. The subsequent government of that territory (now independent Bangladesh) claim that the resulting 'civil war' or 'war of liberation' (the terminology depends on whether you take a West Pakistan or a Bangladeshi perspective) cost up to 3 million lives in attempted genocide. There are many other such presentations of skulls, bones and human suffering in the museums of Rwanda or of the Killings Fields of Cambodia, to name but two. Such places recall a range of genocidal events in which it is estimated that, between 1890 and 2000, 170–200 million people lost their lives – a figure that far exceeds the total number of officially recorded homicides during the twentieth century, but outwit the discourse of criminology. Mainstream criminology, of course, has always been a partial 'world of facts'.

In one of the best-known attempts to frame a 'general theory of crime' capable of overcoming the central ontological problem and provide an explanation for 'all crime at all times' (Gottfredson and Hirschi, 1990), generality was 'achieved' by being faithful to the observed facts of criminal commission, those of mainstream western official criminology. In part, this was also because the atrocities of modernity have mostly gone unpunished. Putting it bluntly, criminology lacked an institutional record of trial and punishment, and therefore did not have a state sponsored data set to work with. The museum is not state sponsored; it is intended as a place where crime is actively 'framed' for an audience whose emotional response, it is hoped, will call justice into play.

What then can replace the state-sponsored categories of mainstream criminology? Among other things, cultural criminology calls for a 'visual criminology', one where a more immediate link is made between social reality and the viewer.

Could visual criminology perhaps provide an alternative way forward? It certainly poses some interesting questions. Could an analysis of images of atrocity put the 'visual human' into the concept of human rights, helping to produce a moral obligation to act, to counter abuse and social harm? Could the type of images featured in this chapter and in museums around the world be used in a liberal aesthetics as a call to action – a visual reminder for us to say 'never again'?

Such questions are unanswerable here, but maybe we can at least start the analysis. However, before we turn to the images themselves, let us pause briefly to consider the existing debates about how we are to read images of atrocity.

In one camp we may see a modernist holding to the image as a new form of capturing reality, of truth telling; in this the positions of the photographer, the subject, the photograph and the viewer have objectivity. Put bluntly, say as by Virginia Woolf, images of atrocities are statements of brutal 'fact', and the facts are simply 'evil' (1938: 21, 260). From this perspective, the photograph is a mute, unbiased witness of reality (Levinson, 1997).

For another camp, exemplified by Susan Sontag (1977), the photograph provides a new medium requiring as much interpretative skills as painting. Sontag warns of putting too much faith in the images as a power for good: 'Images transfix. Images anesthetize'; they can, according to Sontag, 'also corrupt' conscience (1977: 20). In the more extreme versions of postmodern cultural analysis, the photograph even comes to *replace* reality. For example, for Jean Baudrillard (2001: 147) 'reality itself founders' due to an 'endless reduplication of the real'. Consequently, to view the image is to enter a 'relationship of equivalence, of indifference'. From such a position, we witness only the 'extinction of the original' – we are doomed to inactivity and boredom. Faced with such proliferation of the image do we become simply voyeurs, tourists in a mélange of images and texts? What are we to make, for example, of a world where images of mass slaughter in Rwanda or Cambodia are displayed in artistically designed coffee table publications or uploaded onto *YouTube*? In her later work on mass atrocities (such as in the conflict in the former Yugoslavia), Sontag (2003) modified her position and argued that images of atrocities are capable of building bridges between groups. Images, she claimed, can deliver a 'truth' of war, of violence, of suffering in ways that can confront various audiences (including the perpetrators). We may be warned, however, that when putting images into focus, we must remain conscious of their construction.

Focus

Four images

In this section, four images from across the centuries form the focal point. In reading them, we again need to pose a series of questions, including most presciently what actually is being witnessed, and what politics are associated with looking and reading images of atrocity?

Figure 12.2 *Source:* Bartoleme de Las Casas, *Short Account of the Devastation of the Indies.* (Manuscript, 1542, published in the vernacular Spanish 1551. Translation used Griffin, 1992) Image 2 of 18 on page 10 first appearing in a 1598 Latin edition, Frankfurt. Engravings by Theodore De Bry (this image was said to be based on an earlier painting).

Figure 12.2 is one of 18 copper engravings added in a later edition of a short book written in the mid sixteenth century. This work was 'an attempt to press upon the reader the immediacy of the American experience, the importance of 'being there', and of being there with innocent intentions' (Pagden, Introduction in Griffin, 1992). The text alongside the image reads as follows:

> … the island of Hisponiola [current day Haiti and Dominican Republic] was the first to witness the arrival of the Europeans and the first to suffer the wholesale slaughter of its people and the devastation and depopulation of the land…. They forced their way into native settlements, slaughtering everyone they found there, including small children, old men, pregnant women, and even women who had just given birth. They hacked them to pieces, slicing open their bellies with their swords as they were so many sheep herded into a pen…. They slaughtered everyone and everybody in their path, on occasion running through a mother and her baby with a single thrust of their swords. They spared no one, erecting especially wide gibbets on which they could

> string their victims up with their feet off the ground and then burn them alive thirteen at a time, in honour of our Saviour and the twelve Apostles, or tie dry straw to their bodies and set fire to it.... It once happened that I myself witnessed their grilling of four or five local leaders in this fashion... when the poor creatures' howls came between the Spanish commander and his sleep. He gave orders that the prisoners were to be throttled, but the man in charge of the operation detail, who was more bloodthirsty than the average common hangman (I know his identity and even met some relatives of his in Seville), who was loath to cut short his private entertainment by throttling and so he personally went around ramming wooden bungs into their mouths to stop them making such a racket and deliberately stoked the fires so that they would take just as long to die as he himself chose.
>
> (Bartoleme de Las Casas, 1992 [1542]: 10)

The account and the image are deliberately shocking. Understanding their creation and presentation highlights certain foundational issues in the production and critical appreciation of images of atrocity. Our context is the Spanish conquest of the Americas in the fifteenth century which brought shipments of gold and other forms of wealth back to Catholic Spain, at that time, the great superpower of Europe. We also see the emergence of a commensurate counter struggle against these early genocidal atrocities and the first flowering of basic arguments in favour of equal rights for all humanity. Indeed, some now look back on this period as the active birth of the modern campaign for human rights. However, this movement to bear witness to the suffering of fellow humans was fundamentally handicapped.

Firstly, the sociopolitical reality: anyone who participated in the Spanish conquests had a stake in its continuation. The survivors of the massacres were either sold as slaves or given to local Spanish officials as their entitlements. Likewise, the depopulation of the land freed up space for settler colonization (the only weakness in this system being the need for continual labour for the mines and fields, a need that ultimately would require Black Africans to be brought in as slaves). All, including priests, thus had an economic stake in the system. Secondly, there were great ideological, philosophical and doctrinally based arguments that held that the natives of those lands were heathen and inferior to the Christian Spaniards and therefore naturally occupied a lower position in the hierarchy of creation. Some Christian scholars, however, disagreed. Thus emerged a conflict between, on the one hand, the social reality of economic interests and the desire to use discovery for wealth creation, the expansion of national interests and the acquisition of state wealth (primarily required to fund expensive wars in Europe and other overseas interests); and on the other hand, the theological and philosophical recognition of all humanity as worthy of equal respect. An attempt to bridge such contradictions and create a humane doctrine of exploration, encounter and legal protection of differing ethnic groups was embodied in the person of Bartolomé de Las Casas.

If at first a knowing participant in the exploitation of the indigenous people, Las Casas would later renounce such practices, freeing his Indian labour (slaves) and challenging the atrocities he witnessed.[1] He entered the Dominican Order and created a large body of treatises, memorials and testimonies that set in motion a political challenge to the Spanish conquests. Ultimately, he would be appointed the official 'Protector of the Indians' by the crown. Las Casas' arguments against the *encomienda*[2] system (especially his accounts of the cruelty and neo-feudalism of the *conquistadores* in his *History of the Indies*) resulted in the promulgation of the New Laws of 1542 which decreed that no more Indians should be enslaved, and that Spanish officials should no longer depend upon their *encomiendas*. Needless to say, the New Laws were never implemented or enforced as envisaged.

What could Las Casas do? As an intellectual, he wrote complex justifications for treating the Indians with dignity and respect; as an activist known personally in Royal circles he wrote directly to the King informing him of the terror that was happening in the name of the Crown.[3] While these personal appeals resulted in promises from the King to protect the Indians, promises were not enough – Spain's wealth was now inextricably linked to this highly developed system of exploitation. Las Casas's next step was to try to reach the ordinary folk of Spain by turning his manuscript into a popular text – *The Short Account* (without images). He hoped that clearly written evidence of the atrocities would sway public opinion – but once again, he was misguided.

His actions, however, did mark him out as a controversial historical figure. Las Casas is frequently labelled as the creator of the 'black legend' – a narrative used in Protestant Europe to portray the Catholic Spanish as uniquely cruel, vicious and greedy. Here again, though, history has been rewritten. It was not Las Casas's original documents that were appropriated by the Protestants, but later translations by De Bry, a publisher and engraver who produced a series of accounts of the grand voyages of exploration and conflict – only this time the texts were embellished by De Bry's detailed and imaginative copper engravings.

1 Las Casas had first come to the Indies from Spain in 1502, at age 18. After returning to Spain four years later to continue his studies, he was ordained to the priesthood. He then spent two years after his ordination studying canon law. In 1509, he again sailed to the New World, where he served as a chaplain on the Spanish conquest of Cuba and took up residence on Hispaniola. Early in his stay, it is recorded that he participated in the exploitation of the Indians through the system of 'encomienda'.

2 The *encomienda* was a system by which Spanish colonists were given tracts of land and the rights to the forced labour of the native people in return for a promise to instruct them in the ways of the Catholic faith.

3 In writing Las Casas was careful to first grant the King the Divine right to rule but added the caveat that if the right to rule is a gift from God then when the commonwealth suffers from defects or evils the explanation must be that the ruler is unaware of it and will right matters once he is made aware of the reality.

The Inquisition had forced De Bry, a Protestant, to flee his native Spanish-controlled Flanders and set up operations as an illustrator in Frankfurt. After a visit to England in the 1560s, De Bry and his sons planned an ambitious project called *Grand Voyages to America*, a publishing enterprise that reissued previously circulated volumes filled with pictorial accounts of New World exploration. Over thirty volumes were published by De Bry and his sons. Influenced by the Oxford cosmographer Richard Hakluyt, a strong proponent of English colonization of the Americas, De Bry used his Grand Voyages to popularize accounts of French, English and German explorers, generating publicity throughout Europe for a Protestant colonizing project that might potentially compete with that of Catholic Spain and Portugal. The Spanish were depicted as inherently cruel; the Indians as weak almost passive victims. The 18 images included in *The Short History* were of renderings of burnings, flayings, dismemberments, 'savaging' with dogs and other assorted tortures, all fantastically illustrated to provide the largely illiterate audience with clear evidence of Spanish brutality.[4] These accounts of Spanish colonial atrocities generated enough anti-Spanish sentiment throughout Europe (and even within Spain itself) to destabilize Spanish power in the New World (Gibson, 1971); but while impacting upon Spain they did little to stop the destruction of native populations.

Many contemporary intellectuals return to Las Casas for inspiration in a current situation which bears similarities. Echoing La Casas's entreaties to the King of Spain, today, in courts around the world, a marginalized few continue to lobby the power elites (such as the United Nations Security Council) – and just like La Casas, they are greeted with fine words and promises while all the time the atrocities continue. Elsewhere, others engage in popular appeals and significant numbers of the public read impassioned editorials, watch concerts, express their support, but ultimately do little to change the attitude of the powerful. Again, a contrast is drawn between a 'civilized world' that supposedly would not engage in atrocities, and an evil 'other' who does. Indeed, anyone who attempts to link the civilized West to such atrocities (or portray them as causal agents in the actions of the 'other') is seen as disloyal, almost to the point of treason.

Images were added to Las Casas's work, primarily in order to manipulate his message. Was such manipulation simply an outcome of the production techniques of the premechanized age – the painting, the woodcut, the copper etching? Surely, with the emergence of 'modern' images, taken by cameras, such blatant image manipulation is an artefact of history? Susan Sontag (1977), for example, tells us that the photograph is 'not only an image (as a painting is an image), and interpretation of the real, it is also a trace, something directly stencilled off the real, like a footprint or a death mask'. Maybe – but then again, maybe not? Consider Figure 12.3; it is a modern image and thus comes with all the (visual)

4 See Conley (1992) for an in depth interpretation of the images and a detailed analysis of De Bry's publishing strategy.

Figure 12.3 Boy looking at cut up natural rubber vine, rubber extract dripping into pail.
Source: Alice Harris collection Anti-Slavery International, London.

authority afforded by the photograph. Yet, while four centuries have passed, the fate of Las Casas should not be forgotten.

Analysing Figure 12.3, it is almost impossible to read this photograph as an atrocity image, but when contextualized and put into a human rights narrative, it becomes a telling image of the genocidal practices at the heart of King Leopold II of Belgian's personal dominion over the area of land in Africa now known as the Democratic Republic of the Congo (a piece of land larger than Western Europe). During Leopold II's dominion over the region between 1885 and 1908, at least 8 million people lost their lives in exploitative processes. The Congo Free State was given to Leopold by the Treaty of Berlin that carved up Africa among the European Powers in 1884. Leopold waged a media campaign to give out a message of a civilizing mission to open up land for free trade on behalf of global development. Only a few, such as the author Joseph Conrad who played a small part on the fringes of the enterprise as a boat captain on the river Congo came to see the reality. Conrad (1899) gave his account as the novel *The Heart of Darkness* with the memorable line that 'out there, there were no external checks'. No outside body could intervene, no one knew. The reality was a neoslave system of forced labour, of exploitation of the natives to produce for western consumption first ivory and then the rubber that grew wild.

Just as Las Casas had sought to publicly expose the *encomienda,* a committed group of missionaries and campaigners tried to challenge the iniquities of Leopold's regime. Alice Harris and E.D. Morel (who had been a clerk and realized that sending guns and ammunition and cheap trading goods and receiving back ivory and rubber did not add up to 'free trade'), for example, used a series of images to break the hegemony of the official story (see Hoschschild, 1998).

In Mark Twain's *King Leopold's Soliloquy* (1905), an imaginary monologue conducted by Leopold and illustrated with photographs from the Harris collection, Leopold states that the Kodak camera was the only witness he was not able to bribe. Yet, this supposed realism for photography on the side of human rights must be situated, for there was a range of media that supported the official narrative. The popular magazine *Le Congo Illustre: Voyages et Traveaux des Belges dans l'Etat Independent du Congo* (*Congo Illustrated: Travels and Works of Belgians in the Congo Free State*), published between 1892–5, laid out many of the images that would establish the official pictorial framework of representation of the Congo project.[5]

Published in 1904 as a series of Annex to the Annals of the Museum of the Congo under the title *L'Etat Independent du Congo: Document sur le pays et ses habitants,* the series included some 1,500 photographs. The preliminary notes set out the aim as 'bringing reality to the people'. Here the Kodak is used as the instrument of reassurance. There is no explanation of the complex processes by which the images are produced, collected and edited to constitute the evidence of the wholesome nature of the Independent State of the Congo's humanitarian colonial project. The text provides a narrative of a civilizing process, turning the unregulated, instinctive African native into a disciplined body, able to operate in the routinized and well-laid-out new geo-social space which was to be the civilized state. The text functions as an institution of Western authority.

Leopold used these texts (and the construction of the spectacular Museum at Tervuren; see Morrison, 2006, Chs. 5 and 6 for a full account) to gain the approval of the Belgian people. The reader and the museum goer were seduced by the rhetoric of self-congratulation. If, and that was not actually likely, a member of the audience had actually heard the rumours of the 'realty' of the Congo and the measures taken to produce rubber, here was an authentic, tangible rebuff. The images displayed in books and on the walls at Tervuren were studies in 'sustainable agriculture'; images such as Figure 12.3 in which native people are depicted

5 This was later strengthened by the set of volumes *Etat Independent du Congo* (1903-04) published by the Muse du Congo (forerunner of the Royal Museum of Central Africa).

carefully putting cuts in rubber vines to extract the sap. However, the reality of Figure 12.3 is very different. Under extreme pressure to produce increasing yields of rubber, the youth has cut the wild vines into sections, a deleterious practice that will ultimately diminish the return from the vines. Unable to reproduce the initial return, he has essentially signed his own death warrant.

Nevertheless, the modern camera is nothing if not democratic, and other nonstate sanctioned images were also making their way out of the Congo. One of the most dramatic being an image taken by Alice Harris in May 1904 of a local man holding his daughter's hand and foot. The man, Nsala Wala, had come into the mission station at Baringa with a small package containing the severed extremities of his small daughter. Cutting off hands in particular had become fairly common practice by members of the *Force Publique* (the semi military, semi police force) as a way of accounting for the number of cartridges used during their rubber collecting expeditions. It was also a means of terrorizing local people into harvesting more wild rubber. In Nsala's case, both his wife and child had been killed and mutilated, and he had managed to rescue just one small hand and foot to show as evidence. Nsala was photographed seated staring down at the severed human remains in the background two other natives look on. Alice's husband John sent the resultant print back to Britain with the comment, 'The photograph is most telling, and as a slide will rouse any audience to an outburst of rage' (see Thompson, 2007). Under the influence of E.D. Morel, who had formed the Congo Reform Association, the Harrises toured both Europe and America with a Congo Atrocities magic lantern slide show that displayed their array of images. The Nsala image also appeared in printed form in many places, including Mark Twain's pamphlet, several full length books on the Congo atrocities (such as E.D. Morel's *King Leopold's Rule in the Congo*) and in various other newspapers and periodicals. Leopold tried to discredit these images by claiming Harris was a Protestant and ideologically motivated (thus recalling past attacks on Catholic colonialism). However, the tide of public opinion had turned against him and Leopold was forced to 'sell' the colony to the Belgian State in 1908.

In his history of the Congo under Leopold, Adam Hochschild called this the first successful human rights campaign in history, but I am more sanguine. Leopold made a profit, no one was ever prosecuted and when the Congo was later allowed independence, it incurred a national debt (see Morrison, 2006: Chapter 5).

Sontag stated that the camera makes everyone a tourist in other people's reality, and eventually in one's own; this is apt for a whole genre of images I have elsewhere called 'genocidal tourism' (Morrison, 2004b). The advent of the mass produced, relatively cheap camera meant that images could circulate that were taken by the perpetrators themselves in conditions and on occasions that the state authorities would not have countenanced.

In the explanatory literature on the holocaust, there is debate concerning the actions of the men depicted in Figure 12.4. Daniel Goldhagen used the actions and the images of Reserve Police Battalion 101 to argue that only Germans in a

Figure 12.4 Members of reserve Police Battalion 101 looking/smiling at the camera as one of their fellow members takes a memento photo of their 'ackions' against the Jews. (Source: Taffet, 1945) For Daniel Goldhagen (1998): 'These Germans' willingness to make an extensive photographic record of their deeds, including their killing operations, in which they appear with cheerful and proud demeanours as men entirely comfortable with their environment, their vocation, and with the images that are being preserved, is compelling evidence that they did not conceive of themselves as having been engaged in crime, let alone in one of the greatest crimes of the century.'

particular cultural environment, that of eliminatist anti-Semitism', could be the perpetrators of the holocaust – in Goldhagen's memorable phrase, they were 'Hitler's willing executioners'. Sharply opposing this position, Christopher Browning claimed instead that the Reservists were ordinary men situated in a complex of forces, many of which were banal (including peer group pressure) (Browning, 1998 [1992]).

Goldhagen assumes a universal viewer: the image 'illustrates to us, as it celebrated for the Germans, their active disregard for the dignity of Jews … an example of the Germans' use of the socially dead Jews as playthings for their own satisfaction'. Nevertheless, such photographs do not prove this; the existence of similar trophy images in Japanese soldiers' mementoes, among others, demonstrates that Goldhagen had only considered a small sample of the available images of atrocity. For example, what of the trophy images of the abuse of prisoners by US military guards at Abu Ghraib in occupied Iraq? The US President George Bush (6 May 2004: BBC online) stated that he was 'sorry for the humiliation suffered by the Iraqi prisoners and the humiliation suffered by their families', but that he was 'equally sorry that people seeing these pictures didn't understand the true nature and heart of America'. For Sontag (2004) these images revealed a shift: they were 'less objects to be saved than messages to be disseminated, circulated'. The advent of the digital camera enabled images of Abu Ghraib to enter into circulation immediately; they were to be emailed to others, circulated to those not there. However, these US military guards were reservists, lifted from their civilian jobs for their period of service; thus, there was little distance between these perpetrators and us. If the 'perpetrators apparently had no sense that there was anything wrong in what the pictures show', then the processes of authorization and routinization of the brutality done in the name of defending our civilized space implicated not only the Political Military elite but also all of us who voted and acquiesced.

Figure 12.5 also needs to be situated to give it explanatory power – this time in a narrative of racialist scientific procedures. Genocides do not just happen. We are familiar with a pattern of historical processes of stigmatization and labelling in which language becomes an indicator that a group is being prepared for action leading to genocide. The language that portrayed the Jew as a 'parasite', as 'vermin' was buttressed by the 'scientific' findings of eugenics and hereditary characteristics. In posters and in images, the Fatherland (the civilized space of Germany) was to be protected by containing and then solving the contamination problem.

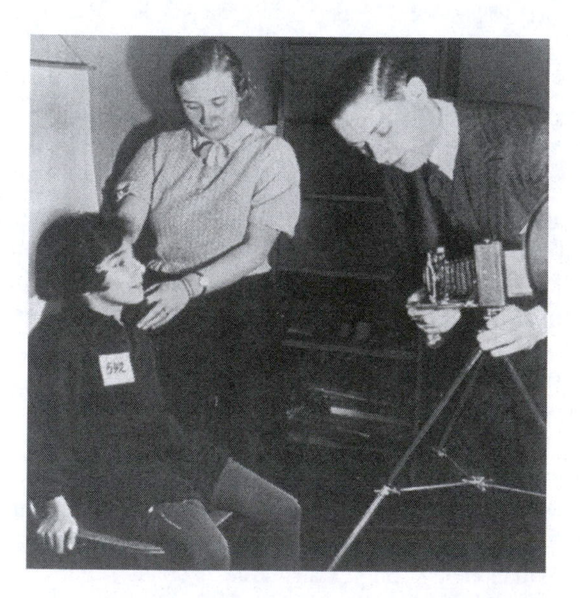

Figure 12.5 A Jewish child being photographed by the 'Institute of Racial Research', a process that formed part of the classification of 'racial types' under the Third Reich. Mid 1930s MEPL/Weimar Archive.

What do we make of this capturing in imagery the characteristics of the out-group? Sontag (1977: 5) states that a consequence of the photograph becoming a primary way of capturing reality is the development of 'bureaucratic cataloguing' in which mobile populations are surveyed and held steady. In one of the Nuremberg Laws, *For the Protection of German Blood and German Honor*, the law legitimated racist anti-Semitism and turned the 'purity of blood' into a legal category' (Dawidowicz, 1975: 63). Likewise Rubenstein (1978: 4) commented:

> The destruction process required the cooperation of every sector of German society. The bureaucrats drew up the definitions and decrees; the churches gave evidence of Aryan descent; the postal services carried the messages of definition, expropriation, denaturalisation and deportation; business corporations dismissed their Jewish employees and took over 'Aryanized' properties; the railroads carried the victims to their place of execution, a place made available to the Gestapo and the S.S. by the Wehrmacht [German Army].

For which side does this image provide evidence? Help comes from a comparative source. When the communist Vietnamese forces liberated Cambodia from the horrors of the Khmer Rouge in 1979, they were treated as invaders of sovereign space by the western powers. In the capital, they found the Tuol Sleng interrogation centre, a building that had first been a school, then a place of torture where confessions were mass produced. (Over 15,000 people who passed through the Tuol Sleng centre were subsequently transported to the nearby infamous 'killing fields'). The centre contained piles of abandoned photos of everyone who had been interrogated/eliminated; these are now central exhibits of Tuol Sleng's new role as a museum of genocide. Each inmate had to sit in a special chair with a protruding and adjustable headrest. They were then photographed from the front and from the side; detailed files along with 'records' of the interrogation and the subsequent 'confessions' were kept. However, for what purpose? They served no functional use at the time apart from providing a record of everyone who had been processed; participation in the record keeping of modernity. One must therefore accept Charny's (1986: 148) statement that: 'the mass killers of humankind are largely everyday human beings – what we have called normal people according to currently accepted definitions by the mental health profession'.

Methodological reflections

Remembering the history of reading the image

The authors of *Cultural Criminology: an Invitation* (Ferrell, Hayward and Young, 2008) hope for a role for a visual criminology. Their hope is that it will help provoke a 'critical engagement with the flow of meaning that constructs late modern crime, in the hope of turning this fluidity towards social justice'

(2008: 13–14). Nevertheless, is there any guarantee that in confronting the visualizations of mass atrocity our response will be one of enhanced social justice?

This essay was prefaced by two quotations and an image. The first quotation dates from a time of great controversy in Europe concerning the power of the image, and in particular of the images of the then accepted source of human life and the structuring of the cosmos: the Almighty, and of the coming together of the divine and the earthly in the figure of Christ. No wonder that the institutional power of the Church had to call the great Council of Trent and lay out guidelines on the role of imagery and arousing the correct form of response. That the image had power was not in dispute, it was for what purpose that power was to be used and in what context a proper appreciation could take place. Between the Council of Trent and a mother leading her young daughter past piles of human skulls, bones and images of atrocities in a small museum of (attempted) genocide in Dhaka, Bangladesh, I placed Mike Presedee's methodological injunction for cultural criminology to break fee of conventional methodological bounds and use as its data and evidence the debris of everyday life. Today, in a range of museums, and scattered memorials around the world, the debris of mass horror, of killings, rapes, torture and genocide are collected, ready for our reading, our 'gaze', and our cultural criminological analysis.

We still share the controversy over the power of the image but no longer attach institutional guidance on where to position images, and how to 'see' them. There are no settled rules as to the methods and processes of reading, nor on how to arouse the desired moral response. If the image is to help criminology face up to the great (nonpunished) 'crimes' it has so steadfastly ignored then we must take into consideration as wide a range of imagery as possible. Whilst I shy away from orthodox 'methods' when it comes to reading and interpreting atrocity images, I offer the following thoughts by way of a starting point for those who may wish to undertake their own research in this area:

- The wide range and location of these atrocity images illustrates the widespread use and extent of mass killing and genocide.
- While humans commit mass atrocities in specific conditions with specific historical and complex explanatory factors, the range of processes and people involved mean that we can take no security from any claims that atrocity can only happen under certain specific conditions.
- We should never lose sight of the fact that, while these images are always 'local', they frequently share certain common characteristics which in turn suggests that terror and state-sponsored violence against the vulnerable may have a universal dimension.
- The fact that we often try to deny the universality of atrocity may be due to the fact that our understanding of atrocities is itself culturally constructed.

Sadly, such statements, of course, suggest no easy methodology. Rather, they tie us to circles of interpretation in which the identities of victim and perpetrator are not easily distinguished. For example, let us consider one final image: when WWII began in the Pacific, Natalie Nickerson, then 20, of Phoenix, Arizona, said a tearful goodbye to her boyfriend, a US Navy Lieutenant. He promised to write and two years later she received in the mail a Japanese skull, autographed by her lieutenant and 13 of his comrades, with a note that read: 'This is a good Jap – a dead one picked up on the New Guinea beach'. Miss Nickerson dubbed the skull Tojo, and on 22 May 1944 a photo of this attractive young woman gazing down on the autographed skull on her table became Life magazine's 'photo of the week' with the title: 'Natalie Nickerson tries to write a sincere thank you note for the Japanese skull her Boyfriend sent to her'. Methodologically, what should we make of this image? We have of course distance; we are not now immersed in the web of ideology that was operating at the time that meant that the actions of the Allies were necessary, while the actions of the enemy 'other' were evil, inhuman and beastlike. The multiplicity of images, as we have examined earlier in this chapter, may display the ordinariness or the extremity of cruelty. The imbalance in recognizing Allied atrocities (as described for example in Dower's [1986] aptly entitled *War without Mercy: Race and Power in the Pacific War)* may demonstrate the still current incapacity of the human in *Human Rights* to have any institutional grip outside of the state.

Conclusion

At the time of the Council of Trent, humans were assumed to be created beings. Our nature had been a gift from God and our final resting place – our place of eternity – would be a return to God's security. Before that, we would face the final judgment. Images and our response to them needed to be controlled so that we would not lose sight of God's power and our need to finally account for our actions.

For great swaths of the world's population, that metaphysical belief did not survive modernity. Facing up to the horrors of the fascist regimes of the 1930s, Walter Benjamin (2008 [1935]) argued that self-alienation has reached such a degree that humankind can experience its own destruction as an aesthetic pleasure of the first order. One of the reasons Las Casas wrote his *Short Account* was his fear for the future of Spain in light of the belief in a metaphysical presence that was greater than that of Man's justice. He feared that God would take divine retribution for the horrors that Spain had visited on itself and destroy its power and bring terrible suffering on its peoples. What have we replaced that fear with today? One could make a case that it has been replaced by the data base of this essay – genocide photo libraries and museums of atrocity, each one full of images of horror and (man made) hell. We have no answer to the question: what does it mean to visit? Those who called the Council of Trent knew that the power of the image and our responses had to be controlled; otherwise we would lose sight of God's message and the common thread creation gave to the world. If today, our world is sceptical of grand stories, we may lose ourselves in an emotional response to the images that in itself becomes all that we can do. Nevertheless, that emotionality needs to be accompanied by critique, by struggle and by action. The sociologist Zygmunt Bauman (1993: 80) states that 'the moral self is always haunted by the suspicion that it is not moral enough'; if so than any idea of a collective 'we' should tremble. To view images of atrocities in the museums of the National War Liberation Museum, Dhaka, of Armenia, of Nanking, of the Holocaust, of Rwanda, of Cambodia, to walk though the Royal Museum of Central Africa Brussels, is to realize that whatever emotion is aroused, that the world – the secular world – does not deliver justice where genocide is concerned. We can, of course, explain this away by saying that modernity was about the nation state and the construction of 'civilized' space within territorial boundaries. In doing this, we can then put out of our minds concerns about rape, murder and the subjugation of the 'other' that were the 'hidden' price that had to be paid for our civilized space. Alternatively, we could say that information scarcity could have been an explanation. Previously, the globe was divided in terms of space, time and form: but we are no longer in that world anymore. First the telegraph, then photography and now the World Wide Web have shrunk the divisions and collapsed the distances. Today, we are now faced with an information glut, a mass of facts and images that many see as meaningless and incoherent. Could there be any grounds for optimism?

I took several photographs at Tuol Sleng in 2007. One was meant to be a photo of a large photo taken by the Khmer bureaucrats of a woman fixed in position so that her image could be recorded side on. The original photo is preserved behind a glass cover and my resulting image has a shadow on it. It is the reflected image of myself taking the photo of the photo, and to the side there is a reflection of another person watching me take the photo of the photo. When I showed this in a presentation someone asked, 'who is that looking, and what are they doing?' Who indeed?

References

Baudrillard, J. (2001) 'Symbolic Exchange and Death', in Mark Poster (ed.) *Jean Baudrilard: Selected Writings* (2nd edn) Cambridge: Polity.

Bauman, Z. (1993) *Postmodern Ethics*, Cambridge: Wiley-Blackwell.

Benjamin, W. (2008 [1935]) *The Work of Art in the Age of Its Technological Reproduction, and Other Writing on Media*, Michael Jennings (ed.), Cambridge, Mass.: Harvard University Press.

Browning, C.R. (1998 [1992]) *Ordinary Men: Reserve Police Battalion 101 and the Final Solution in Poland*, New York: Harper Perennial.

Charny, I.W. (1986) 'Genocide and Mass Destruction: Doing Harm to Others as a Missing Dimension in Psychopathology', *Psychiatry*, 49(2): 144–157.

Conley, T. (1992) 'De Bry's Las Casas', in Rene Jara and Nicholas Spadaccini (eds) *Amerindian Images and the Legacy of Columbus*, Minneapolis: University of Minnesota Press, 1992.

Conrad, J. ([1899] 1988) *Heart of Darkness*, Robert Kimbrough (3rd ed.), New York: W.W. Norton & Company.

Dawidowicz, L. (1975) *The War Against the Jews*, 1933–45. New York: Holt Rinehart Winston.

De Las Casas, B. (1992 [1542]) *A Short Account of the Destruction of the Indies*, trans Griffin, London: Penguin.

Dower, J. (1986) *War without Mercy: Race and Power in the Pacific War,* New York: Pantheon.

Ferrell, J., Hayward, K., Morrison, W. and Presedee, M. (2008) *Cultural Criminology: An Invitation*, London: Sage.

Gibson, C. (1971) *The Black Legend: Anti-Spanish Attitudes in the Old World and New,* New York: Knopf.

Goldhagen, D. (1996) *Hitler's Willing Executioners: Ordinary Germans and the Holocaust*, London: Little, Brown.

Gottfredson, M. and Hirschi, T. (1990) *A General Theory of Crime,* Stanford: Stanford University Press.

Hochschild, A. (1998) *King Leopold's Ghost: A Story of Greed, Terror and Heroism in Colonial Africa*, Boston and New York: Mariner Books/Houghton Mifflin Company.

Levinson, P. (1977) *The Soft Edge: a natural History and Future of the Information Revolution*, London: Routledge.

Lombroso-Ferrero, G. (1911) *Criminal Man, According to the Classification of Cesare Lombroso*, New York: G.P. Putman.

Morrison, W. (2004a) 'Lombroso and the Birth of Criminological Positivism: Scientific Mastery or Cultural Artifice?', in J. Ferrell *et al.* (eds), *Cultural Criminology Unleashed,* London: GlassHouse.

Morrison, W. (2004b) 'Everyday Photography Capturing Genocide', *Theoretical Criminology*, 8(3): 341–58.

Morrison, W. (2006) *Criminology, Civilisation and the New World Order*, Oxford and New York: Routledge-Cavendish.

Presedee, M. (2000) *Cultural Criminology and the Carnival of Crime,* London: Routledge.

Rubenstein, R.L. (1978) *The Cunning of History: The Holocaust and the American Future*, New York: Harper & Row.

Sontag, S. (1977) *On Photography*, London: Penguin.

Sontag, S. (2003) *Regarding the Pain of Others*, New York: Farrar, Straus and Giroux.

Sontag, S. (2004) *Regarding the Torture of Others*, New York Times, 23 May 2004.

Thompson, J. (2007) Capturing the Image: African Missionary Photography as Enslavement and Liberation, Yale Divinity Library Occasional Publication No. 20, New Haven: Connecticut.

Woolf, V. (1938) *Three Guineas*, New York and London: Harcourt Brace.

Zelizer, B. (1998) *Remembering to Forget: Holocaust Memory through the Camera's Eye*, Chicago: University of Chicago Press.

Index

Photographs are given in italics